THE SOUND OF MUSICALS

Amateur Musical Theatre in the South Lakes Peninsulas

Graham Whalan was born and brought up in Ulverston, where his parents ran a Grocery shop on Hart Street. He attended Ulverston Grammar School (now Victoria High School) before moving to Barrow-in-Furness. He then studied Psychology at Birmingham University and worked for many years in the NHS. Although he now lives near Durham he retains an affection for his Furness homeland and recently wrote a history celebrating the centenary of The Coronation Hall in Ulverston.

Stable Door Press

BY THE SAME AUTHOR

FICTION

Mr Tambourine Man

Life is What Happens

NON-FICTION

100 Years of the Coronation Hall

THE SOUND OF MUSICALS

*AMATEUR MUSICAL THEATRE IN
THE SOUTH LAKES PENINSULAS*

Graham Whalan

First published in Great Britain in 2016
by *Stable Door Press*
High Waskerley Farm,
CONSETT DH8 9LJ

stabledoorpress@gmail.com

ISBN 978-1-5262-0596-4

Front cover: Leah Greaves and the Sir John Barrow Monument,
Ulverston (photography by Paul Bryden)

Back Cover: Ladies Chorus from Furness Amateur Operatic Society's
production of *The Rebel Maid, 1936*

Cover design by Sam Whalan

Typeset in Times New Roman and printed and bound in England
by Short Run Press Limited, Exeter, Devon

Acknowledgements

I am hugely indebted to a great many people who have been willing to share their time, their memories, and even their personal memorabilia with me. I am especially grateful to those who entrusted me with such precious treasures as old theatre programmes and scrapbooks which brought past productions alive for me in the way I hope the following chapters will do for you. Among these are: Graham Barker, Pauline Barnes, Ian Bird, Paul Bryden, Margaret Buckley, Steve Carrick, Gordon Crayston, Brian Greaves, Neil Hastings, Ken & Brenda Hindle, Graeme Livingstone, Chris Loveless, Pat Jewell, Aileen Jackson, Jean & Mick Malkin, Maureen Pearson, Elaine & Jack Parkinson, Deborah Powell, Clare Rigg, Jennifer Salder, Colin Smith, Barbara Springthorpe, Len Simm, Bill & Noreen Steel, Paul Williams and Arthur Wilson.

Thanks are also due to the several young performers I met who were willing to share their thoughts and recollections such as: Catherine Andrews, Aydn Blake, Leah Greaves, Tom Halfpenny, Ben Lewis, Sally McKimm, Naomi Shields, Claire Williams, and Chris Wilson.

I am also indebted to the *North West Evening Mail* for permission to reproduce photographs from their archive collection, and to each individual Society for permission to reproduce pictures from their publicity material. Specific details and further picture credits are listed on page 330. My thanks also go to the most helpful staff at the Archives and Local Studies Centre in Barrow, Heather Horner of the *North West Evening Mail*, and to Alan Wilkinson, a fellow obsessive researcher who was most generous in sharing with me his collection of archive material from local newspapers.

And finally thanks are due to my patient and long-suffering wife Helen, for her love and encouragement, and to my son Sam for his skills with the cover design for this book.

CONTENTS

THE SOUTH LAKES PENINSULAS OF FURNESS

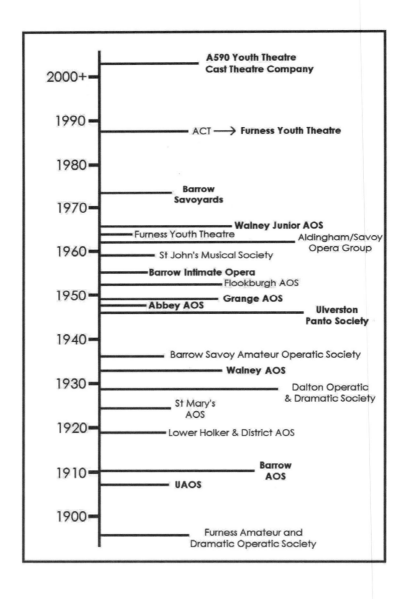

TIME LINE: The year each Society was first established.
Those still in operation are in bold type.

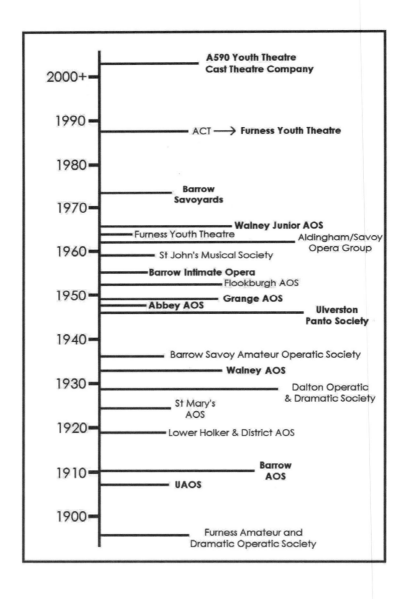

Foreword

During the years that I was Arts Correspondent for the *North West Evening Mail* I occasionally encountered snooty reporters from the *Guardian* or *Times* who would raise their eyebrows and say "Really? Arts Correspondent in Barrow? Where's your concert hall? Where's your art gallery?" I would take pride in replying "the arts in Barrow and South Cumbria are not what people have served up to them, they are what people do."

This is evident in many art forms but perhaps most notably in musical theatre, which forms a significant part of the social and cultural life of the area, offering shows on the doorstep that theatregoers would otherwise have to spend fortunes and travel miles to see. Our musical societies create a can-do culture, encourage creativity and community involvement and nurture talent at any age.

I was first plunged into this world as a trainee reporter on the *Barrow News* Series in 1970. The editor was Bob Strike, who was passionate about amateur theatre and realised its importance to his readers. He was great friends with Ron Metcalfe, the paper's theatre critic who wrote a deliciously gossipy weekly arts column. Mr Strike (I could never call him Bob) would also write the occasional beautifully-crafted review under the name *Talisman*. One of my favourite parts of the week was Mr Metcalfe's visit with his typed copy (no emails then) when I would make him a cup of tea and listen in on the latest news of who was doing which show, who was cast, fall-outs in committee, walk-outs at rehearsal and all the behind-the-scenes goings on that happen in the tense world of the stage.

Sadly, they and their memories are no longer with us, although I'm glad to say that, through their press reviews of past shows, at least something of their spirit is recalled in the chapters that follow. And when I had the chance I was happy to carry on their tradition of making sure the local press was an integral part of the South Cumbria theatre community.

It wasn't until 2012 when I was invited to be president of Walney Junior Amateur Operatic Society that I really began to appreciate the enormous annual task of getting a show onto the stage. By April it really didn't seem possible that a performance could happen in October, there were so many problems and so many people needed to sew hems, put up posters, sell tickets, chaperone dressing rooms and the rest.

But the annual miracle is that shows do go on, and have done in this area for well over a hundred years, touching thousands of lives in many ways. Thank goodness that Graham Whalan has undertaken the eye-watering task of writing their history.

Having spent my career listening to people, taking notes, and trying to make sense of their stories I can appreciate what a task he has taken on. The result is not only valuable social history, it is also a fascinating insight into a tradition which has become part of the social fabric of our district. In short, this history is important to Cumbria and way beyond. I am very glad that Graham has written it.

HELEN WALL
Barrow Borough Councillor
(*Spokesperson for the Arts*)

INTRODUCTION

Bill Bryson, in case his name is new to you, is an American writer who, among other things, writes travel books. In 1995 he published the massive best-seller *Notes From A Small Island* which chronicled a trip he had undertaken around Britain. He has lived and worked in our country and indeed comes across as a committed fan as he writes affectionately about its people, its beauties, as well as some of its frustrations and quirks. In *Notes* he writes about his particular fondness for Durham, close to where I now live. In fact the city found his remarks so positive and uplifting he was subsequently appointed Chancellor of the University, and then a new library was named after him. To be fair this was probably also in recognition of his literary achievements, but his well-received review of the city can't have done him any harm.

I mention all this because, in 2015, he published a sequel to *Notes* entitled, *The Road to Little Dribbling: More Notes From A Small Island*, in which he reports stumbling briefly into Barrow-in Furness. I met him once and found him to be an affable, friendly sort of chap, and I have always found his books well worth a read. But his remarks about Barrow have since forced me to have a re-think. Here's what he says: *'Barrow is just about the most out-on-a limb, end-of-the-line place in England. It inhabits its own peninsula and is miles from anywhere along slow roads. Once it was the seat of industry – for a while its steel mill, now long gone, was the biggest in the world – but these days it is famous for being forgotten and depressed.'* He has a brief walk up what I assume is Dalton Road and describes it as *'more a place for congregating than shopping'* before likening it to a walk through a prison yard. He then drops into Costa for a coffee and concludes that he had *'pretty well exhausted the possibilities for amiable diversion in central Barrow-in-Furness.'*

It's all rather cruel, and I think it probably means he's blown any chance of getting another library named after him in Barrow. Of course he's not the first person to be rude about Barrow, and although it may be true that the town has seen better days, it has always managed to rise above difficult times in the past, and one feels it's currently doing its best. A visit to the Dock Museum could have told him all about that. Instead Mr Bryson moves swiftly on to the Lakes, which he does appear to appreciate, but he fails to give any mention to the other charms and delights of the Furness area. Ulverston seems to pass him by completely – I mean, you'd think that the Sir John Barrow Monument and the Coronation Hall had never been built! But here's the main point – I'm convinced that, if only he'd had the opportunity to drop into the Forum in Barrow, to see one of the many shows performed there by any one of the area's amateur companies, he would come to a very different conclusion. Here he would have seen something very different to his observations in Dalton Road - that is to say he would have been awash with evidence of enthusiasm, energy, vitality, and, most of all burgeoning talent.

Because I now live in the North East you may think I'm something of a defector, but I will assert that my roots remain in Furness, and I still have family and friends here so I visit often and retain much affection for it. It is a wonderful part of the country with a mass of charms and diversions, and I will not have a word said against any part of it. It has made enormous contributions to Britain's economy with its slate quarries, iron and steel industries, and ship-building and has, as its heartland, a vast area of stunning views and natural wonders which has inspired artists, writers and poets for centuries. Did you also know that Cumbria has more local breweries than any other County in England? And in the midst of all that the area really knows how to put on a show, and what's more as you will see, it's been doing this for years. So as well as climbing the hills, or walking the fells, or drinking the beer, whenever I visit Furness I love to go to a show produced by local performers – and I am never disappointed.

I have written previously (*100 Years of The Coronation Hall*) about one of my favourite places in Furness - yes, The Coronation Hall in Ulverston - which as I noted gave me my first experience of live theatre. It was a Christmas pantomime, *Jack and the Beanstalk*, and both my father and sister were in it! My father took on the demanding role of 'Villager' whilst my sister was in Mrs Teagle's dance troupe, The Sunshine Girls. Then, a little later, I was taken to Ulverston Operatic Society's 1955 production of *Goodnight Vienna*, with my father again holding everything together as 'a gentleman of the chorus'. As a 7-year old, although I didn't quite get hold of the story, the explosion of sound, colour and spectacle was magical to me and truly amazing. If you can imagine how, let's say a Kalahari bushman might feel when he first switches on a colour television, the effect was probably something like that. The pantomimes and musicals became a key part of my family's entertainment schedule as I grew up. I was never a performer myself but I knew a few people who were which gave them the status of celebrity in my eyes. One of my friends, John Park, once got the job of 'call boy' which sounded very important and made me very jealous. (I also had an unrequited crush on his older sister Anne at the time – but that's another story.) Then my family moved to Barrow and I had the opportunity to see even more amateur productions there, in venues that are sadly no more – The Coliseum, and Her Majesty's Theatre (affectionately known as 'The Madhouse').

When I was researching material for the Coronation Hall book (of which copies are still available by the way, and a bargain at £5.99) I became fascinated by all the many and varied things that had happened in that small theatre space, not just the celebrities who had paced its boards, but also the many plays, diversions, shows and concerts that had been put on by local performers. I came across lots of reviews of former shows, and became increasingly aware of the output of many local societies – both operatic and dramatic – that were active not just at the Coronation Hall, but all over the Furness area. In fact so much had been done over the years, and so much achieved, that it occurred to me that there was a clear need for all this work to be recorded and celebrated. All the reviews filed away in library archives were fascinating to read, but they were effectively hidden away, and were in need of wider exposure.

If you look around the Furness area as a whole, you will find an amateur theatrical group active almost anywhere, and if you look further you will find others that were active in the past but which have now folded, and that's before you even think about schools and colleges, who of course have always been keen to launch shows of their own and now usually have dedicated drama departments. In the South Lakes such groups as the Ulverston Outsiders, the Elizabethan Players, the Pennington Drama Group, the Northern Drama Association and many others have all made massive contributions to the local scene. 'Am-dram' in general however is not the subject of this book, nor is the Furness area as a whole. My focus is on amateur *musical* theatre in the South Lakes area lying south of Broughton-in-Furness in the west, to Grange-over-Sands to the east. Even in this relatively small geographical area a surprisingly large number of Operatic Societies have been active for many years.

If the smaller Youth Theatre groups are included, then in Barrow alone, a town with a population of around 72,000 there are currently at least 6 active societies. Outside of Barrow, in the area to be covered, there are at least 5 more. Each of those societies of course has its history and its key players, both on and off the stage. And if you then take those 11 societies and add together all the shows they have ever done, and if you then consider all the individuals that have ever been involved, either on stage or in the orchestra, front of house, or behind the scenes, you end up with well, a vast amount of information. By examining the history and development of individual societies and theatre groups I hope to be able to sift through this, set it in context, and review as much of their work as possible in the pages that follow.

The larger context for amateur productions is of course the professional theatre, and there is an interesting and important story to be told of the development of musical theatre as an art form in its own right. I therefore decided to begin, in **Part One**, with an attempt to set the scene by tracing this development from its origins to the present day. Along the way there will be pauses to look at what was happening in Furness at the same time as these developments were underway both on Broadway and in London's West End.

Part Two will then look in more detail at the history and development of the South Lakes Amateur Operatic Societies. They will be considered in chronological order according to their year of origin, Ulverston being the first having been formed in 1907. In doing so I offer immediate apologies to the Millom Society who, although referred to in the text, falls just outside my artificially imposed boundary and so does not get this fuller treatment. All of the South Lakes' Societies I have reviewed have of course operated within the same social context, and the fact that all are still functioning (with the unfortunate exception of Flookburgh) despite the major challenges of World Wars, periods of economic decline, urban re-development, and changes in entertainment tastes, is a huge commendation to the generations of producers, musicians and performers that have kept everything going for so long. As you will discover, their willingness to embrace modern trends and to adapt to these changing times has been the key to such survival.

This survival is also impressive when all the work and effort required to stage a single show is taken into account. This will be examined in **Part Three** followed by some attempt to wrap up proceedings with an analysis of the enduring appeal of musical theatre, and some possible explanation of why it has proved to be such a popular and enduring pastime in the South Lakes area. Of course it is taken as read that the area is awash with talent which needs an outlet, but there is more to it than that.

Two things in conclusion: firstly I hope I have been faithful to the facts as they have been revealed to me, as much as I hope that any interpretations or speculations I have made will also be viewed as more or less accurate. And secondly, whilst many key figures and performers are referred to in the text, I must apologise to anyone who feels that the work of a significant contributor has been somehow overlooked – especially if it's you.

PART ONE:

Reviewing the Situation

God sent his singers upon the Earth
With songs of sadness and of mirth
That they might touch the hearts of men
And bring them back to Heaven again.

Longfellow, *The Singers*

1

THE HISTORY AND DEVELOPMENT OF MUSICAL THEATRE IN AMERICA, ENGLAND AND THE SOUTH LAKES PENINSULAS

Not long ago I was lucky enough to be undertaking a transatlantic sea voyage to New York. To while away the long days of staring at the ocean an American musician was, fortuitously enough, offering a series of talks on – mark – 'The *American* Musical'. At the end of the talks he was besieged by a gaggle of his fellow countrymen, all keen to tell him how instructive and entertaining his talks had been. Indeed they were, but I was disappointed that he had focussed entirely on Broadway productions and I wanted to ask him for his take on amateur theatre, and the interplay between this and the professional world. When I finally managed to get his attention he looked at me as if I was talking some strange Martian language.

"*Amateur*?" he repeated. "What do you mean?"

"Er – musicals that are staged by local groups and enthusiasts."

"You mean … like … Gilbert and Sullivan?"

"Well, partly …. "

Now *I* was perplexed, and began to burble about Operatic Societies and local drama groups in the UK – as if it were some peculiarly British thing. It didn't help. "I recently saw a local production of Sondheim's *Into the Woods*," someone volunteered, helpfully. Except it wasn't, as someone else then chipped in with, "Oh isn't he a genius? Such brilliant lyrics!" As the rest of the group sighed and looked rapturously heavenwards, my man took this as his opportunity to turn his attention from me and, with some relief I suspect, proceeded to rave about Sondheim's qualities as a daring, uncompromising composer-lyricist, and his ground-breaking experimentation of the musical theatre form. I shrank back into the shadows defeated, and slipped away quietly.

I have since realised why it was that my seeds fell on such stony ground. I think it is because the Americans do not have an equivalent word for 'amateur' in their language. Local musical and dramatic societies are plentiful in the States but they are all referred to as "Community Theatre." Please do not imagine that I am being anti-American when I say this – I like the country and its culture – but my experience is that Americans really do think they are brilliant at everything. We know from President Obama's famous Presidential inauguration speech that their prevailing mind-set is that of "Yes we can!" whereas in Britain we are of the more modest "Well, I'll give it a go" variety. The concept of 'amateur' with its connotations of inexpert or unskilled activity is therefore anathema to them, so I think they have dispensed with the whole notion. Hence my man's failure to get to grips with my question. I was puzzled however by his immediate association of 'amateur' with Gilbert and Sullivan. Presumably the explanation is the fact that their operettas were generally the first things to be tackled by non-professional companies both in the US and the UK. But more of that later.

Having carried out further research I have also come to realise that my question regarding the interplay between amateur and professional productions is by no means an easy one to answer. It started out simply enough – the professionals looked down disdainfully on amateurs, who they snobbishly dismissed as unpolished and unskilled, and who they saw as worlds apart from their own elevated standards of performance.

Over time however there was a gradual recognition that the efforts of amateur groups were not only stimulating interest in the dramatic arts, they were generating support for theatrical entertainment at large. The result is that, nowadays, the boundaries between amateur and professional are increasingly blurred. How this change came about is, as you will discover, a long story.

The first task is to understand how the professional musical theatre evolved. As you labour through this you may not feel that such a historical review is relevant to our purpose, but please bear with it. Since professional productions lead the way for the amateur world to follow, this review will provide an important context for the second task – reviewing the changing form of amateur musical productions in our area of concern, the South Lakes peninsulas of Furness. As we proceed the 'birth' of each local Society will be pin-pointed, and some of their productions will be referred to in order to illustrate the new opportunities and challenges they faced as the years went by, but more information on each will follow when we later explore their history and development in detail.

Early Influences

You will recall that my American friend talked about the development of 'The *American* Musical' as if, like Coca-Cola, the Big Mac and Baseball, it is a singularly American invention. Perhaps it is. There is no doubt that, for many years, America was the dominant force in musical theatre with Broadway (New York) as its epicentre. Neither is there doubt that American composers, lyricists and producers have been responsible for major developments and innovations. But the basic foundations and ingredients of the musical are of European origin - namely the continental 'operettas' of the mid-19th century, the Savoy operas of Gilbert and Sullivan, and the 'musical comedies' of the Edwardian era.

The origins in fact stretch further back in time and across various cultures but, for my purpose here, I will take as a convenient starting point the crucial influence of the musical entertainments of the 1850's, 60's and 70's provided in Paris by Jacques Offenbach. Grand Opera had of course been performed for many years prior to this time, but Offenbach wanted to create a form of musical entertainment that was, basically, more *fun*. The result came to be known as the 'Operetta', a musical form which was then embraced and developed to great effect both in the UK and beyond. In the UK Offenbach's work proved to be a powerful influence on two men in particular - William Schwenck Gilbert (1836-1911) and Arthur Seymour Sullivan (1842-1900).

Gilbert and Sullivan were brought together initially by Mr Frederick Clay, an English composer who was first engaged with Gilbert in writing burlesque pieces. Their first joint effort (*Thespis, or the Gods Grown Old*) was something of a flop, although one man, a certain Mr Richard D'Oyly Carte, was an instant convert and saw something special waiting to emerge. After persistent efforts he brought the pair together again to produce their next public offering *Trial by Jury*. It was a runaway success and their future was sealed. In 1881 the Savoy Theatre was built to house their 'comic opera' productions, subsequently becoming known as Savoy Opera. Their appeal has since proved to be timeless, mainly because the social and political parodies, which are a feature of each of their pieces, are very familiar to each age or era. Humour is of course a cornerstone, with the main ingredient being a 'topsy-turvy' world where, for example, pirates become nobles, fairies mingle with British Lords, incompetent men hold high office, and where love matches run far from smoothly.

Meanwhile, in the same period, two other forms of entertainment were appearing in Britain which would also prove to have mass appeal. One was a series of so-called musical comedies, produced by Mr George Edwardes (1855-1915) at The Gaiety Theatre in London, and the other was the rise of the Music Hall. The first of George Edwardes' productions was *Dorothy*, with music by Alfred Cellier and a libretto by B C Stephenson, first performed in 1886 and billed as a 'comic operetta'. It is the story of a young noblewoman who disguises herself as a milkmaid in order to win the attentions of a rakish aristocrat. Subsequent Edwardes' productions appeared, all based on the familiar Cinderella theme of love conquering against the odds, and they came to be known as 'The Gaiety Musicals'. They were specifically designed to appeal to all ages with breezy, popular songs and stylish spectacle. Further examples are *The Geisha*, *The Quaker Girl*, and *The Runaway Girl*.

In America one of the first European imports was Gilbert & Sullivan's *HMS Pinafore*. It opened in New York in 1879 and ran initially for 175 performances but proved an enduring hit with audiences on both sides of the Atlantic. It is reported that it has been produced more often than any other musical in the English language. *The Pirates of Penzance* followed, and then (in 1885) the evergreen *Mikado* was staged, and both pieces enjoyed similar success. *The Mikado* actually ran for 250 performances and was produced by none other than Mr Richard D'Oyly Carte. Home grown American shows were meanwhile not faring so well. For example *The Belle of New York* (1898), written by Hugh Morton with music by Gustave Kerker, managed only 64 performances. When transferred to Europe it enjoyed much better success, and in fact became the first American musical to run for over a year in London.

With regard to the rise of amateur musical theatre in Furness the crucial influence of the Gilbert and Sullivan operettas is also the best starting point for understanding how the early amateur operatic societies came to be. The key decade in this respect is the 1880's when their operatic works were first licensed to be performed outside of the Savoy Theatre. The first sign of something happening in the South Lakes came in 1892 when the already well-established 'Furness Dramatic Society' decided, at their annual dinner to become the 'Furness Amateur Dramatic <u>and Operatic</u> Society.' The express intention was that the members should now extend their talents to the staging of one of these popular new Gilbert and Sullivan operettas. It took them a while to get it together but, sure enough, by 1894 they were ready to put on a performance of The Yeoman of the Guard. It was so well received that a staging of The Mikado followed in 1895, at Barrow's Town Hall. The Musical Director was Mr Alfred S Pass, whose family subsequently ran one of Barrow's premier music shops – 'Pass's' of Duke Street. The society was then very soon to play a major part in a highly significant national development for amateur theatre in 1899.

Such was the popularity of Gilbert and Sullivan at this time that societies similar to Barrow's were being formed all over Britain. In 1897 a society in Lancaster was attempting to stage The Mountebanks, a comic opera written by Gilbert and his later partner Alfred Cellier. It ran into several difficulties and it was only because the afore-mentioned Furness society stepped in and helped them out that the staging was able to proceed. As a result the Musical Director, Mr A P Bulfield was inspired to suggest that a 'Mutual Aid Society' should be formed so that all societies could not only support each other, but also share ideas and advice. He called a meeting of interested parties at The Grosvenor Hotel in Manchester in February 1899, at which representatives from about a dozen *societies turned up. As a result the 'National Amateur Operatic and Dramatic Association' came into being with 41 initial member societies; in 1925 the word 'amateur' was dropped, creating 'NODA' as it is known today. Within 10 years over 100 societies had joined up with further growth being both steady and sure. In 1973 no less than 1,518 member societies attended their annual conference, and at the present time membership stands at over 2,500. Today NODA provides highly valued services and advice to its member societies, monitors standards, and hosts an annual awards ceremony. South Lakes societies, as you will discover, have been recipients of both nominations and awards on several occasions.*

1900 - 1920

Back at the turn of the century it seemed that the American appetite, which had been so ably whetted by the Savoy operas, was solidly for British musical comedy, and a steady stream of London hits crossed the Atlantic. These included *Floradora* (1900), written by Owen Hall and Leslie Stuart, with its alluring 'Floradora Girls' and its musical highlight, *Tell Me Pretty Maiden (Are There Any More At Home Like You?),* and *A Chinese Honeymoon* (1901), written by George Dance with music by Howard Talbot. In London this show had in fact achieved the distinction of being the first musical production in history to run for more than 1,000 performances. Edwardian musical comedy was clearly the hot ticket at this time. A particularly successful show was *The Arcadians* (1909), a musical written by Lionel Monckton and Howard Talbot, with lyrics by Arthur Wimperis. The story, of innocent 'Arcadians' attempting to impose truth and simplicity on to the wicked city of London, illustrated the character of its time perfectly. It is especially notable for its allegorical quality

– just as it sat somewhere between the twee fading world of Gilbert & Sullivan and the more abrasive styles of musical comedy in the Music Hall (such as the comedy of performers like Little Tich, Billy Bennett, and Marie Lloyd) so these old and new styles of musical entertainment were embodied in the show, with the innocent 'arcadians' being contrasted with the brashness of the Londoners. It premiered in London in 1909, before transferring to New York the following year for another successful run.

Having mentioned Marie Lloyd I hope you won't mind if I insert my favourite story about her, even though it is not directly concerned with my subject. She was of course known for innuendo and songs with a certain risqué quality, and this often brought her into conflict with the strict censorship rules of the day. On one particular occasion she performed a song which drew especially sharp intakes of breath from such quarters – it went by the glorious title of "She sits among the cabbages and peas." When reprimanded by the censor for the clang association of 'peas' to well, something else she apologised immediately, insisted she had not wished to cause offence and agreed to change the words. She subsequently came up with "She sits among the cabbages and leeks". Genius. Pure genius.

Meanwhile the British successes in America were soon to be taken over by American shows that were not only home grown but which would be characterised by a distinctly new style. There were key influences in the country which were driving this trend. One of these was the immigration factor – the many ethnic minorities being attracted to its shores at this time brought new, varied and rich cultural influences to bear on the entertainment scene. In particular African-American performers were becoming influential, as were the comedy, sketches and songs from the Minstrel tradition. A diversion also rising in popularity was so-called 'Vaudeville' entertainment. Here the form was basically the same as Britain's Music Halls which had seen a similar rise in popularity in the middle part of the 19th century, where the aim was to provide a cheap form of entertainment that would appeal to the masses. As the man once said – 'a splendid time was guaranteed for all!' It was essentially a variety show where the basic elements of song, dance, comedy and speciality acts were all combined into one show. One minute the audience may be transfixed by a mournful singer emoting a powerful and moving ballad, whilst the next minute they might be booing off some poor unfortunate wannabe who, whilst trying to demonstrate his skill with flaming torches, had accidentally set fire to his beard. Talented composers and songwriters, many of whom had been part of the immigrant influx, were on the ascendant too, such as Irving Berlin, Jerome Kern, and Victor Herbert. They would all subsequently make enormous contributions to the development of musical theatre.

One who was to have a major influence on the future direction of musical theatre in America was George Cohan (1878-1942), a multi-talented song and dance man who emerged from the Vaudeville circuit. His contribution to Broadway's emergence as the epicentre of musical theatre was immense, so much so that he is honoured by a statue commemorating his achievements in Times Square (left). He was a performer, a playwright, a songwriter, director and producer and has been dubbed as both 'the father of the American musical' and 'Broadway's greatest showman' (Hischak, 2008). He brought a new, fast-paced sort of energy and style to musical theatre, and created a new sound by pioneering the art of the conversational lyric. In 1904 he wrote, directed and co-produced the show which characterised all these new developments – *Little Johnny Jones* – the story of a perky American jockey who comes to the UK to compete in the Derby. Two of the many songs he wrote are now hallowed Broadway anthems – *I'm a Yankee Doodle Dandy* and *Give my Regards to Broadway*.

As George skipped joyfully along, the atmosphere was less cheerful in Furness. In 1903 the Barrow group (the Furness Amateur Dramatic and Operatic Society), put on its last Gilbert and Sullivan offering, the less well known The Grand Duke. *Exactly why this was the last isn't known but may well be due to the fact Barrow was in a transitional phase at this time. The steel industry, on which much of its early prosperity had depended, was now in decline, and Barrow was busy trying to reinvent itself as a shipyard town. Anxiety about the town's future was rife, and this would only be deepened by a depression in the economy in 1902. But fear not, Barrow's fortunes rose again, as indeed did the Operatic Society, triumphantly, in April 1911. It was like a sort of 19th century version of Groundhog Day in fact as, when the society reformed under its new name 'The Barrow Amateur Operatic Society' its first production was* The Yeomen of the Guard. *It was so well received the society felt confident enough to stage a second event (yes that's right,* The Mikado*), in November of that year.*

Meanwhile, in 1907, an operatic society had been formed in Ulverston, again with the aim of bringing the joys of Gilbert and Sullivan to the townsfolk. Their first production was the ever-popular Mikado, *in 1908, which by now had been offered so many times it's a wonder there was anyone in the District who hadn't yet seen it. Undeterred, across the bay in Millom, residents there were offered it in February 1910 as the debut production of their new Amateur Operatic Society, founded at the initiative of a Mr Wilf Griffin. Both the Ulverston and Millom Societies then went on to stage a production annually until the outbreak of the Great War in 1914 when their activities were brought to a close. As for the Barrow Society, it too stopped production for a year but then somehow managed to carry on from 1916 with an annual show. As well as providing a source of diversion and entertainment, the aim was, like Ulverston's, to use any proceeds to benefit local charities. All the Societies proved to be very successful in this endeavour for many years.*

With the outbreak of war in 1914 the output on the professional scene on both sides of the Atlantic inevitably abruptly stopped, despite the fact that escapist entertainment was desperately needed. One particular show however did manage to appear before the fighting was over. This was *Chu Chin Chow*, a musical based on the story of Ali Baba and the Forty Thieves and which, according to Derek and Julia Parker (1979), is generally thought of as 'a pantomime for adults.' It was written, produced and directed by Oscar Asche with music by Frederic Norton, and opened in London in 1916 where it ran for 5 astonishing years, setting a record that stood for almost 40 years. When it transferred to America in 1917 however it ran for a mere 208 performances – perhaps George Cohan's influence was already being felt, and this was an early sign that tastes in America were changing.

It is in any case at this point that America takes over the story. All the main ingredients of 'the musical' as we will come to know it are now in place there: from the early operettas we have the basic music score driving a loosely based storyline, and from the Edwardian musical comedies, the Music Halls, Vaudeville and the influence of men like George Cohan we have popular songs, comic sketches and energetic dance routines. Young composers like George Gershwin and Irving Berlin were also making their mark. All these ingredients were now coming together to be interlaced in a new style of show. The driving force at this point was another key influential figure – Florenz Ziegfeld (1867-1932).

Spectacle and lavish production numbers were the speciality of Florenz Ziegfeld (right) and his famous *Ziegfeld Follies*, staged at his New Amsterdam Theatre. Here the emphasis was on the glorification of the American girl in the context of dazzling and extravagant settings. Perhaps the most famous of the 'Ziegfeld girls' was Fanny Brice – a singer-comedienne known for her performances in both revues and vaudeville. (In 1964 the musical *Funny Girl*, based on her life, was produced and from which another star was born – one Barbra Streisand.) In the *Follies* songs and sketches took second place to the spectacle, even though most were written by Irving Berlin, whose songs were to have such an impact on musical theatre as the century moved on. Even so, several popular songs emerged from Ziegfeld's shows, including the famous signature number *A Pretty Girl is Like a Melody*. A musical score, a storyline, comedic interludes, and dance numbers were thus established. If George Cohan underlined the importance of energy, style, and performance to these ingredients, it was Ziegfeld who demonstrated the crucial importance of spectacle and visual impact. All these elements were soon to come together in a new and innovative style of musical, produced by none other than Ziegfeld himself in 1920 - *Sally*.

For *Sally* Ziegfeld spared no expense. Music, songs and dance are of course prominent features of the show (with the hit song *Look for the Silver Lining* being particularly memorable), but it is the lavishness of the production values which makes it a landmark. It was also a key vehicle for a rising Vaudeville performer in the shape of Marilyn Miller who went on to be one of Broadway's brightest stars. *Sally*'s story is the weak Cinderella tale of the orphaned girl who works initially as a dishwasher before finally finding fame in – who would have guessed it? – *The Ziegfeld Follies*. This rags-to-riches story, as you may have noticed, is ubiquitous in almost every musical offering at this time. *Look for the Silver Lining* indeed captured the wishful optimism of the age when all were aspiring to make 'the American Dream' a reality. *Sally* was, in effect, the personification of the American Dream come true.

1920-1930

In the 1920's there was still some clinging to the familiar operettas of the previous era on both sides of the Atlantic, but the dual influences of Vaudeville and the Music Hall were certainly being felt. Typical productions which exemplified this development were *No, No, Nanette* (an American show which achieved the remarkable feat of opening in the West End *before* its premiere in New York in 1925), and *Funny Face* (1927) with music by George and Ira Gershwin, and song and dance provided by Fred and Adele Astaire. In each case, although ostensibly written for the show, many of the songs were written with the primary aim of them becoming popular hits e.g. *Fascinating Rhythm, Tea for Two* and *'S Wonderful*. One other particularly influential show well worth a mention was *Shuffle Along* (1921). It was unique in being the first all-African/American hit on Broadway.

Meanwhile *The Ziegfeld Follies* still held sway with their spectacular routines, sketches, and songs all with little discernible connection. Ziegfeld also found time to produce the hit show *Rio Rita* (1927), which was a large scale operetta with around 100 singers in the chorus and the usual Ziegfeld trademark visual splendour. It was a highly romanticised tale, complemented by comic interludes. RKO produced a film version in 1929 which had the distinction of being the first successful screen version of a Broadway musical. It had Bebe Daniels in the title role. MGM made a second film version in 1942, with the comedy provided by Bud Abbott and Lou Costello.

In Britain some of the new shows from America were produced on the old 'operetta' style however, the big hits being *Rose Marie* (1924) and *The Desert Song* (1926). *Rose Marie*, with its much parodied *Indian Love Call*, ran in London for over 2 years, and achieved equal popularity in Paris. *The Desert Song* has proved to be an all-time favourite with its exotic settings and large helpings of romanticism. It was a hit across the world, including Britain, France and Australia and has, since the 1920's, been revived several times in New York. Both productions have also been staple productions for local operatic companies.

As for Britain's own products the big hit at this time was a show called *Mr Cinders*, which opened in London in 1929, and then played for 528 performances. The plot turns the Cinderella story on its head, and reverses gender roles. It never transferred to New York but its early success ensured a later revival in London in 1983 with first Denis Lawson, then

Lonnie Donegan, and finally Lionel Blair all taking a turn with the lead role.

But a great leap forward in the history of musical theatre was to take place in America towards the end of the decade. This was the seminal production of *Showboat* in 1927, with Florenz Ziegfeld in charge of production. It has been described as the first masterpiece of American musical theatre, and indeed it would change musical theatre forever. It was based on a difficult, sprawling novel by Edna Ferber, which spanned 40 odd years and comprised a complex political plot involving miscegenation, race relations, and the plight of black people in the southern States. Already one's immediate thought has to be, 'That's a *musical*?' And probably one's second thought is then, 'What's *miscegenation*?' (It's inter-racial marriage by the way.) Apart from having black and white folk singing together on stage - a revolutionary notion in itself - the key innovation of *Showboat* is nicely summarised by Jerome Kern, the composer: 'It is my opinion,' he said, 'that the musical numbers should carry the action of the play and should be representative of the personalities of the characters who sing them'. Whereas previously the songs in a musical production had little or nothing to do with the action, now the two would be inextricably linked. The songs would not only progress the story, but would also deepen the audience's understanding of the characters performing them. This was truly revolutionary stuff. Now, as *Showboat* ably demonstrated, a musical could have the same, if not a greater dramatic impact than a play. It was a smash hit and played for 572 performances.

Sadly the optimism of the 1920's was to be followed by the Depression of the 1930's and a subsequent World War, both of which meant that the bright lights of Broadway had to be dimmed. Hollywood took over as the country's main entertainment focus, and Broadway talent all began to drift steadily west. *'Go and become a star on Broadway!'* (somewhat oddly) became the prevailing myth spun by Hollywood, typified by the quintessential backstage movie musical *42nd Street*, which was released in 1933. It was not until 1943 that the Broadway musical would rise again, in the form of the next pivotal production - *Oklahoma!*

Meanwhile, over in Furness, musical theatre was certainly not thriving. The years following the Great War were tough. There had been a savage downturn in the economy of the district as a whole, the markets for iron and steel had basically collapsed, there were nowhere near enough orders for Vickers shipyard, and jobs were being lost almost daily. Between 1919 and 1922 in fact the figure for job cuts at Vickers was just short of 20,000. The Barrow and District Yearbook described 1926 as 'a year of deepening gloom'.

So this was without doubt a tough time for amateur musical companies, and there was the very real fear that they would not survive. And yet, as you will see when we look at the history of individual societies, somehow they did. Church-based groups often kept the flame alive as a development of their choral groups and driven by charitable motives. In Barrow, St Mary's Operatic Society emerged (from the RC church on Duke Street) to stage Iolanthe in 1925. At the same time, perhaps as a vain attempt at boosting morale in the town, an attempt was made to form a new society in Dalton-in-Furness. Councillor John Fisher called a meeting in May 1925 at which he asserted, 'It is a well known fact that Dalton is not behind any town in Furness as regards musical or vocal talent.' Sadly however the town did seem to be behind in terms of interest and sponsors and it took a while before it was possible to mount a production. The Society was destined to have but a short life however, and folded soon afterwards. One that had been formed in Askam suffered a similar fate, while across the bay in Millom, their Society, along with those in Barrow and Ulverston, managed to weather the storms and all are still going strong.

1930-1940

In the 1930's, although American productions were on the ascendant, in Britain there were still key players keeping the flag flying for musical theatre, namely Ivor Novello and Noel Coward. Born David Ivor Davies, Ivor Novello (1893-1951) became, in his lifetime, one of the most popular British entertainers. Starting out as a songwriter (he it was who gave us the perennial *Keep the Home Fires Burning*) he turned to acting and then, in the 1930s, composed a series of extremely popular musicals. e.g. *Glamorous Night* (1935) and *The Dancing Years* (1939). These shows are characterised as a blend of opera, operetta and both modern and classical dance, although some would say they are out-dated and sentimental when compared to the high-spirited offerings of 1930's America. Think of Myrna Rose trying to serenade you with *My Dearest Dear* whilst Ethel Merman is belting out *Anything Goes* in the next room and you get the idea. Still despite some personal troubles, Novello's work retained its popularity as evidenced by one of his hugely successful later works *Perchance to Dream* (1945). He wrote both the music and the lyrics and, as was his wont, took a leading role in the show.

Incidentally this was the show that gave us another of his most famous hits, *We'll Gather Lilacs.*

In a similar vein, and in the same period, Noel Coward (1899-1973) was busy composing several musical works which, despite their popularity, have also been described as old-fashioned. Known mostly for his comedies, plays and witty songs he also wrote comic operettas, of which the most famous are *Bitter Sweet* (1929), the historical extravaganza *Cavalcade* (1931) and *Operette* (1938).

Despite their success in the UK, neither of these two creative forces were to have much influence in America. America, as we saw with the production of *Showboat*, was ploughing new furrows in musical theatre, and it was Noel Coward's dramatic productions that attracted any attention over there rather than either his or Ivor Novello's musical offerings. It is said they were branded as "too British" for American tastes. Another 20 years or so were to pass in fact before Britain's musical creations were to have any real impact on the Broadway scene.

As the 1930s dawned in Furness, two of the major league operatic societies as we know them today – Ulverston and Barrow – were up and running, and then a new one made its first appearance in 1932, the one known today as the Walney Musical Theatre Company. Both Barrow and Ulverston were trying to move away from Gilbert and Sullivan to pastures new (e.g. Ulverston was doing shows like Floradora, The Arcadians, *and* Mr Cinders, *whilst Barrow offered* The Desert Song), *and then in 1936 a newly-formed group, the 'Barrow Savoy Amateur Operatic Society' popped up for a few years clinging to the old favourites such as* The Mikado *and* The Yeoman of the Guard. *If you had a bit of spare cash, you were spoiled for choice. The trouble was of course that, although musical theatre was becoming more plentiful, money was not. The 1930s are not a lot different from the 1920s in being notable for widespread poverty and hunger as by-products of high levels of unemployment. Of course if you could afford the price of a ticket a musical diversion presented by local performers would be quite uplifting for you, it would add to your sense of community, and give you some relief from the rigours of daily life, but if you couldn't, perhaps you could at least benefit via the charities the Societies' productions were supporting. In 1935 for example the Barrow Society reported that, in the 25 years they had been active, the total amount they had handed over to charities was an impressive £1,500 (that's an equivalent of around £70,000 in today's money, about £2,500 per year).*

Such charitable intentions meant, as in the previous decade, that it was often local Church groups who were instrumental in getting new societies off the ground at this time. Indeed this was the motive behind the formation of the new Walney Society in 1932 and later the Abbey Musical Society in 1949. The Walney group actually began life as 'The Walney Parish Church Musical and Dramatic Society' (St Mary's Parish Church) and it was the Abbey Methodist Church which gave birth to the Abbey Society. In the fine tradition of operatic society apprenticeships Abbey cut their teeth on 10 Gilbert and Sullivan productions between 1949 and 1957. Walney on the other rebelled and chose as their first production a comic opera written by two Americans – Reginald De Koven and Harold B Smith. The show was The Mandarin, *which was staged in February 1932, and concerned the love tangles of a Chinese man - so at least they had the good grace to keep things oriental.*

Then it was time for another war, and all musical productions were of course suspended. Some venues were even commandeered for use by the War Office – the Coronation Hall in Ulverston being the local example. In Barrow there was a drive to keep cinemas and theatres in operation, as much as for diversion and morale-raising as anything else, but live entertainment was limited to uncomplicated and cheap forms such as music hall variety shows, or concert parties.

Post-war however local musical societies rose again in force, now with the very important job of morale-raising, although things didn't really get going again till 1947. Both the Ulverston and the Walney Societies put on shows in that year, the Abbey Society as mentioned above started in 1949, and the Barrow Society re-formed in 1950. Licences were also now being granted for amateurs to perform popular musicals from the 1920's, and they did just that, meaning you didn't have to sit through The Mikado *again! (Unless of course you lived in Grange, when a new operatic society got off the ground in 1949. They could not resist the inevitable pull of* The Mikado *and staged it as their first production in 1950.) But, taken as a whole, as far as musical theatre in Furness is concerned, things were looking up.*

THE 'GOLDEN AGE' (1943-1960)

And so we arrive at what is generally known as Broadway's Golden Age i.e. 1943-1960. Think of any of the well-known, frequently revived, musicals and they were probably first produced on the Broadway stage in this period. To give just a few examples - *Annie Get Your Gun, Carousel, Guys and Dolls, South Pacific, The Music Man, The King and I, The Pyjama Game, Paint Your Wagon, My Fair Lady, & West Side Story.* In all cases it was the story that now took precedence over the score. Songs were no longer written with the singular aim of becoming popular hits (although of course many did), they were written to advance the story, to define a character, or even to explore the relationship between characters. And the role of dance changed too – dance numbers now actually became part of the story-telling. And the musical that kicked all this off, and indeed became the model for future productions, was - *Oklahoma!*

The show was the progeny of Richard Rodgers (1907-1979) and Oscar Hammerstein II (1895-1960), a pairing which fortuitously came together when Rodgers lost his former partner Lorenz Hart to failing health. With a focus on the feud between love rivals for a lady's hand, the story examines the wider friction between the farmers and the cowmen of Oklahoma as it strove to achieve statehood. At a time when a weary war was still raging (it premiered in 1943), its images of home, young love, and its underlying emphasis on the American values of an independent and pioneering spirit, all struck a chord. It proved to be an immensely popular show, eventually running for a record-breaking 2,212 performances. According to Hischak's *Oxford Companion to the American Musical* (2008) it remains to this day the most produced Rodgers and Hammerstein musical.

As pioneered by *Showboat* some years before, the themes and topics tackled on the musical stage now became weightier and, in some cases, quite controversial. For example, Rodgers and Hammerstein followed up their *Oklahoma!* success with *Carousel* (1945), which dealt with an intense but doomed romance; Burton Lane and Yip Harburg provided *Finian's Rainbow* (1947) which satirised race relations in the deep South; and *South Pacific* (1949), with its controversial song '*You've Got to be Carefully Taught*', issued a challenge to all to confront racial bigotry.

Lighter fare was to be found in *Brigadoon*, a show which was subsequently to prove very popular with amateur groups. Created by Alan Jay Lerner and Frederick Loewe, it told the whimsical story of a village in the Scottish highlands which magically appeared for only one day every 100 years. It ran on Broadway in 1947 for 581 performances, and transferred to the West End in 1949, for a respectable 685. Then Lerner and Loewe went on to revive the Cinderella story, so favoured by the earlier Edwardian operettas, with their triumphant show *My Fair Lady* (1956). In keeping with the standards set by *Oklahoma,* music, character and plot in both of these shows were all fully integrated, there was a strong storyline, and strong characterisation. In other ways however they belied a British influence. *Brigadoon* was set in Scotland, and *My Fair Lady* was breaking the rules in that there was very little dancing, quite a bit more talking, and the setting was England! It proved to be the hit of the new decade anyway, knocking *Oklahoma*'s record by running for 2,717 performances.

Meanwhile British productions were still struggling to have much impact across the Atlantic. There seemed to be some undefined 'dis-connect' between British and American tastes. Although Ivor Novello was continuing to enjoy success with *Perchance to Dream* (1945) and later, *King's Rhapsody* (1949) in the UK, he was still "too British" to be accepted in America. America's productions meanwhile continued to stream into West End theatres. Improvements were to come in the next decade but in the 1950s only two British shows of any note made it to New York, and each failed to reproduce the excitement they had generated back home. The better known of these is perhaps *The Boyfriend* (1954) which, apart from anything else, marked the debut on Broadway of someone who was to become one of the international treasures of the musical, Julie Andrews. As to the show itself, it wasn't a smooth ride as the show's British writer Sandy Wilson didn't hit it off with the American production team and he was finally banned from the theatre! Although it had been a huge smash in London it enjoyed only moderate success in America running for 485 performances. The other British offering, *Salad Days* (1958) fared even more poorly. Although it had run for a record-breaking 2,283 performances in the West End it only managed a meagre 80 in New York. This was in part attributed to an unfortunately timed newspaper strike which started a few days before opening night, and so deprived the show of the rave reviews the producers were clearly expecting.

Several other notable British shows from this period may not have made it to America, but they nevertheless enjoyed considerable success at home. One such show was *Bless the Bride* (1947), with music by Vivian Ellis and lyrics by A.P. Herbert. It ran for 3 years at the Alephi Theatre in London with a total of 886 performances, and is probably best remembered for the song *This is My Lovely Day,* which went on to become one of the most requested songs on BBC radio. A few years later, in 1951, a show premiered based on the 1902 novel, *Brewster's Millions*. Principally staged as a vehicle for the talents of George Formby, this was *Zip Goes a Million*, with the story and dramatic structure being adapted from the novel by Eric Maschwitz. It ran for a highly respectable 544 performances. And finally there was *Love from Judy*, a 1952 London hit which this time was adapted *by* Eric Maschwitz, from Jean Webster's novel *Daddy Long Legs*. Although this was a musical with a clear American pedigree, with music written by an American song-writing team (Hugh Martin, who incidentally also wrote for the film musical *Meet Me in St Louis*), and had been adapted from a popular American novel, for some unknown reason it failed to get a staging in New York. It was not until 2003 in fact that a small New York theatre company was willing to stage the show, at least for a limited run.

Back on Broadway, the end of the 1950s was to see the appearance of two of the most durable of musicals – Leonard

Bernstein's *West Side Story* (1957) and Rodgers and Hammerstein's *The Sound of Music* (1959). Many aspects of *West Side Story* mark it out as yet another watershed musical. Here neither the story nor the score have precedence – both are equal partners in driving the action forward. The mix of drama, tragic death, and modern dance re-imagined the musical and what could be sung about. It also introduced a new lyricist (and later composer) to the scene – Stephen Sondheim. As for *The Sound of Music,* although it did not have a record-breaking run at the time, the famous film version of 1965, its umpteen regional revivals, plus its popularity with schools and musical groups have all ensured its place in musical theatre history. Sadly it was to be Oscar Hammerstein's last venture as his stomach cancer increasingly took hold. When he died in 1960 all the lights of Broadway were turned off in tribute, and all the traffic stopped moving. The movement of musical theatre however was unstoppable – another sea-change was about to happen as fresh young innovators took over the helm in the next decade.

And as a post script, it is worth mentioning that while all this was happening in the east, over in the American west, Hollywood had also been busy producing a raft of successful musicals on film. Many have since stood the test of time and indeed have eventually found their way on to the stage. Notable examples are: *Meet Me in St Louis, Singin' in the Rain, Calamity Jane, White Christmas,* and *Seven Brides for Seven Brothers.*

Meanwhile as the 1950s and 60s got underway in Britain, an era of promise and new beginnings dawned. Rationing ended in 1953 the same year as a new Queen was crowned, there were signs of greater affluence, and as the frequently used analogy has it, a black-and-white world was slowly transforming into one of colour. If Broadway's 'Golden Age' was well underway across the sea, something similar could also be said to be happening on the local musical theatre scene. As already mentioned, the Abbey Society had been established in 1949, and in the same year there was the revival of a Society in Grange, which was then followed by the revival of yet another one in nearby Flookburgh in 1951. In 1948 the Women's Branch of the Ulverston British Legion began their long run of annual Pantomimes at the Coronation Hall, evolving eventually into the Ulverston Pantomime Society. In fact, all through the 1950's, and the early part of the 60's, the two highlights of the Ulverston year were the annual offerings of the British Legion and Ulverston's Operatic Society. The week of the Ulverston Society's show then became known as 'Opera Week' which always ended with a Grand (celebratory) Ball.

There were also early signs that young people were being encouraged to get in on the act, so to speak. One development important to note for example was the formation of a song and dance troupe, who were made up of youngsters roughly between the ages of 8 and 16, and modestly went by

the name of The Nobody's Concert Party (pictured above). Formed in 1948 they were managed by Bill Davies throughout their life span (of around 10 years), and were trained by Joyce Pattinson. Whilst not a grown-up operatic society they were very popular in their day, performing at both the Coronation Hall, and in village halls and community venues around the district and, in conjunction with other existing local dance schools, undoubtedly did much to stimulate interest in the performing arts amongst its members.

As for the established Operatic Societies, the granting of new licences were providing new opportunities: Barrow could at last put on the seminal Showboat in 1951, to be followed by Ulverston in 1963, and the Walney Society was able to put on 4 of the new Rodgers and Hammerstein's musicals between 1954 and 1958. Both the Abbey Society and Flookburgh finally took their leave of Gilbert and Sullivan, Ivor Novello's London musicals also became available and were given an outing, as were other shows which had had successful West End runs not long before (such as Salad Days, The Boyfriend, and The Pyjama Game).

But it appeared that the appetite for Gilbert and Sullivan in Furness had still not been sated as a correspondent in the North West Evening Mail wrote bemoaning 'the passing of good music' and the loss of 'the old societies' in Barrow. His comments seemed somewhat out of touch with the initiatives of all the local Societies, but he would have been cheered by the fact that a group of former students from the Crosslands Convent School rose to the challenge to give one or other of Gilbert and Sullivan's operas an annual staging all through the 1950's, produced by Mrs M Sharp. Their shows were very favourably reviewed, with the unique feature of their productions being an all-female cast. I suppose, if you had seen The Mikado a few times, this was at least a new twist.

Perhaps also in response to the call for 'good music' a new group was set up in Barrow in this decade which called itself 'Barrow Intimate Opera'. It was the initiative of Esther

Croskery and their offerings were of the higher-brow variety such as The Bartered Bride *(1955) and* The Beggar's Opera *(1957).*

1960 - 1980

At the start of the 1960s major cultural shifts were occurring across America and it was evident that the traditional Broadway musical was somewhat out of step with them. In particular rock music was on the ascendant. Whilst Julie Andrews was trilling about a lonely goat-herd, Barry McGuire was assuring us we were on the 'Eve of Destruction'. The Civil Rights' movements were holding marches and protest rallies, and Americans at large couldn't decide whether the Vietnam War was a just cause or a violent crime against humanity. Old values and certainties were truly being challenged. Insofar as art must reflect the culture of its time, the traditions of musical theatre, firmly established as they were, also needed to adapt if they were to survive. *Hello Dolly* (1964) didn't quite cut it.

But in 1964, hot on the heels of *Hello Dolly*, a musical was staged which, in its way, articulated the above push for change very clearly. *Fiddler on the Roof* is the story of a small Jewish community living in Russia, wrestling with modern challenges to its old traditions. By the end of the piece there is some resolution as the villagers set off for new lives in the 'New World.' In a clear case of art imitating reality, *Fiddler on the Roof* marked the closing of the era of the Rodgers-&-Hammerstein-type musical, as musical theatre itself set off for a new life, embracing new trends and, in a sense, re-inventing itself.

Perhaps the first evidence of this came with *Cabaret*, produced in 1966. This was a musical with dark and unappealing themes – the rise to power of the Nazi party, and the debauchery and decadence of life in Berlin at that time. It was hardly escapist entertainment. Then in 1968 came *Hair*, a musical which featured drug use, a score composed entirely of rock music, and – get this – frontal nudity! Whilst the introduction of nudity into a musical wasn't one to be enthusiastically copied by later producers, *Hair* did open up the possibility of a creative fusion between modern rock music and the traditional form of the Musical. Enter (a bit later) Andrew Lloyd-Webber, but at this time the main innovators, who can perhaps be given most credit for driving things forward were Harold Prince (producer), Michael Bennett and Bob Fosse (choreographers) and Stephen Sondheim (composer and lyricist).

But before moving on to the 1970s mention must be made of the early signs of a growing British influence on Broadway which was evident during the 1960s. Anthony Newley for example had some success with two shows: *Stop the World, I Want to Get Off* (1962), which ran for 555 performances, and *The Roar of the Greasepaint – The Smell of the Crowd* (1965) which ran for 231. Both were produced by David Merrick, the most celebrated American producer of the post-war era, but whilst each show enjoyed moderate success, they were described as 'too offbeat' for American tastes. The most successful British import of this time was Lionel Bart's *Oliver!* which opened on Broadway in 1963, again with David Merrick producing, but this time in partnership with London producer Donald Albery. It achieved a run of 774 performances, and is currently acclaimed as one of Britain's most enduring musicals.

Two years later Tommy Steele then popped up with *Half a Sixpence* (1965), based on H.G. Well's novel *Kipps*, which made 512 performances. The story was quintessentially English and the songs betrayed a strong music hall influence (try *Flash, Bang, Wallop* for example). It was really a vehicle to showcase Tommy Steele's talents as a song-and-dance man but it is also of interest to note that the cast list included a certain John Cleese. One wonders whatever happened to him? And it was to be the last West End show to be transferred to Broadway before the Andrew Lloyd Webber-led invasion of the 1970s, and beyond.

But let's return to the main American innovators who were to have an important influence on the works of the 1970s: in particular Stephen Sondheim, Michael Bennett, and Bob Fosse. Sondheim's musicals are sometimes described as sophisticated, intellectual or cerebral in quality. The plot-lines are said to be 'non-linear' which more unkind people might call chaotic. His themes have a grim, sometimes cynical tone and are usually concerned with the darker side of human nature. All this is perhaps exemplified in the 1970 production of *Company*, a so-called 'concept musical' which consisted of a disparate series of scenes expounding a cynical view of modern marriage and relationships. The choreographer was Michael Bennett, who went on to produce his own concept musical 5 years later – *A Chorus Line*. With music by Marvin Hamlisch it was developed from a series of workshops and taped interviews with actual Broadway dancers, and ably demonstrated the tortured energy dancers not only have to put into each show, but also have to endure in order to win a part in the first place. It certainly found its audience and subsequently ran for 14 years. In the same year as *The Chorus Line* opened, Bob Fosse, another innovator who had already made his mark on the Broadway scene, was providing the distinctive choreography for another new show, *Chicago*. Again the themes were somewhat tawdry in nature as it dealt with America's obsession with murder, sex, and celebrity.

But it was Stephen Sondheim in particular who really got into his stride at this time. His other major success of the decade was *A Little Night Music* (1973) in which he produced his most popular and well-known song, *Send in the Clowns*. He then ended with the grisly and ghoulish *Sweeney Todd, the Demon Barber of Fleet Street* (1979). One wonders how his pitch to Harold Prince, the producer, went for this one: "I'm thinking about doing a musical about slaughter and cannibalism. I want to scare the audience half to death and, through the medium of song and dance, give them a truly disturbing experience. What do you think?" Even so, although its track record performance-wise reached nowhere near the heights of say, *Oklahoma*, it is still regarded as Sondheim's biggest achievement.

By now you probably get the idea with all these developments – musicals are now exploring form over content, more is being demanded of audiences, and the themes they are tackling are both challenging and uncompromising. As I say, this is partly the work of the bold innovators mentioned, but I think it is also a response to the huge social changes of the 1960s and 70s. The next developments however are to come from a different source altogether – they are to come from across the Atlantic.

An early salvo of this impending British invasion was shot in 1971, with the first musical of Andrew Lloyd-Webber's canon to play on Broadway – *Jesus Christ Superstar*. Already familiar to audiences through the innovation of a prior-released concept album it became a Broadway favourite and ran for 720 performances. In the same year another British import was revived - Sandy Wilson's *The Boyfriend* – which you may recall had first appeared on Broadway in 1954. Richard O'Brien's *Rocky Horror Picture Show* opened in 1975, although didn't really catch fire. It returned to Broadway in 2000 when its status as something of a cult classic had been established by the film version, released in 1975. As a result it fared rather better on its second outing and ran for 356 performances.

Then the next of Lloyd-Webber's London hits came to town in 1979 – *Evita*. In a possible case of 'if you can't beat 'em, join 'em' the innovative Howard Prince, Stephen Sondheim's chief collaborator, was the director and his artistic contributions are reported to have added significantly to its success. Then, as the new decade arrived, there was a clear foretaste of what was to come when another Lloyd Webber piece, *Joseph and the Amazing Technicolour Dreamcoat,* was transferred from an off-Broadway theatre, where it played for 747 performances. It was already a well known piece as it had previously been staged by many schools and amateur companies across the country. In that respect it has the distinction of being an amateur piece first, before being staged on Broadway with a professional company. Whatever next?

On the local scene in Furness the 1960s and 70s proved to be a period of mixed fortunes for amateur musical groups. Because of the steady march in popularity of television, and the increasing range of leisure and entertainment opportunities, support for live theatre was waning. Barrow, for example, actually lost two of its finest veterans in the 1960s – The Coliseum in 1964, and Her Majesty's Theatre in 1967. (The subsequent demolition of both of these grand old theatres has been much mourned in the town ever since.) The impact of these losses on the output of the Furness Societies will be considered in more detail in later chapters. This situation was also not helped by the fact that amateur players were not communicating with each other regarding their performance dates. As a result there were times when 3 societies (i.e. operatic and dramatic) were all putting on shows in the same week. It actually took some time before each Society signed up to an agreement for regular fixed time slots for their shows.

The shift towards more gritty material and rock music scores, which was the main feature of many of the new shows in the professional world, could not of course be reproduced in

Above: *The Coliseum Theatre, Abbey Road, Barrow*

Below: *Her Majesty's Theatre, Albert Street, Barrow*

local offerings as societies had to wait until such shows were made available to the amateur stage. When reviewing the amateur productions of this period therefore, one sees a mix of the old attractions and the new favourites – from the 1910 Edwardian comedy The Quaker Girl *to* My Fair Lady *from 1956, with more or less all points in between.*

It is worth noting however that several shows also made their first local appearances in this period. For example, the Walney Society was the first to stage Oliver! *in 1969, Barrow had already been first with* Oklahoma *in 1955, and now gave the town the premiere production of* My Fair Lady *in 1969, whilst the Ulverston Society premiered* Fiddler on the Roof *in 1972. Barrow also tried to woo audiences to live theatre by staging a series of* 'Black and White Minstrel Shows' *between 1974 and 1977. This was a show that had somehow achieved mass appeal on television, so presumably the hope was to attract a fan-based audience, much like today's tribute acts try to do. Let's just say that if you were to try the same strategy today it's unlikely that a Minstrel Show would be your first choice.*

A couple more church-based groups appeared, St John's (based on Barrow Island), and the Aldingham Parish Church Operatic Group, with the usual Gilbert & Sullivan repertoire, but these had both fizzled and burned by the mid-60s. The noble charitable causes supported by such groups were, at least for the time being, now a thing of the past. The Societies themselves now needed charitable donations in order to survive, but recruiting patrons and players was becoming problematic. Then came the demise of Barrow's old theatres, which prompted James Hay, Chairman of the Abbey Society, to express the worry that was in everyone's mind. 'One day,' he said, 'our children's children may be asking what a theatre was really like.' On a practical level the loss of these venues also meant that the Barrow Society, together with both the

Abbey and Walney Societies, were all rendered homeless. In order to carry on they had to make a reluctant shift to Barrow's Public Hall where sound and lighting facilities were

nowhere near as good. Some production years were lost as a result. Indeed life was hard.

The Abbey and Flookburgh Societies fared somewhat better, even though both tended to stage mainly older shows, such as the evergreen Goodnight Vienna *and*

Public Hall, Barrow

The Desert Song. *Such shows were favourites of the so-called 'hats and handbags' brigade who were now making up most of the audiences for musical shows. The younger element was presumably patronising the pubs-turned-discos of the 1960s or Barrow's new night spot –* The 99 Club.

Then, in 1969, the new kids on the block arrived – Walney Juniors, a newly-established Society specifically for 8 to 16 year-olds – with their first show, guaranteed to appeal to all generations – The Wizard of Oz. *The founders were in some way all associated with the Walney seniors but, from the start, they asserted that this was not to be merely a 'junior section' but an independent Society in its own right. Perhaps the move was a reaction to James Hays' fear that live theatre could be lost to future generations. If so it was to prove a timely development as, in the years following, it has grown from strength to strength and, as you will discover, has spawned a considerable amount of new talent.*

Another new force arriving on the scene in this period was the redoubtable David Marcus who made his first appearance in the early 1970's, oddly enough in a Walney Juniors' production (albeit as an adult cast member). You will be hearing a lot more about him in later chapters but, for the moment suffice it to say that he was instrumental in giving the Savoy operas a re-birth in 1973 with his part in the formation of the Barrow Savoyards.

It is interesting to think of these two new developments as a sort of pincer movement on any flagging interest in amateur theatre – that is to say there was the freshness and liveliness of youth on one hand, with the Savoyards back-to-basics manoeuvre on the other. All bases covered really.

1980s-1990s

On the American musical stage the 1980s had opened with a production of *42nd Street*, a strange sort of celebration of Hollywood musicals in the context of a love letter to Broadway. It had started out as a Hollywood movie as far back as 1933 but was still one of the first to be adapted for the stage. The producer was again the notorious David Merrick, a master of promotion and publicity gimmicks. He is described as one of the last great showmen of Broadway as corporate production and big budgets came to supersede the era of the sole producer. But more of that point later.

In 1983 one of Broadway's more traditional shows appeared, *La Cage Aux Folles*, although its subject matter was very non-traditional in that it was the first show to have gay men as the lead characters. The score was written by Jerry Herman who had enjoyed previous success with *Hello Dolly*. Although it initially became a mainstream hit, it also became a victim of the 1980's AIDS scare which made its story questionable and unattractive to audiences (as the Ulverston Society was later to discover.) Nevertheless it managed to run for 1,761 performances.

Then in 1982 the formula for a successful musical theatre production was again re-drafted by a new show, this time imported from the UK. It was co-produced by Cameron

Macintosh and David Geffen, adapted from T.S. Eliot's *Old Possum Book of Practical Cats*, with music by the irrepressible Andrew Lloyd-Webber. This was of course the phenomenally successful *CATS*, an entirely unconventional show whose appeal reached across generations and was to become the longest running show in Broadway history. As the line from its most famous hit song *Memory* has it: "Look, a new day has begun."

The 1980s and 1990s were indeed to be yet another explosive period for the musical as, in response to increasing competition from cinema and television, shows had to become more exciting, even more lavish, and more spectacular. In other words this period saw the birth of the so-called mega-musical characterised by a rock-influenced score, impressive sets, and spectacular stage effects. *CATS* was indeed only the beginning. Cameron Macintosh is given major credit for spear-heading a great revival of British musicals in this period. Under his shrewd guidance several mega-musicals were imported to Broadway with huge success, each having already been gigantic hits in London's West End. Perhaps the most famous of these are *Les Miserables* (1987) and *The Phantom of the Opera* (1988). The story goes that he first became a fan of musical theatre when, as an 8-year old boy, he was taken to see *Salad Days*. Soon he was singing and acting in musicals himself and the rest, as they say, is history.

The emphasis now was on emotionally powerful story-telling, stirring ballads, and colourful spectacle. The principle seemed to be that huge issues merited equally huge visual statements to have the necessary impact. So *Phantom* needed a crashing chandelier and an underground cavern, *Les Miserables* needed a massive barricade, *Miss Saigon* (1991) needed a helicopter landing on the stage, *Starlight Express* (1987) was to be performed entirely on roller-skates in a gothic setting complemented by stylised costumes, and huge orchestrations were required for *Sunset Boulevard* (1994). Hence, as mentioned earlier, the need for corporate help with their bigger budgets.

The impact of such influences was demonstrated to very beneficial effect when the Disney Corporation impacted on Broadway. The famous New Amsterdam Theatre which in many ways had kicked things off with the *Ziegfeld Follies* (1913-1927) had fallen into considerable disrepair, and was located in an equally dilapidated, run down, and unsavoury part of New York city. In 1995 Disney Theatrical Productions signed a 49-year revenue based lease, and within 2 years had restored the theatre to its former glory. Disney had already been enjoying considerable success with a series of animated musicals, and one in particular had been successfully transferred to the Broadway stage in 1994 – *Beauty and the Beast*. *The Lion King* was to be the next mega-hit as it was to be a dazzling theatrical version which opened the New Amsterdam Theatre in 1997. It ran for a decade before moving uptown to the Minskoff Theatre to make way for Cameron MacIntosh's lavish theatrical production of the 1964 film, *Mary Poppins*.

There was still room however for smaller scale productions. 1986 saw the opening of a British show which had been staged in London's West End the previous year. This was a revival of a 1937 musical *Me and My Girl*, which had had a successful West End run at that time, and had even spawned a later feature film. With music by Noel Gay and lyrics provided by L. Arthur Rose and Douglas Furber, it was the story of an unrefined, carefree cockney who inherits an earldom. The Broadway bods weren't interested however in 1937, and it was only when it was revived as a massively popular West End production in 1985 that it was brought to New York. It subsequently ran for 1,420 performances. In London its run lasted for 8 years.

Another British import, again on a smaller scale, came from none other than Andrew Lloyd Webber in the shape of *Aspects of Love* (1990). It opened in London's West End in 1989 where it played for 1,325 performances. The Broadway production opened a year later in 1990, but the reviews were unenthusiastic and it lasted for the much more modest total of 377. It was not forgotten however and much later, in 2007, it completed a successful 36-week tour of the UK with David Essex in the lead role.

As you may well have noticed by now a hit show in London may in turn wow America but such success is by no means guaranteed. One case in point is Willy Russell's *Blood Brothers*. It started out as a school play before being developed, at first somewhat reluctantly by Russell, as a West End musical in 1983. It then had only a short run before returning, triumphantly, in 1988. It has since proved unstoppable and, with currently more than 10,000 performances to its tally, is now the third longest running musical in West End history. And what was its fate in New York? On Broadway its performance tally was a mere 840. The songs reflect an earlier era, reminiscent of the 60s and 70s, and its story is predominantly working class and northern. Perhaps you have to be British to really relate to such themes.

As to what was happening in Furness during this period, the 1980s echoed the previous decade in many ways as amateur companies were not permitted to stage new shows whilst they were still being performed on the professional circuit. Accordingly some of the old favourites turned up such as Mr Cinders, *staged by the Walney Society in 1985, and* The Quaker Girl *from Flookburgh in 1984 (which by now was challenging* The Mikado *as the most produced show in Furness.) The Barrow Society however did achieve something*

of a coup when it obtained permission to mount Jesus Christ, Superstar *in 1984 – the first production in the area by an amateur company. They then followed this up in 1988 with another step into ambitious territory with Sondheim's blood-fest* Sweeney Todd.

Then as the 1980s turned into the 1990s, although there was the explosion of interest in musical theatre in America, the steady march of the Lloyd Webber machine and the overall boost to the scene there afforded by Disney dollars, local amateur theatre could only look on with envy, and hope that their turn would come. Meantime they could at least benefit from the excitement that was being generated. They may have again had to fall back on tried and tested shows for the most part, with occasional 'compilation' or 'greatest hits' shows thrown in, but that didn't mean there wasn't some effort being made to keep pace with modern developments. Then again, such efforts weren't always appreciated. When Ulverston chose La Cage aux Folles *for example as their production show for 1992, they had no idea of the outrage it would cause – Ulverston sensibilities were apparently not yet ready for the sight of two gay men singing a love ballad to each other. Undaunted they came back with a vengeance and, between 1993 and 1999, the Ulverston Society managed to put on two shows each year.*

Otherwise, for all the local Societies, there was the usual highs and lows with the perennial problems of finance, and how to achieve a happy balance between familiarity and freshness in the choice of shows. For the Barrow groups at least the usual anxieties about a suitable and reliable performance venue were finally put to rest with the opening of 'Forum 28' in 1990.

David Marcus had also by now really got into his stride and was proving to be a major force in the development of local musical theatre. Perhaps aware of the increasing emphasis on visual effects and spectacle, he spearheaded a revival of The

> **16 — EVENING MAIL, THURSDAY, AUGUST 16, 1990**
>
> VISITORS to the Festival of Furness Abbey which starts on Monday could be rubbing shoulders with continentals. The Box Office for Jesus Christ Superstar and the all-star events, reports enquiries from as far away as the continent. By DEBORAH KERMODE
>
> ## They will come in their hundreds from all parts of the country
>
> Coaches have booked in Devon and Norfolk; hundreds are coming from London and Middlesex, and some events are already sold out.
>
> The most popular 'celebrity' nights have proved to be the Hallé Orchestra on September 8 and Ronnie Scott Quintet/Humphrey Lyttelton line-up with Helen Shapiro on the 4.
>
> Pasadena Roof Orchestra on Sunday, August 26, has also proved popular.
>
> Some performances of Jesus Christ Superstar are almost fully booked, despite extra seating being arranged for the last week.
>
> Festival of Furness Abbey 1990 was the brainchild of director David Marcus, following the success of the Furness Mystery Plays two years ago.

Furness Abbey Mystery Plays in 1988, and then in 1990 created The Festival of Furness Abbey, an ambitious outdoor event which included performances of Jesus Christ Superstar *by a mixture of local and professional players.*

2000-PRESENT

From the year 2000 to the present day it is perhaps possible to group the musicals either newly produced or currently running (whether in New York or London) into three groups: the revivals (*Guys and Dolls, Gypsy, The King and I, Chicago*), the mega-musicals (*The Lion King, Les Miserables, The Phantom of the Opera, Wicked*), and the newbies (*Hairspray, Matilda, The Book of Mormon, Hamilton*). A further sub-division of the newly-produced is the so-called 'Jukebox Musical', a show with a minimal plot contrived to fit a collection of the hit songs of one particular artist or group. (e.g. the music of Carole King is celebrated in *Beautiful*, The Kinks in *Sunny Afternoon,* Abba in *Mamma Mia!,* The Four Seasons in *The Jersey Boys,* and Queen in *We Will Rock You*).

As well as a nostalgic nod to the past the popularity of the **revivals** also demonstrates, at least in part, a reaction to the horrors of the 9/11 terrorist attack on New York. Familiarity and a wish for happier times are always welcome in times of great upheaval. On this basis it is perhaps no surprise that the newer musicals of this time were lighter, feel-good shows. *Hairspray* for example first appeared in 2002, a show based on the musical comedy and escapism of old. *The Full Monty* had already appeared in 2000, and then came a masterful offering from Mel Brooks in 2001 – *The Producers*. It was simultaneously both a satire on Broadway and a love letter as it harked back to a silly and irreverent vision of 'how things used to be done.' **Mega-musicals** perhaps need no further comment, but both the **new productions**, and the Jukebox musicals are said to be set more as a tourist attraction than an outlet for the creativity and innovations of previous times. It almost doesn't matter who the performers are – it's the production itself that is now the star. According to figures quoted by Kenrick in his book *Musical Theatre: a history* (2008) 60% of those who currently attend Broadway shows are tourists, 17% are New Yorkers, and 23% are sub-urbanites. There is no reason to believe it is any different in London. Staging a new show is now no small matter, with the necessary budget in America said to be in the region of $14 million. It is no wonder that corporate sponsors now dominate the scene.

The 'big bucks' which were financing such highly advanced and ambitious production values and spectacle in London and America were sadly not available on the local scene (although David Marcus' productions at Furness Abbey were a bold attempt). But where financial resources may have been lacking there was certainly no shortage of enthusiasm, talent, energy and commitment. All the local societies we will shortly examine have succeeded in putting on annual shows of consistent quality, judging by the many positive reviews I have read. And there is certainly no lack of daring and ambition, with complex shows like Sweeney Todd *and* Les Miserables *making first appearances in 1988 and 2005 respectively. In fact, when looked at together, the Societies' production lists from 2000 onwards make up an extremely rich and varied programme, literally catering for all tastes. There are inevitably occasional struggles to find an audience and, for some societies, particular difficulties in recruiting. Young people proved to be a problem for a while though the rise and rise of Walney Juniors and Youth Theatre groups seems to be solving this one by inspiring and training up a new generation to take the place of the old stagers.*

I hope, in reviewing the developments in local musical theatre that I have not given an impression of competition between the various societies. That's not to say that there never was such a thing as some friendly rivalry is almost inevitable. There have been 'moments' of difficulty, as you will discover shortly, but my over-riding impression is that all local societies currently operate in a spirit of mutual cooperation, with much cross-pollination, much sharing of ideas and resources, and in a culture where performers feel free to move from one society to another and back again. On the other hand, each society has its own individual character, its own history, highlights and achievements. Some of these have already been alluded to, but now its time to give each society its own space so that their activities over the decades can be looked at in much more detail.

ACT TWO
Thank You for the Music

A590 Theatre Group

fyt **Furness Youth Theatre**
www.furnessyouththeatre.com

ABBEY MUSICAL SOCIETY

Walney Musical Theatre Company

Walney Junior Amateur Operatic Society
(Affiliated to the National Operatic and Dramatic Association)

Ulverston Amateur Operatic Society

Barrow Operatic & Dramatic Society
BODS

Flookburgh and District Amateur Operatic Society

GRANGE and DISTRICT AMATEUR OPERATIC SOCIETY

ULVERSTON PANTOMIME SOCIETY

Barrow Savoyards

CAST THEATRE COMPANY

2

ULVERSTON AMATEUR
OPERATIC SOCIETY (Founded 1907)

As we explore the history of local Societies in detail it seems logical to take a chronological approach. In this the Ulverston Amateur Operatic Society, formed in 1907, pips Barrow's official birthday of 1910 by a few years. It is true however that one or two groups had got going in Barrow before 1907 but as they were short-lived they don't really merit a full chapter, so we will consider their story when we get on to the Barrow Society itself. So it is Ulverston's debut performance of *The Mikado* in 1908, the year following the Society's inauguration, which accords it the honour of being the oldest amateur operatic society in the district still in existence.

As far as Ulverston is concerned, it has always been a town to embrace music, dance and drama. From the concerts staged at the old Theatre Royal on Theatre Street (built as far back as 1801) to the modern-day International Music Festival, musical appreciation has long been at the heart of the town. A predisposition for song has been satisfied through the years by a thriving Choral Society, a Male Voice Choir, and lately by a group known as the Ghyll Singers. As for dance, a 'Monster Whist Drive and Dance', the forerunner of very many future dance events to be organised at the Coronation Hall, was one of the first events to be offered when the Hall opened its doors in 1918. And today the majority of the groups taking part in the annual Ulverston Carnival Parade are dance troupes. And finally, a local drama group The Ulverston Outsiders, regularly stage drama productions, again at the Coronation Hall, as they have done since their formation in 1936.

Having mentioned the Outsiders, although my focus is on musical theatre, it is worth noting that this group has had occasional forays into this genre over the years. Its back catalogue of drama productions is very impressive but I have found at least 5 occasions when they demonstrated their ability to not just act, but to dance and sing at the same time. The productions in question are: *Toad of Toad Hall* (1955), *Lock Up Your Daughters* (1972), *Cabaret* (1983), *Carousel* (1985), and *Blood Brothers* (2007). There is of course a major crossover between drama and musical theatre anyway, and many local performers are adept in both arenas. You will hear more about some of them as we proceed.

The up and downs of the early years

Against this background the formation of an amateur operatic society was inevitable and, as is the case with every such society formed at the start of the 20th century, it was also inevitable that its first production would be a Gilbert and Sullivan operetta. Yes, it was *The Mikado*, which was performed at the Victoria Hall in Mill Street (now the Emmanuel Christian Centre) in 1908. Following *The Mikado* the Society then moved to the Drill Hall for their next production of *The Gondoliers* in 1908, and by the outbreak of the Great War in 1914 they had produced 5 more successful light operas. The last of these was the now forgotten *Haddon Hall*, which did have music by Arthur Sullivan, but it had been written with a new collaborator Sydney Grundy, after he and W S Gilbert had parted company.

Haddon Hall played to packed houses and was judged to be 'a great success' by the *North West Daily Mail*, and 'greatly enhanced the local reputation of the Society earned by

its previous productions.' The 'Coach and Manageress' was the redoubtable Mme. Margaret Forbes-Wilson (pictured left), "late of the D'Oyly Carte Opera Company", as she always liked to be billed. She is said to have directed productions 'with a rigid firmness of purpose' but was always popular and in great demand. When the Great War was over she produced and directed more shows for the Ulverston Society, as well as for societies in Whitehaven, Workington, Maryport and Cockermouth.

One cast member in *Haddon Hall* is also of note, Mr Thomas Rawsthorn, as he was to play an important part in the work of both Ulverston's and many other local Operatic

Societies post-war both as actor and producer. He had embarked upon a stage career at an early age, and in his youth was initially a member of a celebrated drama company of the age, the Fox Stock Company. He then decided to study all branches of stage work with a view to becoming a vocal coach and producer, and for a time was associated with George Edwardes (of the famed Gaiety Theatre in London) and his schools of musical comedy. On arrival in Furness he immediately became involved with local Societies and, like Mrs Forbes-Wilson, eventually produced shows for Societies all over the Furness area. By day he ran a successful tea shop (not a cheap commodity at this time) in King Street, Ulverston. Temperamentally he was, in contrast to Mme. Forbes-Wilson, known for the quiet, kindly approach he took towards the task of production, demonstrating rather than demanding of his players what he required. Ronald Metcalfe – actor, singer, producer, and future Arts correspondent for the local press - described him as 'one of the greatest ... a producer and a gentleman.'

The Great War necessarily brought productions to a halt – until April, 1918. Although the War had not officially ended then, the impetus for a new production came from the newly-built Coronation Hall. The story of the building of the Hall is recorded in my book *100 Years of the Coronation Hall,* so I will not repeat it here, save to say that it was on the initiative of local musician and choirmaster Mr Edmund Telfer that a proposal was put forward to stage a show, partly to bring the Hall into use but also to help fund the purchase of a Fire Safety Curtain. From that moment on, the Coronation Hall was to become the Ulverston Operatic Society's permanent home providing a sense of stability and belonging, factors which have been of great significance for the Society's progress over the years.

The Mikado – what else? – was the chosen show for the Society's revival in 1918. A few minor events had already taken place at the Coronation Hall but the Ulverston Society's 1918 *Mikado,* as well as having the distinction of being the Society's very first production 10 years earlier, also holds the distinction of being the first fully-staged production to be presented at the Coronation Hall. The Society officials probably hoped that the novelty of the brand new building would be enough to draw in the crowds but, as if anticipating a groan of indifference from the townsfolk the publicity material pleaded, "*The Mikado* is a show that gains rather than loses by repetition." In the event everyone rallied round – performers from Ulverston, Grange, Dalton and Barrow all took part, the two leads from the 1908 production (Mr H Eden Smith and Miss Marjorie Dempster) reprised their roles, Mr R Nott, the Art Master from the Grammar School marshalled his students to provide the scenery (aided by the Coronation Hall's renowned architect Mr Dean Brundrit), Edmund Telfer wielded the baton, and Mrs Forbes-Wilson pulled everything together. The local paper hailed it 'an unqualified musical and dramatic success', and the Ulverston Society was once again back in business. It has remained so ever since. The aims were subsequently stated clearly in the Barrow and District Yearbook: *to develop and foster a taste for operatic music by the study of good operas and their adequate representation, to provide a source of intellectual and instructive amusement for its members and the public generally, but chiefly to assist deserving charities.*

For the next few years the productions returned to familiar territory, with Mr Telfer and Mrs Forbes-Wilson mainly in charge. In 1925 however things started to unravel somewhat when receipts for *The Rebel Maid* unexpectedly fell quite a bit short of expectations. For the following year the Committee then made the rather odd choice of staging *The Emerald Isle*, another Arthur Sullivan creation (this time with Basil Hood), but one that was not known as a universally popular piece. Sullivan had been unwell whilst working on it and presumably it even caused *him* to lose the will to live as he had passed away before the score was fully complete. The plotline, of attempts to re-educate an Irish patriot in the ways of the English, was also unappealing to many. Audience response was unenthusiastic, the show made a substantial loss, and clearly the previously proudly stated aims of the Society were not being met. The post-mortem at the Annual Meeting in

March 1926 argued that too little had been spent on advertising, scenery and costumes. Of course because of the poorer receipts for *The Rebel Maid* in the previous year the budget had been too low to permit this anyway, but perhaps also a bit of complacency had set in.

With their confidence weakened the Society retreated to safer ground with *Iolanthe* in 1927, and then to tried and tested popular operas (though new to the district) such as *The Quaker Girl* (1928), *A Chinese Honeymoon* (1930), and *The Belle of New York* (1931). Tom Rawsthorn had by this time taken over as Producer, and gradually audiences responded and the Society's balance sheet got firmly into the black again. In fact in the programme for *A Chinese Honeymoon* in 1930 they felt in good enough spirits to mount a competition with spectacular prizes: 1st prize was a 1931 Saloon Car, 2nd Prize was a suite of bedroom furniture and 3rd Prize was 10 Tons of coal! Which all sounds splendidly generous, until you get to the small print, which comprises a series of jokey conditions ending with: *It is a condition of entry that the above prizes will only be awarded*

provided we get them given. It was surely a sign of the Society's restored self-confidence.

Cast members from the 1928 production of The Quaker Girl

Pre-war Productions

The Society's productions in the 1930's were generally those that had proved successful both at home and in America in the early part of the century. Unless you were lucky enough to afford the odd trip to London, this was definitely an opportunity to see locally something new and different. The 1930 show *A Chinese Honeymoon* was packed even on the opening night – unusual as numbers generally grew as the run went on. Then *The Belle of New York* in 1931, said to be a show designed to 'showcase young women in lavish costumes', proved a clear hit, and in fact became one of the few shows to be revived 3 times in the Society's history (in 1953 and, unwisely as it transpires, in 1969). *Mr Cinders*, a London show only having its premiere in 1929, was then successfully staged in 1935. It is reputedly a challenging show which demands considerable versatility on the part of cast and chorus, but all went well and it pulled in the crowds. It also required new skills in terms of creativity with special effects – how about the illusion of an express train crossing the stage amid plumes of smoke?

Then, in 1936, they tried their luck with Florenz Ziegfeld's *Sally*, the show which had famously wowed American audiences in 1920. It had a similar effect in Barrow and was a runaway success – 'the principals and chorus were called again and again by the appreciative audience', says the *North West Daily Mail*. Following the final performance the Society's president Mr E L Hartley and the producer Tom Rawsthorn both made enraptured, congratulatory speeches. 'Stars may come and stars may go,' said Mr Hartley, 'but if only the public will continue their support of this Society, it will go on forever.' Such a plea for public support echoes down the ages of course, an issue as alive today as it ever was in 1936. Mr Rawsthorn meanwhile praised 'the boys and girls' of the cast, Mr V Dilks the Musical Director, and Jack Gelderd, the Stage Manager. 'The applause broke out with renewed fervour.'

The creative team for the majority of these early productions were: Tom Rawsthorn and Harry Yates (Producers), Mr V Dilks (Musical Director), and regular performers (among many others) were Harry Jarvis, Charles Chester, and Dorothy Fell. Cyril Braithwaite also made an early appearance, later to progress to chorus master, and to roles in many of the post-war British Legion pantomimes.

The Society was undoubtedly moving from strength to strength at this time which, given the high levels of unemployment and difficulties of the age, was quite an achievement. And then, yet again, another global conflict was to intervene and put a stop to everything. The 1939 planned production of *Rose Marie* was cancelled, and the Society did not perform again until 1947.

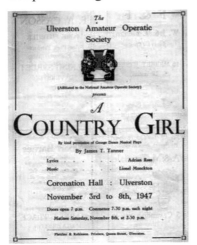

Post-war Producers and Performers

But marking a clear return to form in 1947 came *The Country Girl*. This was the first show to be produced by Robert Bowker, whose name will become more familiar as our story unfolds, and it also marked the debut of at least three men who were subsequently to have a long association with the Society – Leslie Thompson, Donald

Johnson and Donald Helme. On the other hand the show also featured the last performance of Tom Brown who had provided the comedy in many of the Society's pre-war productions. *The Country Girl* was a very popular production and heralded the start of something of another purple patch for the Society as its annual productions became a regular highlight of Ulverston life, and were always keenly anticipated.

Jessie Barbour   *Gene Anderton*

Jessie Barbour took over production duties in 1949, and continued until 1955 before handing over to Mr Gene Anderton. She again was an early starter on the stage, having first appeared as a 10-year old. She went on to study music, and performed in both London theatre and provincial repertory, before turning her hand to producing. In this regard she was involved with almost every local Operatic Society in the North, from Leeds to Newcastle. Her shows were always very successful. *Rose Marie* (1950) for example was hailed as 'the most spectacular show ever undertaken', and at the time set a record for the most advance bookings in the history of the Society. As for Gene Anderton he was a professional producer with an impressive background in theatre as both actor and director, chiefly in the London area. From 1955 he produced a total of 9 shows for Ulverston, until 1963 when he handed over to Joyce Warrington (1964-1966) from Morecambe, who also did a lot of work with the Flookburgh Society. The fact that they were all in demand perhaps gives some indication of the expertise they brought to Ulverston's productions at this time.

And as ever there were changes in personnel as loyal supporters retired and new blood took their place. In 1951 for example, Harry Jarvis, a Society member since the very early days, played his last acting role in *The New Moon*. He had first performed in 1920, and had subsequently appeared in principal roles in the majority of all subsequent productions. In 1959 he was appointed Society Chairman, succeeding another elder statesman Wilfred Randall, until illness finally forced him to retire. He passed away, a much-missed loyal 'trouper' in 1965. New blood appeared meanwhile in the shape of Joan Park (later to become Joan Eddevane) Brenda Burrow, Joan Teper, Victor Sharp, Fred Stowe, Elaine Parkinson (nee Wilson), and Ronald Metcalfe. All would become much valued members and regular performers for the Ulverston Society. Derek Jenkinson, now a regular member of the orchestra for several local productions, also popped up in the 1952 production of *Katinka* as a choirboy.

Joan Park made her debut as a dancer, also in 1952, in *Katinka* and took on her first principal role in 1957 in the Society's Golden Jubilee production *Love from Judy*. In the following year she took the lead in *The Quaker Girl* and then took second female lead in *The Arcadians* in 1959. Incidentally whilst this production would see the last comic performance of Charles Chester, a regular player since the late 1930's, it also saw the debut of a young Elaine Wilson (now Elaine

Parkinson) who was to make a significant mark herself in future years in local drama, musicals, and pantomime.

Charles Chester in his last comic role as Peter Doody in "The Arcadians"

Joan Park in the 1958 production of "The Quaker Girl"

Elaine had first joined Joan Bradley's dance classes at the tender age of three, and then 5 years later graduated to Joan Pattinson's song and dance troupe, The Nobody's Concert Party. (This was the group made up of youngsters up to the age of 14 or so, which had been first put together in 1948 to tour village halls, hospitals and community groups.) Elaine then joined the Ulverston Society and following her debut in *The Arcadians* in 1959, has since performed in many of their shows both as a chorus member and in leading roles. Her acting skills also impressed Ronald Metcalfe, another UAOS stalwart, who enrolled her in his amateur dramatics group The Furness

Drama Association. She appeared in many of their subsequent plays, winning a *North West Evening Mail* 'Oscar' in 1963 for her performance in *A Shot in the Dark*. And as further proof of her versatility she made her first appearance in pantomime in 1961, becoming one of the regular players before succeeding Bridget Turner as Producer in 1980, a role she fulfils to this day.

The 1950s and 1960s

Returning to the Ulverston Society of the 1950s, of course each show staged had its own special quality, but perhaps 2 or 3 are worth singling out mainly because, post-war, Ulverston is currently the only Society ever to have staged them. The afore-mentioned *Katinka* (1952) is one such, famous for its lavish costumes, its chorus of Cossacks, and a range of stage sets designed to represent Russia, Istanbul, and Vienna. *Chu Chin Chow* (1954) is another - first produced in London in 1916, it famously ran all the way through the Great War and beyond, notching up a total of 2,238 performances, a record which

stood for almost 50 years. Although a hugely popular show of its time Ulverston remains the only local group to have staged it. Perhaps it was the costliness of putting it on that was the deterrent. The Society spent £1,200, a prodigious sum in 1954, but the show demanded even more elegant scenery than *Katinka* had done, brilliant costumes, and creative choreography. With Leslie Thompson (left) in the title role and Brenda Burrow as leading lady the show attracted a rave review from 'Talisman' (aka Bob Strike) in the *Barrow News* – 'more than three hours of undiluted pleasure.'

Then finally, the 1956 show *Zip Goes a Million* is worth a mention. This had been produced in London chiefly as a vehicle for the popular comedian George Formby. When Ulverston decided to stage it, Beryl Formby sent her best wishes. 'What a pity we are not at home,' she said, 'otherwise we would have popped up to have a look at you.'

So by now it seemed as if the Society could do no wrong. Except it could. On the second night of *The Quaker Girl* in 1958 the stage manager, the chorus and orchestra were all thrown completely off kilter when one of the principals skipped over 10 pages of the libretto. Patricia Jewell, who was involved in the production, told me that, although at the time it felt very chaotic, somehow or other they managed to carry on and in the end everything passed off successfully. Then she added brightly, in the way of a seasoned professional, 'I don't think anyone noticed.'

Already well-known on the amateur scene Ron Eddevane (pictured right) played his first lead role with the Ulverston Society at this time. He had been nurtured in his stage career by his early association with St John's Church Youth Club when he appeared in plays, musicals and pantomimes they put on in the 1950's. He then joined their senior society (St John's Operatic Society) which was not only a popular  exponent of Gilbert & Sullivan operas for a period (see the Savoyards history) but also spawned several other performers who were to make their own mark on the amateur scene e.g. Harold and Florence Melville, and Bill Steel (see the Abbey Society history). For Ulverston Ron Eddevane first appeared in *The Vagabond King* (1961) and then in *Annie Get Your Gun* (1962). He performed many times subsequently, and also appeared in drama and pantomime. The Society was also to play a part in bringing him together with Joan Park (are you keeping up?) who he married in 1964. Remember she had played lead in *Love From Judy* in 1957.

Then through the 1960s the evidence suggests that the Ulverston Society was trying to cater for popular tastes with a choice of shows which reflected the post-war rise of American musical theatre. So from Broadway's Golden Age there came to Ulverston such shows as *Oklahoma*! (1960), *Annie Get Your Gun* (1962), *Showboat* (1963), and *South Pacific* (1966). It was a winning formula as, by the mid-1960s, according to Ronald Metcalfe writing in the *Evening Mail*, Ulverston had attained 'the happy position of being the strongest society in the area, both from a financial and playing point of view.' Certainly the aim of raising donations to local charities was now being consistently met. Mr Metcalfe's comment was a considerable compliment and quite an achievement since 4 other local Societies (Barrow, Walney, Abbey, and Flookburgh) had all appeared on the post-war scene, and there was the inevitable competition for audiences. *Bless the Bride* (1967) and *The New Moon* (1968) did particularly well, both produced by Ron Metcalfe, with notable performances from many familiar names such as Leslie Thompson, Wendy Jackson, Joan Teper, Marie Worrall, and Colin and Terry Leech. All were to feature in many later shows.

The choice for 1969 – *The Belle of New York* - was therefore questionable. The Society had already performed the show on two previous occasions and, although all the individual performances were highly praised, the show itself received press criticism for being 'dated, creaky and antiquated.' It was suggested that the Society had lost the sense of adventure it had once shown and was in danger of losing touch with its audience. Indeed, despite the usual popularity of the Ulverston shows, audience numbers were becoming more variable with considerable competition arising from the growing number of entertainment alternatives available, the productions of other local Societies, and the ever-increasing pull of stay-at-home television. To keep shows attractive, production values had to be enhanced which inevitably meant higher costs. And if this were not enough a wider range of entertainment was beginning to be offered in the Society's homeland, at the Coronation Hall. In this regard, there were two important developments to note. Firstly, following the late-60's demise of Her Majesty's Theatre in Barrow the Renaissance Trust, which had evolved from there as an arts promotion body, was to be responsible for promoting a wide range of events at the Coronation Hall, designed to cater for all tastes. And secondly, with the local government re-organisation of 1974, the new managers of the Hall, the South Lakeland District Council, declared their intention to bring it into more frequent use as a concert venue and conference centre. In short, audiences now had a great deal more choice of where to go and what to see.

New Shows for the 1970s

Perhaps the discontent surrounding *Belle* was a turning point as during the next decade there was certainly evidence of the Society making a more sustained attempt to meet the challenges of the day by again staging shows which were new to the area. *Half a Sixpence*, which had only premiered in London 5 years earlier, was staged in 1970 and its reception proved a triumphant contrast to the one *Belle* had received. It was Ronald Metcalfe's fourth production for Ulverston, ably assisted by Mary Lumb, described in the show's programme as 'one of the best choreographers in the North West.' The show was reviewed as 'bright, modern, breezy, and colourful with high praise being given to the principals Terry Leech ('a tour de force') and Wendy Jackson ('a natural'). Joan and Ron Eddevane also featured, as did Joan Teper and Les Wilde. A young man named Fred Hool also featured in his first principal role, having moved up from the chorus. He was to become a regular performer around the district, as was another player making her first appearance with the Society, Barbara Springthorpe. She had recently moved to the Furness area with her husband Bill, and both were to become regulars in future shows, with Barbara later graduating to the role of Producer. You will encounter them later in their work with other Societies, especially Abbey and the Barrow Savoyards.

Emporium owner Mr Shalford (played by Les Wilde) keeps the shop girls in check, played by Linda Newton, Hazel Fisher, Barbara Springthorpe and Sonia Sturgess

(Half a Sixpence, 1970)

Half a Sixpence was followed by two more shows new to the area, *Brigadoon* (1971) – which incidentally the Barrow Society had to abandon for reasons which will later become clear - and *Fiddler on the Roof* (1972), which saw Terry Leech again in the cast, this time accompanied by his two young daughters, Kim and Tracy. *Brigadoon* and *Fiddler* were both produced by Ron Metcalfe, though sadly they were to be his last and his sudden death early in 1973 was much mourned. He had produced all of Ulverston's shows for the last 6 years and, as has been noted, had been a major force as a performer, producer, supporter and, as arts correspondent for the *Barrow News* and *Evening Mail*, a promoter of amateur theatre in all its forms. So now is probably a good time to pause and say a word or two more about him.

Born on Walney Island, his career started early when, aged 11, he had appeared in a school musical called 'The Magic Key', which was produced by another prominent figure in the history of local amateur theatre, Charles Thompson (see the histories of the Abbey and the Flookburgh Societies.) At the age of 16, in 1931, he then had a brief association with the Barrow Society when he appeared in *The Marriage Market*, under the direction of the afore-mentioned popular local Producer, Tom Rawsthorn. Subsequently he embarked on a professional stage career as a singer, and toured extensively all around the UK. In 1935 he married a sister of George Formby, but sadly this marriage failed and he subsequently moved back to Barrow. Here he met an Ulverston girl, Bunty Thompson, who was to become his second wife, and together they had a son, Neil who would later follow in the family tradition and become a popular local performer in his own right. Meanwhile Ron and Bunty began to appear in many local drama productions and musicals, before they founded the Furness Drama Association, a kind of local repertory company which recruited actors from all the local societies and staged plays throughout the district.

As a talented actor and singer he also regularly appeared in musical productions, mainly for the Ulverston Society, and occasionally took on the role of Producer. In 1955 Ronald and several others became the first local performers to appear on the new and exciting ultra-modern form of entertainment, television. They were all taking part in the BBC inter-town talent show *Top Town* when Ulverston took on Stockton-on-Tees (and sadly lost). In short, he was a man clearly dedicated to the stage, and it wasn't long before the local press invited him to be their regular arts correspondent and theatre critic. His reviews and his weekly column 'Stage Spotlight' were to become regular features in the *Barrow News*. Although his sharp observations weren't always appreciated, his reviews were generally regarded as fair and constructive. As I have mentioned, when he died in 1973 his passing was recorded as a major loss, as he was without doubt an energetic promoter and rabid supporter of amateur theatre in all its forms throughout the Furness area.

In 1963 he persuaded the local press to instigate the *Barrow News* 'Oscars', "to serve as a permanent reminder of a portrayal or production that has been extremely well accomplished." He took pride in the fact that the *News* was "the only newspaper in the North West promoting such a tangible show of interest in live theatre." It was a well-timed move, which probably gave all the local societies and players a

boost of self-esteem when morale was low. Like their Hollywood counterparts the Oscars were gold statuettes, mounted on a small plinth (pictured left), and were awarded at a special annual ceremony, hosted by the *Barrow News*. The system persisted for many subsequent years, being managed after Ron Metcalfe's death by Bob Bowker, his successor. Eventually they became superseded by the annual nominations and awards presented by NODA.

Other losses were also keenly felt at this time as Albert Higgins, Musical Director for more than a dozen previous years had died 3 years earlier in 1970. Mr H Earnshaw, Chair of the Society paid the following tribute, 'His quiet efficiency proved him to be a master of his craft and his complete imperturbability instilled the utmost confidence in those who worked with him.' Also lost were two members who had worked hard for the Society for many years both backstage and front of house, Norman Park (father of Joan Park) and Anne Scrogham. Of course the early 70's were tough all round, being chiefly remembered as a period of nationwide economic decline and industrial unrest. In February 1972, because of the famous '3-day working week' and associated power cuts, preparations for *Fiddler on the Roof* were hit when all rehearsals were "cancelled until further notice." There was also a shortage of male recruits, not an unfamiliar problem for amateur societies, but perhaps a reflection of the mood of pessimism and disillusionment sadly prevalent at this time. In the event *Fiddler* went ahead as scheduled, its theme of social change proving very pertinent. Musical productions designed to cheer followed – *White Horse Inn* (1973), *No No Nanette* (1974) and, always a popular choice *Rio Rita* (1976) - all playing their part in raising morale.

The 1977 production of *Carousel* saw Joan Eddevane (nee Park) taking over the mantle of Producer, already as we know a popular actress and singer from many previous shows. With a career dating from the mid-50's she had established herself as a talented and versatile performer in a range of roles from the sweet and demure (*The Quaker Girl* in 1958), to the ebullient and more raucous Ethel Merman-type delivery in *Annie Get Your Gun* in 1962. In 1964-65 Ronald Metcalfe awarded her his 'Oscar' for her role as Kathie in *The Student Prince*, the same year as she married Ron Eddevane. As for *Carousel*, Bob Bowker, who had now succeeded Ronald Metcalfe as *Evening Mail* correspondent, rated the show highly and noted 'a happy progressive atmosphere' and 'improved standard of dance routines' under Joan's guidance. It went on to win the Ronald Metcalfe Memorial Trophy for the year's best local show. Joan herself went on to produce a further string of shows which included *Finian's Rainbow* (1978), *My Fair Lady* (1979) and *Oklahoma!* (1980). Raymond McIlroy had now taken over as Musical Director, assisted by the long-serving Harry Garstang as accompanist. Mr Garstang in fact served as the Society accompanist for more than 20 years before he passed away in 1984.

New Faces and Further Progress

The new decade brought new faces and new ideas. Among these on the production side were Shirley Britton (Producer), Doreen Dunlop (Musical Director), Elizabeth Waller (Accompanist) and Choreographers Helen Corkhill and Jean Lancaster.

Shirley Britton had appeared on stage many times and taught drama at Summer Schools run by Cumbria County Council alongside Gerald McNally. In the 1980s, for Ulverston she directed *Camelot* (1985) which featured Ron Metcalfe's son Neil as Arthur, and which fittingly won the Ronald

Metcalfe Memorial Trophy that year, and *Kiss Me Kate* (1986) at which Cyril Braithwaite and his wife Joyce were presented with 50-year long service awards. Through her collaboration with Gerald McNally she then decamped to Newcastle to take up a teaching post at the Newcastle School of Performing Arts where such budding Geordie stars as Ant & Dec and Ross Noble passed through her hands. When she returned to Furness in the late 1990s she immediately became involved with local societies once more directing shows for the Barrow Society, Ulverston Outsiders, and Walney Juniors. Then, coming full circle, she again produced *Kiss Me Kate* for Ulverston in 2002.

Doreen Dunlop served as Musical Director for most of the Ulverston Society's shows throughout the 1980s, and into 1990s. Born in Kendal she trod the boards herself at the tender age of four, and then subsequently trained in Manchester where she studied the violin, the art of conducting and voice production. She later played with the National Youth Orchestra, the BBC Northern Orchestra, and then the Hallé Orchestra. There is no doubt that the local scene has benefited greatly from her talents and experience as, in addition to Ulverston, she has orchestrated the music for the productions of almost every local group. She is known affectionately as 'the sparkly lady at the front' with her glittery baton and an outfit to match.

Elizabeth Waller, the accompanist for more than 30 shows, came to Barrow in 1983 and, as an accomplished musician, worked with the Walney Operatic Society as well as Ulverston's. She was also a key contributor to the Barrow Savoyards' productions for more than 15 years before, sadly, she passed away in 2001.

In 1986 the Society suffered the loss of one of its staunch supporters and contributors Mr Leslie Thompson. A member since 1947, he had played several principal roles and served as Vice-Chairman for many years before becoming the Society's President in 1970. Before coming to Ulverston he had also been involved with Societies in Kendal, Blackpool, and Burnley and had previously been honoured for his long years of service to the amateur stage by the *Barrow News*.

But, as mentioned there were new faces and, despite the losses, there was a sense of renewed vigour within the Society. Certainly energy levels seemed to be at an all-time high in this period as, between 1985 and 1999, the Ulverston Society managed to stage two shows a year – one in spring and another in autumn. Given the challenges of the times in terms of audience choices, this must be recorded as a considerable achievement, requiring as it does more or less year-round involvement by all members whether on stage or not. And in order to sustain audience interest there was an attempt to cater for as wide a range of tastes as possible by bringing to the stage a mixture of the traditional and the familiar with shows that were more adventurous. As an amateur operatic society Ulverston was to prove as willing as any other to take risks with many new shows which were 'firsts' for the district's amateur scene.

Even amongst the traditional choices there were shows which the Society had not previously staged – for example, *Guys and Dolls* (1987), *The King and I* (1988), and *Oliver* (1989). Shows which might be described as adventurous were more a feature of the 1990s, although some which were staged in the 1980s possibly fall into this category e.g. *Camelot* (1985) *The Merry Widow* (1988) and *Die Fledermaus* (1989). The biggest risk however came in the spring of 1992 when the Society announced its decision to stage *La Cage aux Folles*, a musical about a middle-aged gay couple. It was perhaps unfortunate timing as the global panic about AIDS was only just subsiding, and fears were soon voiced that the show might corrupt, deprave or offend the sensibilities of the Ulverston audience. The issue went before the South Lakes Council who, having consulted both Section 28 of the Local Government Act and Section 2 of the Theatres Act, decided censorship was not warranted and gave the show the go ahead. But the damage had been done and people took fright and stayed away. Helped by a very positive press review, numbers picked up slowly as word got round that the show was actually lively, funny and quite inoffensive, but the overall response was poor and disappointing.

Russell Palmer (Georges) & Allan Lewis (Albin)
in the 1992 production of La Cage aux Folles

Perhaps by way of apology, the choice for the autumn production was Cole Porter's *High Society*, a good, old-fashioned traditional musical, although still one that was new to the district. It was the first show to be produced by Ulverston regular Barbara Springthorpe, with Lindsey Jackson taking the leading role of Tracy Lord and Allan Lewis as Dexter Haven. Long service awards were also presented at this time to several members including Gordon Crayston (30 years), and Leslie and Pat Jewell (40 years). Gordon will turn up again later in our story since his expertise with performance lighting has been, and still is, a feature of every amateur production in the district. In another life however he had also featured as a regular performer in some productions, especially during the 1970's. For the Abbey Society for example, he

Gordon Crayston, Marie Allmark (nee Worrall) & Colin Smith in a scene from the Abbey production of The Merry Widow, 1978

appeared in (among others) *The Vagabond King* (1973) *The New Moon* (1975) and *The Merry Widow* (1978). Leslie Jewell had first joined the society in 1952 with his then girlfriend, and later wife, Pat. Together they played a significant part in the Society's growth and development both on stage and, in later years, at front of house.

The treading of safer ground continued for the next few years with more playful, innocent pieces such as *The Wizard of Oz* and *Annie*, both staged in 1993. If this was an implicit appeal to a younger audience it paid dividends as, in preparing for the

1994 production of *The Music Man* over 70 young hopefuls turned up to audition for 12 places. The show was another ambitious effort with both challenging staging, and musical numbers. Barbara Springthorpe even had to launch an appeal for the loan of brass or woodwind instruments to be used as props in the famous marching band sequence. There was a particular need for a golden cornet which had a special significance in the script. Generous support was forthcoming from all quarters, with Ian Whiteley of Ulverston Outsiders eventually providing the essential golden instrument. The show was very successful although its requirements had added to the Committee's concerns about production costs which were rising all the time, and doubt was expressed about the Society's ability to continue with an output of two shows per year. As things turned out, with new sponsors and energetic fund-raising events, there was enough support and goodwill to allow the Society to carry on producing two shows a year until 1999. By then production costs had risen to £15,000+ for a week's run. Still two shows a year for 15 years was pretty good going.

Despite this, the intention remained to present as much novelty as possible. In 1995 the Society staged *Calamity Jane* which, perhaps surprisingly, it had not done before. The production team comprised the well-established quartet of Barbara Springthorpe, Doreen Dunlop, Jean Lancaster and Liz Waller. Kerry Willison-Parry played Jane, supported by such regulars as Russ Palmer, Lindsey Jackson, Bill Springthorpe and Elaine Parkinson. Then in 1996 came *Singin' in the Rain,* a brave venture not yet attempted by any local amateur group, not least because of its technically demanding rain effects, among other things. Don Johnson, a veteran performer since 1947 was even talked out of his retirement to play the policeman in the famous rain-soaked song and dance number. A specialist firm from Suffolk was drafted in to manage the

Bob Needham, Terry Leech, Bill & Barbara Springthorpe in a scene from
Singin' in the Rain, 1996

rainfall and, for the first time, the production team made use of filmed inserts. These had been filmed at Stone Cross Mansion, the former home of Myles Kennedy, one of the founding fathers of the Society's own 'home', the Coronation Hall. The show was a triumph and a real coup for Ulverston.

The following year Don Johnson was still not allowed to rest but was persuaded to take part in the Society's spring production of *Brigadoon* (1997). With Russ Palmer in charge it went on to present *The Hunchback of Notre Dame* in the autumn, featuring the new young talent of Michelle Larcombe as Esmeralda, a future regular presence in both local theatre and, nationwide, in great demand as a soloist. As a point of interest, another cast member Dave Diggle, was to meet his future wife Nicky during this production.

Both *The Hunchback of Notre Dame* and *Gentlemen Prefer Blondes,* which followed in 1998, were also shows which were new to the district's amateur scene and which explored new ground. Sue Little, who had made her debut with the Society 20 years earlier, played the Marilyn Monroe role (from the 1953 movie) Lorelei Lee.

Given the precarious nature of the changing times, a particularly courageous choice for the autumn of 1998 was *Children of Eden*, a lesser known musical written by Stephen Schwartz (of *Godspell* and *Pippin* fame) which portrayed the first 9 books of Genesis. The cast was a nice mix of both fresh and familiar faces such as Russ Palmer, Lindsey Jackson, Tracy Jackson (nee Leech), John Brice, and Michelle Larcombe, together with a dozen or so children, aged from 4 to 13, who played Noah's animals, a butterfly and two elephants - in wellies, of course. As well as the costumes and characterisations, a lot of attention was paid to creating imaginative sets which all added to the spectacle of movement and colour in the show which was much praised. The sets were created by a team led by Ken Hindle who, by this time had been with the Society for several years and had appeared in many shows. He had been the set coordinator for several previous shows and, when not performing, building sets, or designing programmes, he found time to appear as the Dame in the Pantomime Society's annual shows. He became Chair of the Society in 2000.

A new century

As fresh faces appear so the world turns and a new century dawns. The Society kicked off with *Oliver*, produced by another long-standing member, Brenda Sweeting (later to be Brenda Hindle). One hundred children auditioned for the coveted title role which finally went to 13-year old Daniel Serra. Russ Palmer played Bill Sikes with Steve Freeland as

Fagin, a role he was to repeat for the Barrow Society's production in 2005.

Consider Yourself – One of Us. Oliver, 2000

In 2003 Brenda Hindle, now Ken's wife, took over as Producer/Artistic Director for the next series of shows. She had been an active Society member for many years, having helped backstage in almost every aspect of production – make-up, wardrobe, props, publicity, fund-raising etc. Among her successes were *Guys and Dolls* (2003), *The Secret Garden* (2004), *Goodnight Mr Tom* (2006), and *Meet Me in St Louis* (2007) all being notable for being more firsts, not only for Ulverston, but for the district's amateur scene. Other points of interest are that both *Guys and Dolls* and *The Secret Garden* featured local performer Yvonne Patterson, together with her two children Daniel and Vicky Serra, who have now both advanced to the professional stage.

Goodnight Mr Tom (2006) was particularly ambitious as there was no standard set available, and the music was totally unknown. Although neither challenge was especially new for the Society the subject matter was a lot more weighty than usual, with a wartime theme, evacuees, mental illness and child abuse all stretching the acting talents of the 60 strong cast. Veteran performer Allan Lewis played the title role, with Ben Yorke as the troubled young evacuee Will Beech who, grudgingly at first, 'Mr Tom' takes in. The gamble paid off as the show drew in large audiences during its run.

The 2007 production *Meet Me in St Louis* was important for another reason. It was the Society's centenary production. The story centres on the life and loves of a turn-of-the-century American family as they anticipate the wonders of the 1904 World's Fair. Naturally it featured many performers who had appeared in several previous productions and, with a

Grandpa Prophater (Bill Springthorpe) with Agnes (Kim Little) and Tootie (Clarissa Isaacs)

Meet Me in St Louis, 2007

story centering on family life, it was nice that the cast also included members from the same Ulverston family. Terry Leech, a stalwart since the 1960's, appeared with his daughter Tracy, also a regular performer since her debut as a small child back in 1972, whilst Terry's wife Rita continued to beaver away backstage, especially in the wardrobe department, as she had done since the 1960's! The show itself was a shrewd choice, having the desired effect of transporting the audience back in time 100 years. Many aspects of the Society's history had also been revived a few months earlier with a reunion cabaret and buffet evening. Old programmes, photographs and reviews of past shows were on display as the group of specially invited guests shared anecdotes and reminisced.

In the years following, renewed energy was as ever provided by new faces, often inspired to perform by following in family footsteps. Among these new rising stars were Ben Lewis and Connor O'Hara, Coby Barker, Demi Cole and Mathilda Kenny who all appeared in the shows produced from 2008 onwards. The problem of course, and one which every Society has to bear, is that these youngsters are inclined to move on to college or University, leaving hard-to-fill gaps behind. And of course there is the inevitable loss of older members. A particularly sad loss in 2009 was the death of Leslie Jewell.

As for the more recent shows, although 100 years old, the Society has been keen to demonstrate that it is still a vibrant force. *Scrooge*, the modern musical version of *A Christmas Carol* was chosen for 2008, followed by a super-modern show for 2009, *When It Rains*. This was a musical play which aimed to take the lid off the 'am-dram' world by focussing on the trials and tribulations of the fictional Pharaohs Amateur Dramatic Group. It is described as 'a luvvie story' and depicts all the usual backstage squabbles, petty rivalries, and ego battles that are apparently a standard part of the territory in the am-dram world. (Really? Sad to say, in my research for this book no-one told me about this. So I can only conclude that *When It Rains* portrays an exaggerated made-up world, far removed from the real world of am-dram, where the rivalries, airs and graces, and backstage sniping are contrived and engineered entirely for comic effect. I'm sure that's the case.)

The kudos for Ulverston was that it was one of a very select set of amateur groups to put on this show, as well as the fact that the show's creators, David Shannon and Marc Folan, came to see Ulverston's production for themselves. In keeping with the *Barrow News* review they were very pleased with what they saw.

The Ulverston Society was however now caught up in the same dilemma as other local groups. What was best to pitch to an audience – a well-known musical of old, or a modern, untried production? *Scrooge* (2008) and *When It Rains* (2009) fell into the latter category but, although novel and fresh, had attracted smaller audiences than usual. Would a traditional one be more attractive, or would it be dismissed for being old-school and out of fashion? It was a difficult choice, but eventually the decisions were to present *The King and I* in 2010 and *Camelot* in 2011. Both productions bore the usual features of a strong cast and high production values, and equally benefitted from a stable and consistent production team. This consisted of the all-female team of Brenda Hindle, Doreen Dunlop, Jean Lancaster, and Elizabeth Greaves, all highly experienced.

As we know however the survival of a Society also depends on its ability to attract new talent, and its production choices for 2012 and 2013 reflect this with shows that are essentially built around a younger cast – namely, *Annie* and *Whistle Down the Wind*. Mathilda Kenny successfully carried off the part of Annie, supported by almost 20 young 'orphans', two of whom were later to feature in *Whistle Down the Wind's* lead roles. There was then a sort of compromise in 2014 with a staging of the ever reliable *Fiddler on the Roof,* which featured a creative mix of both newcomers and the more experienced. Russ Palmer played Tevye, with Allan Lewis as Lazar Wolf, the embodiments of tradition, with the spirit of youth and change represented by Tevye's daughters played by Hannah

Mitchell, Ella Boardman, and Frances Harley. The 'Fiddler' was played by none other than Leah Greaves, the daughter of stalwart Society member Elizabeth Greaves. In fact sisters Leah and Phoebe Greaves both featured in the cast, having already appeared in several previous productions both within the district's youth theatres and the Ulverston Pantomime Society. When not on stage, Leah can usually be found playing violin in the orchestra pit. Phoebe meanwhile is happier on stage, taking a main character part in the 2015 production, *42nd Street*, and is due to appear in the 2016 show, *The Wizard of Oz*.

In Summary…

Having been a constant presence in the town for more than 100 years Ulverston Amateur Operatic Society is as much a part of Ulverston as the St John Barrow Monument. I might also include the Coronation Hall in this since they both have their origins at the start of the last century and, being the Society's home base, they are inextricably linked. It has of course been an advantage to have such a reliable venue, although equally may have occasionally placed limits on the Society's production choices. Even so its development over the years has been prudently managed in that the greater part of its resources, from artistic direction to stage management, set design and front of house services, have all come from in-house sources. The Society has also demonstrated a talent for innovation, whether it be the use of 'side stages' to make more efficient use of their performing space, the building of a complete Noah's Ark for *Children of Eden*, or the addition of cochineal to a borrowed fountain to double as pink champagne in *Die Fledermaus*! The verdict of one past Chair of the Society speaks for itself: 'Never before,' he says, 'have I come across such whole-hearted cooperation from all sections of the Society or such enthusiastic teamwork.' As can be seen, the Ulverston Society has a proud history, having treated audiences to an eclectic mix of musical entertainments, both classical and modern, scoring several 'firsts' along the way.

The key to survival, as Charles Darwin pointed out to us long ago, is of course evolution, a willingness to adapt and move with changing times. It is strange to think that, early in its history, the Society was gently mocked as the parochial 'country cousin' of more serious-minded musical groups, characterised by a sort of casual heartiness. I couldn't say if this was ever the case but, if it was, how things changed.

During the centenary celebrations none other than Lord Andrew Lloyd-Webber sent the Society his personal congratulations: 'I wish you every success for the future,' he said, 'and trust that the Ulverston Society continues to flourish for many years to come.' Up to this point the Society had not produced any of his shows, but this was to change in 2013 when the Society secured permission to stage *Whistle Down the Wind*. With a chorus of 14 children and 3 others playing leading roles it was, as already noted, perhaps a sign that a new generation was taking over. And sure enough, as if it were planned, the 2014 show forecast that such a change was coming with *Fiddler on the Roof*, the musical with the principal theme of a new order taking over from old traditions. I like to think that, symbolically, its theme was heralding a new chapter for the Ulverston Society with the old traditions giving way to something new. The energy unleashed in the 2015 production *42nd Street* with its novel dynamic dance numbers was perhaps the first sign of new things to come. Certainly the story told by this musical could be interpreted as driving the message home. After all, it depicts a director creating a hit show in uncertain times. And what is the underlying message? That, no matter what, the show must go on.

3

BARROW OPERATIC AND DRAMATIC SOCIETY (Founded 1910)

Origins

At the end of the 19th century, as an industrial working-class town, it would be easy to assume that the people of Barrow-in-Furness had little time for the arts. Serious drama and operatic singing in particular were thought of as middle-class pastimes, so presumably the uncultured masses of Barrow were happily being entertained down at the Music Hall. Not so! As early as 1877, with a population of only around 35,000, a few members of the Furness Railway Company got together to form 'The Furness Railway Company Amateur Dramatic Society.' It operated for several years in a fairly casual sort of way, until 1892 when it re-invented itself as 'The Furness Dramatic and Operatic Society'. The Gilbert and Sullivan operas were by now well known and, having been newly licensed for amateur performers, and with a newly-built Town Hall (1887) as a suitable venue, there were sufficient conditions for this Furness Society to get going more formally. By 1896 they had successfully produced such pieces as *The Yeomen of the Guard*, *The Mikado*, and *The Gondoliers*. They all went down very well and it is reported that *The Gondoliers* actually ran for 8 performances and raised a massive profit of £487-14s-2d (massive as it staggers in at around £50,000 at today's value) which was distributed among various local charities. (As mentioned in Part 1, it was this group who, in 1899, had come to the rescue of the Morecambe Society and inspired the formation of the modern association of amateur groups known as NODA).

The 'leading mainstay and backbone of the Society' (as he was described in the *North West Daily Mail*) was one W S Whitworth, who had first become involved in 1881, and operated as Producer and Stage Manager. He was still in charge when the Society staged its final performance in 1903 when it was subsequently disbanded, probably because of a lack of support arising from a severe downturn in Barrow's economic fortunes (although the death of Mr Whitworth may also have had something to do with it.) Coincidentally the Society's swansong was also the final collaboration of Gilbert and Sullivan – a piece entitled *The Grand Duke,* in which Mr Charles Halle Pass took a leading role and Mr Alfred Pass was Musical Director. As already noted, the Pass family became well known in the town as the owners of Pass's Music Shop on Duke Street, one of the two main music shops in Barrow. (As a matter of interest I bought my very first record there: *I Love You Baby* by Paul Anka) The other was Kelly's of Dalton Road, established by another local musician/violinist, Mr William Kelly who often featured in local Society orchestras. (I bought my first guitar there).

There was then a lull, and it was not until 1910, in a context of increasing optimism, that the artistic community once again dared to express itself. A band of enthusiasts led by Mr Walter Iliffe, started things off, and soon, with additional support forthcoming, and local dignitary Sir Alfred Barrow appointed as its first Chairman, the Barrow Amateur Operatic Society was re-born. With a remarkable display of self-confidence the Society booked the Royalty Theatre (located on the corner of Cavendish Street and Dalkeith Street) for a week-long run of *The Yeomen of the Guard*, and the curtain went up on opening night on Monday, 24th April, 1911. Principal players were Tom Brown who was described as a natural comedian and Len Worrall, both of whom were to have a long association with the Society in future years. Mr Roland Johnstone was Musical Director, and amongst the chorus members was Tom Pearson who, in addition to performing in later minor parts, was to become a long-serving Secretary and Vice-Chairman of the Society. The full cast list is shown below:

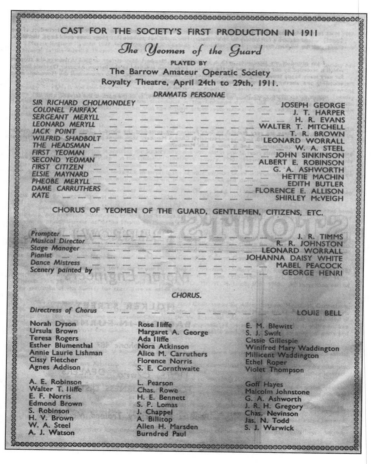

CAST FOR THE SOCIETY'S FIRST PRODUCTION IN 1911

The Yeomen of the Guard

PLAYED BY

The Barrow Amateur Operatic Society
Royalty Theatre, April 24th to 29th, 1911.

DRAMATIS PERSONAE

SIR RICHARD CHOLMONDLEY	JOSEPH GEORGE
COLONEL FAIRFAX	J. T. HARPER
SERGEANT MERYLL	H. R. EVANS
LEONARD MERYLL	WALTER T. MITCHELL
JACK POINT	T. R. BROWN
WILFRID SHADBOLT	LEONARD WORRALL
THE HEADSMAN	W. A. STEEL
FIRST YEOMAN	JOHN SINKINSON
SECOND YEOMAN	ALBERT E. ROBINSON
FIRST CITIZEN	G. A. ASHWORTH
ELSIE MAYNARD	HETTIE MACHIN
PHEOBE MERYLL	EDITH BUTLER
DAME CARRUTHERS	FLORENCE E. ALLISON
KATE	SHIRLEY McVEIGH

CHORUS OF YEOMEN OF THE GUARD, GENTLEMEN, CITIZENS, ETC.

Prompter	J. R. TIMMS
Musical Director	R. R. JOHNSTON
Stage Manager	LEONARD WORRALL
Pianist	JOHANNA DAISY WHITE
Dance Mistress	MABEL PEACOCK
Scenery painted by	GEORGE HENRI

CHORUS.

Directress of Chorus ... LOUIE BELL

Norah Dyson	Rose Iliffe	E. M. Blewitt
Ursula Brown	Margaret A. George	S. J. Swift
Teresa Rogers	Ada Iliffe	Cissie Gillespie
Esther Blumenthal	Nora Atkinson	Winifred Mary Waddington
Annie Laurie Lishman	Alice M. Carruthers	Millicent Waddington
Cissy Fletcher	Florence Norris	Ethel Roper
Agnes Addison	S. E. Cornthwaite	Violet Thompson
A. E. Robinson	L. Pearson	Goff Hayes
Walter T. Iliffe	Chas. Rowe	Malcolm Johnstone
E. F. Norris	H. E. Bennett	G. A. Ashworth
Edmond Brown	S. P. Lomas	J. R. H. Gregory
S. Robinson	J. Chappel	Chas. Nevinson
H. V. Brown	A. Billitop	Jas. N. Todd
W. A. Steel	Allen H. Marsden	S. J. Warwick
A. J. Watson	Burndred Paul	

The production received an extremely enthusiastic reception with the packed house 'applauding vigorously and demanding numerous encores,' according to the *North West Daily Mail*. At the AGM in May, 1911 profits of £69 7s 2d (which today would be about £7,000) were reported, of which £50 2s 0d (around £5,000) was to be distributed amongst local charities. Unsurprisingly the biggest expense had been on theatre rents and services, i.e. £64 18s 6d (approx. £6,500 today). The meeting also discussed the formal dissolution of 'the old society' (i.e the erstwhile Furness Dramatic & Operatic Society) and a handing over of its effects was agreed. "There was the very kindest feeling of the members of the old society towards the new one," says the report, "and there was not one single bit of jealousy." So that's good to know. A small cash balance of £4 16s 1d (about £500) was also handed over which the old group still had in hand. So flushed with success and good feeling the Society went on to perform again in November of that same year with a production of *The Mikado* – a feat they were unable to repeat for more than 70 years.

In 1912 they stayed with Gilbert and Sullivan for *The Gondoliers* but then, in 1913, abandoned them for an ambitious French comic opera entitled *Les Cloches de Cornville*. A lesser known work, and one which was French at that, was a definite risk, but perhaps it was the sheer novelty that pulled people in as it again played to enthusiastic houses. In fact it realised a total profit of £51-18s-5d, which was distributed among 11 local charities. At the AGM in 1914 it was reported that, in its first 4 years, the Society had distributed a sum total of £210 to charities – which equates to around £20,000 in today's value. That's quite some going.

The Great War was then to over-shadow everyone and everything although, miraculously, the Society was somehow able to carry on staging productions from 1916 onwards. Mrs T

Bourne, a music teacher and leading light in, amongst others, the Barrow Madrigal Society, had now taken up the baton as Musical Director. She led her Barrow choristers to many titles over the years and in fact so impressed Hugh Robertson from Glasgow, a composer and founder of the Glasgow Orpheus Choir, that he dedicated his song *All in an April Evening* to her and her choir. The song has since become a very famous choral piece. Mrs Bourne herself held the position of Musical Director with the Barrow Society until 1921 and was highly praised for her contribution. And in 1917, at the Society's AGM, Walter Iliffe, in recognition of his services, was imaginatively presented with a furniture catalogue from which he was asked to 'choose something that would be suitable.' Thankfully IKEA had not yet made its bid for world domination. Furniture was built to last in those days, and not a cheap item, so I like to think his choice was a mahogany cocktail cabinet or some such. In any event the gesture provides us with more evidence of a pretty healthy financial situation, although all this was about to change.

At the AGM in 1920 the first ever loss (of £57) was reported, followed by another in 1921 when *The Gondoliers* produced barely enough receipts to cover costs. Why was this? The fact that the Ulverston Society was producing the same show at the same time can't have helped, but the Barrow productions were also becoming quite repetitive (*The Yeomen of the Guard* 1911 & 1918; *The Mikado* 1911 & 1920; *The Gondoliers* 1912 & 1921). But perhaps most importantly, the damaging consequences of wartime were being felt at this time as the fortunes of Barrow took a downward slide with a general decline in trade and a decrease in population numbers. As a result productions ceased for 3 years, and it was not until 1924 that the Society felt sufficiently confident to stage another show. Perhaps inevitably Gilbert and Sullivan pieces were the first choice, but those which they had not previously attempted – *Trial by Jury/The Pirates of Penzance*. The Musical Director was Robert Pass, a position he held right through till 1938 when World War Two finally stopped the Society in its tracks.

Meantime, in the years following 1924, the Society's fortunes picked up. According to the proceedings of the AGM in 1928 a lot of the credit for this is given to a gentleman named Engineer-Captain A E Lester DSO, RN. He had served as the Society's Chairman since 1925, and was being presented by Mr Tom Pearson, Secretary, with an inscribed gold match-box, marking the Society's gratitude to him as he left the town to take up an Admiralty position in Malta. The contributions of his wife and daughter to the work of the orchestra were also commended. Mr Pearson reported that, since Mr Lester had taken up office, the Society had handed over £116 to local charities, and had the grand sum of £197 in hand. "He leaves us at the high water mark of prosperity", he said to a cascade of cheers and applause. Quite what he did isn't recorded, and even though a gold matchbox isn't exactly a mahogany cocktail cabinet, it's clear he was extremely highly thought of. Perhaps he encouraged them to take some steps away from their Gilbert and Sullivan comfort zone, as there is evidence of some change of direction from 1924 onwards with comic operas such as *Tom Jones* (1925), *Merrie England* (1926), and *Toreador* (1927). This trend continued with *The Marriage Market* (1931) at which a certain Bob Bowker made his debut, *The Geisha* (1932), and *Katinka* (1933) which was produced by a man we have already met, and whose name runs through the story of many of the early societies, Tom Rawsthorn. You shall hear more of both Mr Bowker and Mr Rawsthorn as we proceed.

Another bold step was the move to a larger capacity, and more prestigious theatre, the Coliseum on Abbey Road for the 1934 production of a new style of show, *The Desert Song*. 'No point of difference has occurred between us (and the

Royalty Theatre)' explained the Society Chairman Mr Thomas Pearson, with an air of both apology and pride, 'but a more costly production demands a larger patronage and with a more numerous cast, a stage of increased proportions is imperative.' There were voices of doom however warning everyone that the Society was now over-reaching itself, but in fact the show was hailed as the Society's 'greatest triumph.' The takings amounted to £808 which, when one considers that the highest priced seats were 3s-6d (that's 17½p to you and me) was a considerable achievement.

The Silver Jubilee production *Viktoria and her Hussar* followed in 1935, which was produced and directed by a professional producer, Mr Horace Manger of Torquay. The Society was now really flexing its muscles. This story begins in Japan, goes on to Russia, and ends in Hungary so you can imagine the variety of sets, costumes and dances that were needed. Principal roles were carried off by Bob Bowker and Dorothy Steel (above) with support from Joseph Simm, another prolific local performer across several societies. The dances, under the management of Miss P Devine and always a highly praised aspect of these early shows, were singled out for special mention in the press review. More successes followed. *The Maid of the Mountains* in 1936 for example was described as 'an entertainment which ranks with the best in the history of the Society,' and which incidentally featured a rare appearance by Joseph Simm's wife, Abbie – more notable, as you will hear, for her later contributions as a skilled musician. But sadly, after *The Street Singer* in 1937 and *The New Moon* in 1938, just when things were getting going, everything came to an abrupt halt with the outbreak of World War Two. The 1939 attraction was to be a show called *Wild Violets* but, despite 6 months of rehearsal, it was never staged. The Society would not perform again until 1950.

Meanwhile during the 1930's the town had given birth to another operatic society. This was 'The Furness Amateur Operatic and Dramatic Society', not to be confused with the one that had been formally dissolved in 1911. This was an entirely new group whose origins are somewhat obscure, as indeed is its ultimate fate. However it managed to stage at least 3 light operas from 1935 to 1937. These were *Rose Marie*, presented at the Coliseum in October 1935, *The Rebel Maid* staged at the Royalty Theatre in 1936, and *The Quaker Girl* presented at the Palace Cinema (which once stood opposite the Town Hall) in 1937.

Some of the names associated with this initiative (e.g Alderman Bram Longstaffe, President and Mr A J Middleton, Chairman) are unfamiliar, whereas the man responsible for the production is not. This was again Thomas Rawsthorn, assisted on this occasion by Mr H H Thomas, Musical Director and Miss Edna Parkinson, Dancing Mistress. All of this Society's shows were enthusiastically supported and highly praised – indeed, at the close of *Rose Marie*, all the cast were treated to a Civic reception at the Town Hall. But then, after 1937, I can find no further trace of them. I assume like every other amateur group they were stopped in their tracks by the outbreak of war in 1939, and then afterwards never came to life again.

Revival

What then of the Barrow Operatic Society? Barrow had of course suffered much during the War with Vickers shipyard and engineering works being a prime target for German bombs. There was bomb damage almost everywhere in fact and the town faced a severe housing problem. A state of weariness and general exhaustion was prevalent. Throughout the country a spirit of hope and optimism was gradually restored, although this perhaps took a little longer to arrive in Barrow. Theatrical entertainment was always going to be a healthy distraction and morale-raiser however and in 1950, despite only having a leftover bank balance of £19, the Society felt confident and optimistic enough to mount a revival. With a cast of about 80 people, almost all of whom were new recruits, it staged a production of *The Vagabond King*.

There were familiar figures in the cast however – Robert (Bob) Bowker, who played Francois Villan, 'King of the Vagabonds', John Myers as King Louis XI, and Eric Gaudie as Guy Tabarie, the comedy lead. Hubert Bramhall, who had once sung with the 1930's 'Savoy Amateur Operatic Society' (to be reviewed in the chapter concerning the Barrow Savoyards) and who had helped to get the new Abbey Musical Society up and running was also in the cast, as were other regular pre-war performers such as Eva Ward and Mamie Saunders. Production duties were in the hands of Mrs Jessie Barbour, and the Musical Director was now William Kelly, both familiar names in our history.

Throughout the rest of the 1950s the spirit of optimism grew. The gloom-lifting Festival of Britain was held in 1951 (and incidentally a section of this was to act as a show-piece for amateur drama), and in 1953 it was as if a new era was beginning with the Coronation of a new young Queen. The chosen production for Coronation year was *The Arcadians*, a favourite piece from the Edwardian period and with an appropriate theme of innocence and optimism working against an old order. It was described in the press as 'one of the Society's finest productions.' But there were difficulties and challenges to be faced. At the time the Barrow Society was re-treading the boards again there were three other major societies on the scene – Walney, Abbey, and Ulverston – and, bothered at this stage with a sense of vulnerability, members' loyalty to their particular Society was an unspoken rule. In fact Society hopping was nothing less than sinful, totally unlike the more fluid situation which exists today. A famous example is the skirmish which broke out in 1951, which you will hear more of in the history of the Abbey Society, when Bob Bowker a veteran performer for Barrow agreed to produce the Abbey's production of *The Gondoliers*. Infamy! In some sense the demand for such loyalty may have been understandable in a climate of increasing competition. There was the novel pleasure of home entertainment for example, in the form of television, which was becoming an increasing threat, and the audiences who had grown up with live theatre were now ageing. A youth rebellion was brewing, driven by young people who were no longer content to follow in their parents' footsteps. In other words all the Societies had to work hard in order to survive.

In order to woo their audience the Barrow Society embarked on a series of quite risky productions – risky because they were geared towards an older audience, and because they were lavish and therefore costly productions to stage. The first of these, in 1952, was *Glamorous Nights*, a show which had first appeared in 1935 and had been written, devised and composed by Ivor Novello. The key feature of the show was spectacle, to be created by colourful stage groupings, sets and costumes. Thankfully, despite some teething troubles on opening night, the Society scored a resounding success. In leading roles, and much praised for their efforts, were Marion Pearson, Eric Gaudie and John Myers, and in all, the cast comprised a total of 81 people. In charge of production was Jessie Barbour.

Emboldened by this success, they repeated the experience with other Ivor Novello pieces, *The Dancing Years* in 1954, and *Perchance to Dream* in 1957. For *The Dancing Years* they also broke new ground by engaging a Producer from outside the area, Mr John Denis (pictured left). He had had a successful career in professional theatre, having been associated with the Royal Shakespeare Company in Stratford, with the famous tenor Richard Tauber, and with Hermione Gingold in the West End. His production credentials with amateur companies were also impressive. The show was a triumph and goes down as one of the Society's most memorable productions – not least for its spectacle but also for the unprecedented £1,700 it cost to put on. Much credit was of course given to Mr Denis who went on to produce the Society's next 7 shows, until 1960.

As for *Perchance to Dream* (1957) it fared less well in terms of audience numbers, mainly because its performance dates coincided with a shipyard strike, two rugby semi-finals, and the arrival in Barrow of Chipperfield's Circus. This was a shame as both its production values and individual performances drew considerable praise from John McDonald, the *Barrow News* theatre critic.

Perhaps under John Denis' influence the Society then took another unprecedented step by engaging a professional singer for the lead role in their 1959 production of *The Merry Widow*. This was Joseph Ward, a 25-year old baritone from Preston who was a member of the Sadlers Wells Opera Company. His appointment prompted some anxieties as to how much of a diva he might be, and whether he might look with contempt on the non-professionals. In fact such fears proved to be unfounded as he soon showed himself to be not only a team player but also a modest and affable soul to boot. Box office takings were boosted too, so overall his engagement was viewed as a very good thing.

Although the emphasis at this time seemed to be on catering for more mature tastes, there was some attempt to engage the youth in an initiative led by Mr Terence Dilks, a teacher at Risedale Secondary School, and son of Mr Victor Dilks, a frequent Musical Director for both Barrow and Ulverston. Together they wrote and produced a fairytale fantasy entitled *Sprookje*, which was staged at the Public Hall in December 1956. It was billed as the premiere production of "the youth section" of the Barrow Society although, so far as I can tell, it was not a venture that took flight. Even so, *Sprookje* was a successful production that enchanted the audience, and is also notable for the appearance of one Ron Eddevane in the cast. Presumably inspired by this experience he went on to be a regular local performer appearing, if you recall, in Ulverston's shows and in a host of local productions.

The Society's Golden Jubilee year, 1960, was celebrated with a 6-day run of *The Desert Song*, a show they had previously staged in 1934. The show featured a certain Noreen Steel (pictured left as Clementina) who, along with her husband Bill, was later to be a key figure in the development of the Abbey Society. It was to be John Denis' last show as Producer, with William Jacobs as his Musical Director and Sylvia Hardy in charge of the dancers. Although she was to continue in this role for the next three productions different Producers now followed in the wake of Mr Denis: Freddie Collier, a professional actor from the London theatre scene, was engaged for *The New Moon* in 1961, then Donald Sartain from Her Majesty's Theatre handled *The Boyfriend* in 1962, and the Society's last ever show at the Coliseum before it closed for good, *Me and My Girl* (1963).

It was an unsettled period. As well as the lack of a fixed, reliable producer there was now equal uncertainty about venues, as this period marked a tough time for live theatre in general. As commercial theatres both Her Majesty's and the Coliseum depended on good houses week on week, and both had been struggling for some time, despite the Coliseum's brief attempt to re-invent itself as a cinema. Following its closure, as every Barrovian of a certain age can recall, the poor Coliseum was eventually demolished, and the space once occupied by this grand, ornate building became well, just that, an empty space. The same fate was eventually to befall Her Majesty's but, at least for now, it was available so *Salad Days,* perhaps with a touch of irony, went ahead there. It was also notable for being the first show to be produced for the Society by Ronald Metcalfe, and won two of the first *Barrow News* Oscars to be awarded – to Delia Elliot, for best female lead, and to Jack Fisher, the best male. Sadly it was also to be the last show from the Society for a while.

Troubled Times

Together with the abiding uncertainty over the future of Her Majesty's Theatre, the Barrow Society was feeling the loss of the Coliseum keenly, and they were unable to put on a show for the next two years. It is fair to say that, around the town, there were real fears for the future of amateur theatre. Without an appropriate venue, where were they to perform? There is even some evidence to suggest that some felt the heyday of amateur theatre was over anyway. In a 1966 *Barrow News* article, for example, Ron Metcalfe writes about his encounter with a group of people who had talked about the diminishing quality of local society productions, and who had described several local performers as 'fly-by-night' players of dubious talent when compared to the 'masters and craftsmen' of old. In the article Mr Metcalfe mounts a furious defence: "I could not stand idly by and hear the present generation of amateur players unfairly pilloried," he writes. "We have today some outstanding performers who can more than hold their own with the players of the past." This sort of debate seems to me like a symptom of the times when, in a pervasive atmosphere of anxiety and uncertainty, it is perhaps usual for people to hark back to earlier, less troubled times and to eulogise 'the good old days.'

In any case, far from being downcast, the flame still burned in the Barrow Society and after the lull of 1964 and 1965, it returned in 1966 with a production of *No No Nanette*. A new man had arrived at Her Majesty's in the shape of Donald MacKechnie and, determined to reverse its fortunes, he worked closely with the Barrow Society to get this new show off the ground. It felt like a new start for all, with an almost entirely new company from the one who had last performed in 1963. The sad reality however was that, despite everyone's best efforts, the lure of alternative forms of entertainment (especially television) meant that live theatre was in decline. Undeterred the Society tried again with *Guys and Dolls* in 1967, again at Her Majesty's Theatre. It proved to be a troubled production however and, although it had an experienced local producer at the helm in the shape of Joyce Warrington, it was said to 'lack pace' and was subject to a critical press review. It also ran into a number of technical difficulties with the handling both of the scenery and the lighting. The review described the distracting noise of scene shifting during the show, and how, at one time, the stage staff could even be seen moving stuff around in the background while the singers performed at the front. Presumably, given the lack of support, it was all a reflection of the company's loss of heart.

Sadly these few years comprised Her Majesty's last gasp as Donald MacKechnie finally had to admit defeat and, the following year, the curtain came down for the very last time and the theatre closed for good. A combination of rising costs, insufficient box office returns, and reduced subsidies (in the form of Arts Council grants) had sealed its fate. *My Fair Lady* therefore, the 1969 production, now had to be staged at the Public Hall, a much less suitable venue. A spat then broke out between the Society and Ron Metcalfe, almost as if they had displaced the frustrations of the time on to each other. Mr Metcalfe maintained that the Society officials had failed to forward advance information to him and, being clearly miffed, he took them to task in his weekly column for what he called their 'myopia'. He went on, perhaps unwisely, to attribute their omission to the critical review of *Guys and Dolls* which had actually been written by his colleague John McDonald. Whether it was because of this spat I couldn't say, but certainly when it came to Show Week audience numbers were down on expected and *My Fair Lady* ultimately suffered a financial loss.

But as the 1970s rolled in, significant challenges for both live theatre in general, as well as the Barrow Society in particular, remained. It was of course the chief question of rising costs and how to secure sufficient audience numbers to cover them. From now on the engagement of a professional, either in a producing or performing role, was to be a thing of the past. Remember also that the 1970s was a decade of unrest and austerity, the era of strikes and the 3-day week. For the annual productions the limitations of the Public Hall as a venue also had to be factored in so, for all such reasons, the proposed production for 1971, *Brigadoon*, was eventually cancelled as it was felt to be over-ambitious. It was replaced by *How to Succeed in Business Without Really Trying* – an antidote perhaps to the times.

Then finally, in 1972, there was some light at the end of the tunnel with the completion of the first phase of the new town centre development. It meant that a new theatre space, in the shape of the newly-opened 'Civic Hall' was available, and was in fact to be the Society's new home for the next 15 years or more. Still, the challenges remained. By now there were 3 other major amateur societies operating in the town – Walney, Abbey and (since 1968) Walney Juniors – and they all needed audiences. Barrow's response was to stage a succession of popular, 'safe' musicals such as *The King and I* (1972), *South Pacific* (1973), *Carousel* (1975) and *Hello Dolly* (1976).

It was around this time however that a certain Jack Fisher came into his own. Together with his wife Joan, they had both been a part of the theatrical landscape for some time – Jack as actor, producer, and set designer and Joan both as a performer and skilful costumier. Indeed, during the run of *Hello Dolly* in 1976 they proved to be a literally inseparable force. Much to everyone's horror Joan, who was playing the lead in the show, lost her voice and could not perform. Without an understudy there was only one thing for it. Jack, who was producing the show and knew it inside out, promptly donned wig, dress and make-up and went on in her stead. It is said that no-one could actually tell the difference!

What is certain is that Jack and Joan Fisher both played a key role in the development of the Barrow Society at this time and, as well as the *Hello Dolly* story, these latter years of the 1970s provide good examples of just how their creativity drove things forward. In 1977, the Queen's Silver Jubilee year, Jack produced *Camelot*, and in so doing managed to persuade the Committee to dig deep into its pockets to allow the creation of a truly spectacular show. The same production team of Jack Fisher, Saxon Winship (Choreographer) and Frank Crayston (Musical Director) and the ever faithful Betty Newton as Accompanist, was then appointed for the following year's production of *Mame* (a Musical first for Barrow), although this show was soon to hit difficulties. Rehearsals had no sooner begun when Frank Crayston fell seriously ill, and there was the inevitable period of anxiety and uncertainty until Derek Judge offered to step in. Then rising costs became an issue, particularly after the outlay for *Camelot*, and there was real panic over whether it would be possible to afford the fees required for the hire of costumes and sets. Mercifully Jack's wife Joan then saved the day. Armed with her talents as a costume designer, and with the support of several willing Society members, she managed not only to source authentic period pieces for the show but also to design and, with her team of helpers, create the costumes needed. All in all some 250 outfits were subsequently created by Joan and her team.

In-between times, from 1974 to 1977, in addition to the annual musical, Jack Fisher drove forward a series of *'Black and White Minstrel Shows'*, for which Joan Fisher's costume designs again became a spectacular feature. It was a bold move, with the aim of prising people from their homes by offering a local version of what was then a hugely popular television attraction. It's not the sort of initiative that would be applauded today, but it worked very well at the time.

Then in 1979 Jack Fisher was interviewed and subsequently appointed by Barrow Corporation to the post of General Manager of The Civic Hall and the Markets Department. Within a week however he had resigned 'for personal and private reasons.' Apparently both the *Barrow News* and market traders were shocked and disappointed by this turn of events, and there was much speculation on what his reasons may have been. Although they were of course not disclosed they are perhaps not that difficult to work out. The appointment had been made on condition that Mr Fisher "relinquish all his existing business interests … involving the supply of any goods or services by any firm in which Mr Fisher … has any pecuniary interest." Ever a man with big dreams, he was about to launch his own theatre company 'Jack Fisher Productions'. He had become somewhat frustrated by what he called the 'restrictions' of a normal amateur Society and declared that the aim of his new company would be, as he modestly put it, 'to bring lavish Las Vegas style entertainment to the Furness area.' As his proposed company, to all intents and purposes, would be based at the Civic Hall, it presumably fell into the category of 'goods and services' in which he had a clear personal interest.

As it turned out his theatre company had a short, albeit successful life. With a hand-picked cast, which included local professional entertainer Danny Patterson, he presented a series of summer 'extravaganzas' and then, in June 1981, its first and last full-scale musical, the Stephen Schwartz musical *Pippin*. As one of the new breed of 'rock musicals' it hit Barrow audiences firmly between the eyes (and presumably ears) with its reported 'kaleidoscope of colour, magic, and tricks,' chiefly comprising the costumes, wigs and masks created by Joan Fisher and her team. Peter Goude, a previous recipient of a *Barrow News* Oscar played the title role. Shortly afterwards Jack and Joan left Barrow for London where their flair and artistic eye enabled both of them to forge successful careers. Their daughter Abigail advanced to the professional stage and, it is reported, appeared for a time on the TV soap *Emmerdale*. And having spoken to a number who recall their work in Barrow, they are remembered with much affection, and it is clear that their contribution to the amateur scene is highly regarded.

For the next two shows another key local figure, David Marcus took over as Producer, this time supported by Liz Dunn's choreography. For *Oliver!* (1979) Derek Judge acted as 'Guest Musical Director' supported by Doreen Dunlop as 'Leader of the Augmented Orchestra.' Then in 1980, for *The King and I*, she was to take on the full responsibility for the first time, at least for the Barrow Society. David Marcus' vision was ambitious and although ultimately described as 'visually stunning' it all came at a price, with final costs coming in at around £5,000, a record figure for the time. But despite the sleepless nights of poor Tim Melville, the

Hon.Treasurer, the shows were winning many plaudits. *Oliver!* for example was awarded 'The Ronnie Metcalfe Memorial Trophy' for the best all-round production of 1978-79, and Eileen Millard won a *Barrow News* Oscar for her portrayal of Anna in *The King & I.*

Onwards and Upwards

If it's true to say that, at the end of the 70s the Barrow Society was limping along, by the end of the 80s they had broken into a veritable gallop. The 1980s was to prove a decade of major change for the Society with new faces and new initiatives sweeping in a new order. The decision to stage *Fiddler on the Roof* in 1981 was therefore very appropriate since the principal theme of the show is that of changing times and the subsequent challenge to old traditions. Then, perhaps underlining the point, the chosen production for 1982 was *The Man of La Mancha*, the story of Don Quixote, the man who dared to dream 'The Impossible Dream.'

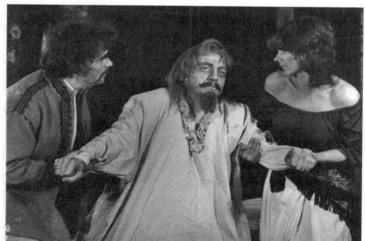

Bill Calvert (Sancho Panza) David Marcus (Don Quixote) & Liz Dunn (Aldonza): The Man of La Mancha, 1982

However, appropriate as it may have been it was by no means a safe choice – it had never been staged in the district before and, compared to its time on Broadway, had not fared that well in the West End, so audience response was unpredictable. In addition the action takes place entirely in a dark, claustrophobic dungeon.

Unfortunately the gamble didn't pay off, as the show attracted audiences that are best described as thin. Bob Bowker, writing in the *Barrow News*, was impressed however, referring to 'the extraordinarily high standard of production and performance' and praising the choreography and acting talents of Liz Dunn, and the portrayals of Don Quixote and Sanch Panza given by David Marcus and Bill Calvert. In fact the show was so highly thought of it was awarded the Ronald Metcalfe Memorial Trophy for 'best show.' Nevertheless with public support being so disappointing it was perhaps no surprise that there was a retreat to safer ground in 1983 with *My Fair Lady*.

But the major coup for the Society, and the event which seemed to set the Society up on a new plane, came when permission was granted for the staging of *Jesus Christ Superstar* in 1984. Up to this time a very select few amateur companies nationwide had been granted such a licence. The show had opened in London in 1971 and although initial reactions were mixed it had gradually evolved into a global phenomenon, a show which everybody wanted to see. Artistic Producer for the Barrow production was David Marcus with Doreen Dunlop as his Musical Director, and a show of this stature needed no half measures. Under the guidance of the much experienced Tom Hendrie and his crew the Civic Hall underwent a major re-design to create a set that was similar to the one used in the show's hit run at the Palace Theatre in London. Ramps were installed to create a split-level stage, incorporating a cross that would be raised by an unseen motorised apparatus.

There were many familiar faces in the cast, with some having been recruited from other Societies - Gerald Babb for example from Flookburgh, played Pontius Pilate; Steve Freeland of the Barrow Savoyards played Simon Zealotes; and Bill Calvert, late of the Walney Society, played Annas, a priest. David Marcus himself took on the role of King Herod with Pam Birkby as Mary Magdalene. Chief honours however went to two new arrivals – Ian Bird who played Jesus, and Steve Carrick, who played Judas Iscariot. Both were to feature in many of the Society's subsequent shows. The chorus featured others who were either already very involved in amateur theatre or were soon to become so, e.g. Ken Hindle, a major player in the Ulverston Society, Pauline Barnes, Andrew Bond, and Shirley Britton.

Ian Bird had been spotted by Shirley Britton performing with a local band 'Toccata', and she encouraged him to audition for the show. At the time he had been content to perform in local bands, and hadn't considered a career in musical theatre. Shirley Britton had other ideas however, and he was eventually cast in the title role. Steve Carrick on the other hand had considerable previous stage experience. He had first performed with Arnside Players in the early 70's, was a regular member of Ulverston Outsiders, and had appeared in several of Ulverston's Pantomimes. He was to go on to perform in many subsequent productions for the Barrow Society, eventually assuming the role of Producer for *The Wizard of Oz* in 2011.

To say the show was well received is an understatement. It broke all records, queues for tickets extended the length of Duke Street, extra performances had to be hurriedly negotiated, and each performance elicited a lengthy standing ovation. It was as if the West End had finally arrived in Barrow. All members of the cast excelled in their roles, and at the *Barrow News'* annual Oscar award ceremony

Judas (Steve Carrick) places the Crown of Thorns on Jesus (Ian Bird)

held later in September the show swept the board. The show itself won the Ronald Metcalfe Memorial Trophy for 'best musical', whilst Doreen Dunlop won The Renaissance Trust Special Award for her musical direction, Gordon Crayston won the *Barrow News* discretionary award for outstanding technical achievement, and of course Ian Bird won the Oscar for 'best leading actor in a musical' for his remarkable debut performance. Pam Birkby and Steven Carrick had also received nominations for their performances. Ian Bird himself went on to perform in several later productions and, as with most loyal Society members, had a spell as Society Chairman.

The problem then was how to follow such a massive success. The answer, perhaps surprisingly, was a show of complete contrast – *Annie*. Again David Marcus and Doreen Dunlop were in charge, now assisted by choreographer Liz Dunn who, incidentally, also took the part of the monstrous Miss Hannigan. David Marcus himself played Daddy Warbucks and, for the sake of the part and for the benefit of a local charity, he even agreed to shave his head. Fortified with a glass or two of whiskey, the 30 minute ceremony was performed at the former Barrow nightspot *The 99 Club*. The distinctive feature of the show however was the fact that it gave a younger group of performers the chance to showcase their talents. 150 hopefuls auditioned for parts in the show with eleven-year old Claire Twynam coming out on top, cast in the title role. She had first appeared in a Barrow show in 1980 when, aged just 6, she had played one of the young princesses in *The King and I*. Her talents were soon recognised when, the following year, she was awarded a Barrow News Oscar for her portrayal of Bielke, one of Tevye's five daughters in *Fiddler on the Roof*. In the role of Annie she charmed the audience and impressed everyone with her mature singing voice but, sad to record, her young life was cut short only 5 years later when she died in a tragic accident. When the Society staged a repeat production of *Annie* in 1999, the show was dedicated to her memory.

Despite the success of these shows however, according to the Chairman Shirley Britton, dark clouds were looming. In the programme notes for *Annie*, she drew attention to proposals which she said had been put forward for the demolition of the Civic Hall in 1987. Although it was to be replaced ('at some point in the future' she notes wearily) by a building which would include some performing space, she felt this would not only be small and prove inadequate, it would also seriously limit the scope of future shows. She went so far as to express the fear that the 1986 show might be the Society's last. Still, undeterred, the Society gamely continued with its policy of bringing new and untried shows to the town. *Sugar* was the choice for 1986, a musical version of the Hollywood film *Some Like It Hot*, which gave Steve Carrick and Andy Bond the

opportunity to explore their feminine sides (with unnerving conviction).

Shirley Britton produced, with Doreen Dunlop and Liz Dunn looking after the music and choreography. The Marilyn Monroe role was taken by Julie Lloyd, yet another local talent who will figure more prominently in our story as we proceed. For a start she would direct the first Autumn show staged by the Society in 1987, *Andy Capp*, a musical version of the Daily Mirror comic strip, written by Alan Price and Trevor Peacock. Steve Carrick relished the role of Andy, with Shirley Britton as his long-suffering wife Flo, and Bill Calvert as best friend and drinking partner, Chalkie. It was performed 'in the round' which helped the audience to feel fully involved.

But wait. The Civic Hall was still standing! Following a public meeting and a period of consultation it had been decided that, rather than be demolished, the Hall would eventually be re-furbished, giving breathing-space for the Society to bring another West End show to Furness for the first time, *Sweeney Todd* (1988), which would then be followed by *Funny Girl* in 1989. For *Sweeney Todd* Steve Carrick was the eponymous barber, with Julie Lloyd as Mrs Lovett, the pie shop owner. Also of note is the choreographer, Judith Barrow. A veteran of previous shows, she subsequently graduated to the professional stage and, at the time of writing, is Stage Manager for the touring production of David Walliams' *Gangsta Granny*. Also noteworthy is the fact that the razors and famous tilting chair were borrowed from the actual West End production. As far as I know the blood used was from local sources.

So thankfully, despite a couple of years of uncertainty, Shirley Britton's earlier Cassandra-like predictions had not been realised and, to the delight and relief of all local groups, by 1990 a new improved theatre space had become available, in the shape of Forum 28. It has since become home to all the local amateur groups, and is now one of the district's prime theatrical venues.

The Storey Square era

In the meantime, fired with optimism for a brighter future the Society had invested in a dedicated rehearsal space in Storey Square to avoid the cost and inconvenience of room hire. This was the former United Free Methodist Church, a building which, in the 1970s, the Society had once rented until costs had become prohibitive. They had since re-located to the Co-op

Hall in Trinity Street, on Barrow Island. This had not proved a happy arrangement however, especially as far as local residents were concerned. An *Evening Mail* article of 6th December 1985 quotes one resident complaining that, 'The hall is used day and night. We have to put up with banging and music going full blast – just a few yards from our homes.' Another points out, 'I didn't have to go to see *Jesus Christ Superstar*. I knew all the words off by heart!'

Clearly not wishing to alienate their public, the Society swung into action. Through the initiative of Tom Hendrie, Tim Melville and many others, plus the support of the Sir John Fisher Foundation, it eventually became possible for the Society to purchase their former 'home' in Storey Square.

Much needed to be done, but ambitious plans were drawn up to bring the building up to standard. The hope was for it to be offered as a facility to other community groups, and perhaps be developed into an Arts Centre. Sadly it was to prove a money pit. There was no heating, an insufficient number of doors, a leaky roof, broken windows and, to cap it all, dry rot was discovered. Yet again the Society's finances were put under considerable strain. Then the 1989 show *Funny Girl*

came in with a loss, and the show planned for 1990 (*Seven Brides for Seven Brothers*) had to be scratched when Barrow Council finally decided it was time for the Civic Hall's refurbishment. In its stead a revue show *The Double Feature Show* was put on, which thankfully proved to be very successful.

As luck would have it 1990 marked the Society's 80th birthday, but not only that, also saw the grand opening of the new performance space 'Forum 28'. When the Society staged *The Double Feature Show* there as its 80th birthday celebration it must have felt like a new beginning. Directed by Julie Lloyd and Ian Bird the aim was to chart the Society's 80 year history in music and dance. It was actually performed in a candlelit cabaret setting in the Forum's ballroom. The first half cleverly linked news items with songs from past shows, and then the second half presented songs from shows the Society hoped to stage in the future. The highlight though was a turn from veteran performer Bob Bowker who had made his debut with the Society back in 1931. Now aged 88 he sang 'Lover Come Back to Me' from the 1938 production of *The New Moon*, a performance which elicited more than a few tears.

The sense of 'a new beginning' was then reinforced by an initiative which was to run through the 1990s and into the new Millenium – productions of straight dramatic productions. These continued annually until 2007 and gave players the opportunity to step away from the musical genre and showcase their acting talents. As our focus is different I won't chart their progress here but it should be noted that their output gained an impressive degree of success both locally and in various nationwide Drama Festivals.

But back at Storey Square, having received hefty investment, came the hotly anticipated event – the formal opening of the Society's new rehearsal rooms (and possible

Arts Centre) on 21st December 1992. Ian Bird, the Society's Chair, hosted the proceedings and invited the Mayor Councillor Joyce Fleet to do the honours. Also honoured that evening was long-serving Society member Betty Thompson. Her memories went back to the Society's post-war revival in 1950 when she had performed in *The Vagabond King*. Subsequently she had proved invaluable back-stage as a dresser and wardrobe mistress.

As for the musical productions these continued with vigour through the 1990's, chiefly with David Marcus producing, backed by a new Musical Director Peter Dyer, who was involved with the Society's shows right through to 2009. He had moved to Cumbria in 1975 and was appointed Head of Music at Dowdales School, Dalton in 1979. He was also a favourite with other local societies, especially the Barrow Savoyards. And in this period, true to the promises made at the *Double Feature Show,* the Society continued to stage several shows new to the Furness area. e.g. *Chess* (1994), *42nd Street* (1995), and *Moll Flanders* (1998).

The production of *Chess* was a clear indication of the Society's renewed confidence. It was the first amateur group in the country to acquire the performance rights of a show that was described as fiendishly difficult to produce both in terms of the staging and the complexities of the musical score. Written by Tim Rice and the boys from Abba, it is almost entirely an operatic piece, with little spoken dialogue, so it is perhaps not surprising to find two well-known Savoyards in the cast, Helen Troughton and Phil McIntosh, along with Ian Bird, Steve Carrick, and Sarah Flanagan (soon to become Mrs Carrick). She had come from a musical family as her parents, Olive and Tony, had been part of the local music scene for many years. Tony Flanagan in fact played the drums in Chapter Five, a rock group that was one of Barrow's answers to the Merseybeat boom of the 1960s. All three had previously performed in the Society's production of *The Pyjama Game* in 1993.

But back to *Chess* - in order to promote the show and to raise funds Bill Calvert and David Marcus played a 24-hour marathon game of chess in the window of the Oxfam shop on Dalton Road. Their stunt managed to raise in excess of £1,000 which was shared with Oxfam. And in recognition of *Chess*'s Furness premiere Tim Rice sent a letter of congratulations and good wishes to the Society, and apologised for being unable to attend in person. 'It unfortunately clashes with an opening of *Beauty and the Beast* on Broadway,' he says, 'to which I contributed several songs.' Excuses, excuses.

Neil Metcalfe & Sarah Carrick as Julian Marsh & Peggy Sawyer
42nd Street

42nd Street was another coup as again Barrow was the first Society in the area to be granted a performance licence. This really put the Ulverston group's nose out of joint as they had also applied. 'It's a decision we can't comprehend, but good luck to Barrow,' Allan Lewis is quoted as saying, presumably as he gnashed his teeth, as only the previous year his Society had been pipped by Barrow's Abbey Society in their bid to stage *Barnum*. Anyway the show had a very successful run, complemented by costumes direct from the West End! Presumably David Marcus, who was in charge of production, had something to do with this.

1996 saw the re-staging of *The Man of La Mancha*, last performed in 1992, with principal parts being taken by Steve

Freeland, Bill Calvert, and Julie Lloyd. It was hailed 'best musical of the year' by the *Barrow News*. Then 1999 saw the return of *Annie*, this time with young Sally Kemp in the lead role, and Steve Carrick (unshorn), as Daddy Warbucks. The demand for tickets was so great an extra matinee had to be arranged at short notice.

Sally Kemp, Pauline Barnes, Sarah Carrick
*& Bill Calvert (*Annie, 1999)

Julie Lloyd as
Miss Hannigan

Also of particular note is that several of the young cast from this show eventually went on to study drama and/or musical theatre and subsequently to forge careers on the professional stage. Among these were Sally Kemp herself (who, for professional reasons, later became Sally Ann Ramage when she enjoyed some success in London and Leeds), Paige Cook, Brogan Rae Anderson, Amy Larcombe, and Julie Lloyd (or Julie Edwards as she is now known). As the latter has figured largely in our story so far, before moving on to the next century, perhaps this is a good place to pause to say a word or two more about her.

She is clearly highly thought of in the district as both an actress and director, and I have heard her variously described as 'the best actress the district has produced,' 'multi-talented', and 'a one-woman repertory company.' She made her debut as a 12-year old at Her Majesty's Theatre with the Furness Youth Theatre. Subsequently she studied Drama and English at Newcastle and, on returning to Furness, performed in, and directed numerous musicals and plays from *Andy Capp* to Shakespeare. She first performed with the Barrow Society in 1985 when, at the time married to Ian Bird, played the part of 'Lily' in *Annie*, and then, as you will have noticed, was associated with many later productions. As an accomplished actress she was also active in local drama, memorably taking the one-woman play *Shirley Valentine* on tour in 1996. In 2014 she undertook further training with ALRA (Academy of Live and Recorded Arts) in Manchester, and latterly, under the name Julie Edwards, has been seen on TV in commercials and in a part in *Emmerdale*. Currently she is with the Box of Tricks Theatre Company in a touring production of Becky Prestwick's play, *Chip Shop Chips*.

Her enthusiasm for the stage has also inspired her daughter Rachel, and her step-daughter Deborah, who are both regular local performers. Rachel had her first adult role with the Walney Society, before joining the Barrow Society's production of *Oliver* in 2005 when she played the ill-fated Nancy. Paul Boyce was cast in the lead role with Steve Freeland as Fagin and Luke Mooney as the Artful Dodger. Deborah was also in the show, building on her earlier experiences in productions staged by both the Abbey Society, and Walney Juniors. Later both sisters would be found performing together in several other shows including *Anything Goes* (2007), which incidentally was directed by Julie Lloyd, the re-run of *Sweeney Todd* (2008) and *The Music Man* (2009).

Both sisters had already made an important contribution to another of the Society's famous leaps in the dark when it staged a musical that had not only never been seen in Furness, it had never been seen outside of its homeland New Zealand. This was *Rush* (2006), a dark and sinister piece about the search for gold in the mid-19th century. With scenes involving rape, murder, and hanging it was a long way from the jaunty feel-good themes of *Annie* and *My Fair Lady* but, with David Marcus as Producer, the Society's officers must have thought it was a worthwhile risk. As it was, the acting talents of all the cast rose to the challenge and it was ultimately highly praised and, according to the *Barrow News* was 'played to perfection.' Kevin Lynch, the composer, even flew from New Zealand to add his support and congratulations. (Eat your heart out, Tim Rice.)

Despite these success stories on-stage, all was not well off-stage. Storm clouds were brewing that would threaten the very future of the Society. It was all to do with the Storey Square building which, if you recall, despite its advantages and undoubted charm, was proving very costly to maintain. By 2008 it was agreed that the drain on funds could not be sustained, so the proposal was to sell it on with outline planning permission for it to be demolished and replaced by housing. But then English Heritage stepped in, claiming that, as one of Barrow's finest brick-built buildings, this former church was part of the town's heritage and should be protected with 'listed' status. A period of mounting anxiety followed until, mercifully, after English Heritage had carried out a thorough inspection, they announced that they had changed their minds – the building was not of great historical significance after all. Everyone breathed a huge sigh of relief. Martin Craig, Chairman at the time, was quoted as saying, 'This is brilliant. If English Heritage had decided to list it we would not be in a position to look after it, and that would probably result in a long period where the building would slowly deteriorate.' Presumably the same fate would also have befallen the Society. In the end, as per the original plan, the building was finally sold on to a local builder who promptly demolished it to make space for housing.

A new beginning

Now – in case you haven't realised, the year that marked the 100th birthday of the Barrow Amateur Operatic Society, 2010, had arrived. To mark the occasion all current members, past officers, and officials from neighbouring Societies were invited to a grand Centenary Ball which was held at 'Chequers' in Dalton. There were photos and memorabilia on display before a three-course meal was served with each table named after favourite shows. As other groups were doing at this time it was also decided to drop the 'amateur' tag from their name and to re-brand the Society, complete with a new modern logo, as The Barrow Operatic and Dramatic Society (i.e. BODS).

Some thought had already been given to the approaching centenary in 2009 when the then Chairman Martin Craig, perhaps prompted by the Storey Square crisis, noted a need to look to the future and announced an intention to step up

efforts to encourage the younger generation to join the world of amateur theatre. *The Music Man* had been part of this drive that year which had leading parts for 3 young actors and also needed a back-up children's chorus line. Then, for the centenary year itself, the Disney classic *Beauty and the Beast* was chosen with Deborah Bird as Belle, and Mark Johnson as the Beast (pictured left). It was such a success it was followed by the perennial favourite *The Wizard of Oz*, this time with Rachel Craig (nee Bird) in the leading role. Both shows generated a lot of excitement and, as expected, attracted an audience heavily populated by youngsters. When Andrew Barrow took over as Chairman that same year he re-asserted the new 'outreach' policy: 'You will be seeing a lot more of us,' he said, 're-branded, and taking our style of drama, music, and entertainment out on tour to smaller venues, delivering live theatre to the community and diversifying into projects outside the bounds of the Society's structure.' Such a plan had already been set in motion a couple of years earlier with a series of additional concerts which had been staged to promote the Society, and to showcase its talented membership. *A Real Story of Song and Dance* had been staged in September 2008 which was basically a musical trip through some of the most popular and successful shows of the last few decades, compered by Martin Craig and Andrew Barrow. It also featured a certain "boy" band called Take Fat, seen preparing for their next World Tour. It all went down so well the idea was repeated in 2009. With the ball now rolling it gathered more speed in the following years as extra bonus concerts became a regular autumn feature of the Society's programme: *Great Music, Great Songs* (2011), *And the Winner Is ...* (2012), *The Phantom of the Musicals* (2013), and *Now That's What I Call Music* (2014).

Then, true to the outreach aims there were further initiatives to help the Society to integrate more with the local community. Some activities from 2013 for example include singing at the Vintage Christmas Fayre at Barrow's Dock Museum and performing for the staff and residents in Risedale Nursing Home at Abbey Meadow.

Although, as I have shown, the Barrow Society (now re-branded as BODS) has been producing shows of considerable quality and energy for some time, there was a sense in which, since its centenary, everything now picked up an even stronger pace. It's not just that the shows that followed were ambitious – that has generally been Barrow's style – there also seemed to be an even greater emphasis on high production values, particularly through the use of imaginative sets, and the embracing of modern technologies.

Chess (2012) typified this approach, advancing even the innovations of the 1994 production by pushing everything to a totally new level with disco-type lighted flooring, background projections, and simulated live TV feeds onto giant on-stage screens. Back projections had been used before but this was something on quite a different scale. The effects were orchestrated by Rachel Lawrence, with the lighting and sound as usual in the capable hands of Gordon Crayston and Alex Linney. The show won 3 North West NODA nominations for Choreography (Sally McKimm), Best Leading Male (Joe Kaye), and Best Musical. Then the following year came *The Witches of Eastwick*, another first for Barrow, necessitating the use of a hair-raising flying rig to literally sweep the 3 witches (played by Sarah Carrick, Michelle Larcombe, and Rachel Craig) off their feet. This show was also nominated for 3 NODA awards for Director (Steve Carrick), Best Leading Male (Martin Craig), and Best Musical. In fact it was such a success the cast were invited to perform excerpts from the show at the 2014 NODA conference.

And in keeping with the trend of bringing modern new musicals to Barrow, the Society's most recent productions have been *Jekyll and Hyde* (2014), and *Sister Act* (2015). These have proved to be brave but popular choices, and both have been successful in stirring up excitement and anticipation prior to 'Show Week'. At the time of writing another modern show, *Legally Blonde*, is being planned for 2016. Among the Society regulars in a leading role for all these productions was Louise Marshall (nee Wells) who had actually made her stage debut at the age of 7 for the Walney Juniors' 1982 production of *Sing a Song of Sixpence*. Since then she had progressed to appear in many of the later BODS and the Walney Theatre Company's productions.

All of these recent shows, from 2011 onwards, have been directed by Steve Carrick (pictured left), following his retirement from a long career in teaching. He takes an easy-going, democratic approach to the task which is clearly appreciated and, as he says, allows for an atmosphere of creative collaboration between himself and the cast. His career in teaching is a clear advantage, as indeed is his long association with the Barrow Society. 'It often happens,' he told me, 'that when the cast come together I realise that I've known a lot of them since they were kids!' (and probably inspired many of them to join the Society in the first place.) Alongside him there have been two other constant members of the production team, viz. Paul Blake, Musical Director, and Sally McKimm, Choreographer. Paul was initially an experienced rehearsal accompanist for the Society, and was in charge of musical arrangements for the centenary concert (*100 Not Out*), before picking up the baton for his first full-scale musical. Sally McKimm's first outing with the Society was as a 14-year old in the Dream Ballet sequence for *Oklahoma!,* and then, following her professional training, first took on the role of Choreographer in 2008. She has since choreographed all subsequent shows and her creativity has attracted considerable recognition. In 2010 she was awarded the Sylvia Barrow Award for *Beauty and the Beast*, and was nominated as Best Choreographer for *Chess* in the 2013 NODA awards.

So as we finally reach the present day, the Barrow Society can surely look back with a great deal of pride on all it has achieved. Like other local Societies it has had its high points, but has also had to ride the storms, weather periods of uncertainty, respond to the challenges of changing times and, perhaps most of all, take risks. In researching this book I have spoken to several experienced Producers who lament the problems of predicting whether a show will be a success or not. A good house on opening night is usually the key indicator. The dilemma is that the novelty of an unknown show may well be a draw, but it can also work the other way and put people off. Equally the well-known and popular shows are not necessarily safer options as they run the risk of being shunned as 'old hat'. As far as the Barrow Society's choices over the years are concerned, a successful balance seems to have been struck between the traditional and the modern, and certainly the policy in recent years of presenting a series of ambitious modern shows seems to have really paid off.

But before moving on, a point worth repeating and one which applies to all local societies, is never to under-estimate the amount of work and effort that goes into producing each individual show. I saw this for myself as, whilst researching this book, I was privileged to be invited to a rehearsal of BODS production of *Legally Blonde* in 2016 (more of this later). In this context however, I should also say that my survey has tended to focus on the performers and immediate production teams, but behind them there is a whole army of helpers, patrons and supporters. Again, I will be highlighting their essential contributions later, but in the meantime consider all the people that have been involved with the Barrow Society since its beginnings, and marvel at the extent and variety of all the entertainment opportunities they have provided over the years. But best of all, look out for the next 'BODS' production and go and buy a ticket.

4

WALNEY MUSICAL THEATRE COMPANY
(Founded 1932)

"The Walney Parish Church Music and Dramatic Society is intent on establishing itself quickly as one of the leading amateur operatic bodies in the town." So rang out the battle cry of the group we know today as the Walney Musical Theatre Company in 1932. They declared themselves to be the first such society on the island and were promoting their first production *The Mandarin*.

The man chiefly responsible for kicking things off was Cyril Dent (left), a Walneyite for at least the first 60 years of his life. He had joined St Mary's (also known as Walney Parish Church) youth group as a youngster and then, aged just 26 but with the confidence of youth on his side, decided that something more ambitious was required. Remember that live theatre was premium-style entertainment at this time, there was no such thing as domestic TV, and films had only just begun to talk so, presumably having seen the onward march of the Barrow Society, he was inspired to start a similar movement on Walney. He soon recruited other church members to the cause, such as Sid & Phyllis Bundy, and a steering committee was set up. Keen to establish a point of difference from the start the committee decided to avoid the usual Gilbert & Sullivan curtain-raiser and went for a light opera written by Henry de Kloven, *The Mandarin*. Mr de Kloven was a prolific American composer who actually patterned his work after good old G & S so, in a sense, it was the same idea, only different. The Producer was Charles Thompson (you will be hearing more about him as a man also at the forefront when the Abbey, Grange and Flookburgh Societies got going), so the show was in good hands. Cyril Dent sang in the chorus, along with others who were to remain with the Society for many years, such as Sid & Phyllis Bundy, who were to give more than 60 years of service. The show ran for 3 nights only but received an enthusiastic reception.

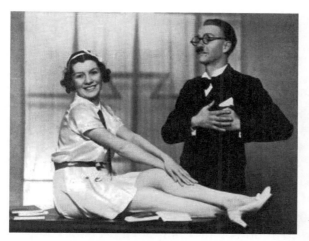

Emboldened by the success, the Society staged *The Rose of Araby* the following year, and they were on their way. By 1935 Cyril Dent had taken over as producer for *No No Nanette* and, under his guidance, a series of popular, modern shows followed. One that was viewed as a particular high point was *The Girlfriend*, staged in 1937, and again starred players who had already become regular performers such as those pictured above, Hilda Entwistle and Harry Fell, and others such as Emily Smith and Albert Stubbs. 'Lilting, popular melodies, robust humour, scintillating chorus work,' ran the review in the *North West Daily Mail*, 'and, above all, outstanding team spirit.'

Other forces from the local scene then arrived – Dora Marshall, a local dance teacher, was engaged, Mr V Dilks became Musical Director and, for *Goodnight Vienna* in 1939, Tom Rawsthorn was appointed as Producer. And all would no doubt have proceeded apace had it not been for the outbreak of World War Two. Rehearsals for the next production, *The Belle of New York*, were in fact well underway when all activities were called to a halt, resulting in a significant financial loss for the group. As for Cyril Dent, to his credit he turned his attention to the war effort and set about organising a number of concert parties for the benefit of rehabilitating servicemen. For this purpose he recruited all available local performers and established a group known as 'The Walney Highlights Concert Party.'

After the war, amateur theatre had a nationwide re-birth and the Walney Society, in the same year as the Ulverston Society, re-commenced activities in 1947 with *Tulip Time* under the direction of Cyril Dent, Dora Marshall, and Mr W E Kelly as Musical Director. As with all the pre-war shows, *Tulip Time* was staged at the former Walney Theatre, on Dominion Street and the reaction to it was so positive, it was as if they had never been away. The Society breathed a huge sigh of relief as its financial situation was pretty poor following the war, and the show was produced in a tense and uncertain atmosphere. *Maritza* followed in 1948, a light opera from an Hungarian composer, and then, presumably with a view to the Society's further development by pooling a wider audience, proceedings were moved to the Coliseum on Abbey Road, Barrow for *Wild Violets* in 1949. It was a bold but successful move, as well as a sign of improved confidence, and all future productions were staged there until – well, you know the rest. But at least for now the Society was doing very nicely, thank you very much.

Boom Years

The year 1950 then saw the revival of the Barrow Amateurs, and the birth of Abbey Musical Society. The Grange and Flookburgh Societies were also to become re-kindled at this time. In other words there was now more competition for audience attention. The Walney Society responded with a series of north-west premieres. An early one was *Magyar Melody*, with music and lyrics supplied by the same writing team who had created *Goodnight Vienna*, Eric Maschwitz and George Posford. The pair actually sent their best wishes to the

Society for the success of the show with a warm-hearted, if somewhat over-blown message of congratulation: 'We are proud and happy that the North-West premiere of this show should be given by your outstanding Society,' they said. 'We believe in all sincerity that 'The Amateurs' are the life-blood and backbone of the English Musical Theatre.'

Rio Rita followed in 1951, a reprise of the show the Society had previously staged in 1938, but this time with Bob Bowker as Producer for the first time. Then came *Balalaika* in 1952, another first in terms of being previously unseen in the district, but also for the fact that the Musical Director was new

– though he was not an unfamiliar face on the local scene. This was Wyn Large who would be a popular choice for both Walney and the Flookburgh Societies in several later productions. He had come to Barrow from Liverpool in the 1920s, and soon became a well-known local musician. He first appeared as an accompanying pianist for the old silent films being shown at the old Palace cinema on Duke Street. Then when the talkies came he could be found in the orchestra pit of the Royalty Theatre before moving to His Majesty's Theatre in 1937 when the Royalty closed. Once enlisted by local amateur societies he continued to act as a popular Musical Director until ill-health forced him to retire. He died at the age of 94 in 1998.

Meanwhile, back to 1952 and *Balalaika*, this show was also a first for someone else who had recently returned to the area post-war, and who was to make his own mark on the amateur scene as the years progressed – Ronald Metcalfe. The cast also included Society 'regulars' Hedley D Smith, Frank Farish, and Irene Livingstone and, because of the success the Society had enjoyed, many new members had joined the throng. All in all there were as many as 75 performers in the *Balalaika* cast!

Ronald Metcalfe then soon progressed to the Producer's chair for *Floradora*, staged in 1953. Described as 'the queen of musical comedies' it was the Society's contribution to the celebrations of Coronation year. And in case you didn't know (I certainly didn't) it was the show which gave birth to two songs that have become the perennial favourites of those of a certain age: *Lily of Laguna*, and *Tell Me Pretty Maiden (are there any more at home like you?)*

In 1950, when Eric Maschwitz and George Posford had sent their goodwill message they had added another thought: 'America has recently presented the West End of London with several great new musical shows in the modern sophisticated transatlantic style,' it ran. 'But we firmly believe that the amateurs of Britain, whose singing far transcends anything that we can achieve in the professional theatre, will always prefer the colourful costume play with a light operatic score.' One wonders if they could have laid it on any more thickly. Old cynic as I am, I'm inclined to read it as, 'I hope you'll keep putting on our stuff instead of that new-fangled American tosh.' But this was Broadway's Golden Age, the age of the new transatlantic style indeed and, as far as the local scene was concerned, a group of amateur players would ignore such developments at its peril. In fact, as things turned out, the Walney Society was to be the first to bring something of the Broadway experience to town.

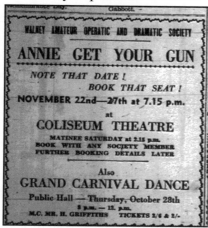

In 1954 they produced the first in a series of 4 such musicals: *Annie Get Your Gun* (1954), *South Pacific* (1956), *Carousel* (1957), and *The King and I* (1958). All were really quite new at this time. *Carousel* had only been premiered in the US twelve years earlier, and the others less than eight. When *Annie Get Your Gun* opened in Barrow the queue for tickets was unprecedented. It was clearly the show to see and as such was a real coup for the Walney Society. 18-year old Hazel Thompson took the lead role, with Hedley D Smith as Buffalo Bill.

Bumps in the Road

In the early 1960s the Walney Society continued to stage shows from the modern era, now joined by the other local

Societies who had adopted a similar policy. The offering for 1961 was *The Pyjama Game*, with Wyn Large still wielding the baton as he had done since 1952, but with a new Producer. This was Verne Morgan, a professional actor from London who came with impressive credentials. He had appeared in David Lean's film *Oliver Twist* in 1947, and had played on the West End stage with, among others, Anthony Newley. He had now turned his hand to producing and, having worked with several amateur companies around the country, he arrived in Barrow in 1961.

Both *The Pyjama Game*, and his next show *The Flower Drum Song* (1962) were hailed as major successes. His next, *The Music Man* (1963), was seen as something of a gamble, a brave choice perhaps, and was certainly produced under trying circumstances. If you are familiar with the show you will know that it is a demanding production with a very tricky, if innovative, musical score and something of a bizarre plot. This was also the time of venue disruption, when the Coliseum was being shut down and alternative venues were either under threat themselves, or offering limited facilities. The show even suffered the sudden indisposition of cast member Shirley Morgan, and Vera Illingworth had to step in at short notice. She had been a member of the Society since 1947, having first performed in *Tulip Time*, but had retired from performing several years earlier to concentrate on administrative and committee duties for the Society. Overall anxiety and low morale amongst the cast were prevalent and, although the show went down reasonably well, it was said to lack the exuberance it needed.

As for the venue disruption the upshot for Walney was that between 1964 and 1967 the Society was only able to stage one show, *Calamity Jane* in 1965. Verne Morgan returned to produce the show but sadly the expertise of Wyn Large had been lost as he had been forced to stand down because of failing health. Then two more fallow years followed. 'A lay-off that caused the committee and members a considerable amount of inconvenience, heartache and tribulation', says Ronald Metcalfe, writing in the *Barrow News*. It was indeed the toughest of times for the Society, so much so that its very continuation was called into question. But who better to save the day than the indomitable Cyril Dent? In 1968 he took on the task of producing *Oklahoma!* ironically enough a show about (among other things) the formation of the new State, in other words a new beginning. Mr Dent was as tenacious as ever but had a very difficult task on his hands. He had no replacement for Wyn Large as Musical Director for some time (Bob Bowker gamely filling in until Mr William Crawford was available to take his place), several backstage helpers had bowed out during the fallow years, Barrow's theatres were slowly disappearing leaving only the more limited space of the Public Hall for performances, but worst of all, where was his cast? Some Walney 'old reliables' were available (e.g. Irene Livingstone and Frank Farish, and Emily Smith who had performed in the very first show back in 1932) but it was chiefly the input and support from other Societies on which the viability of the show ultimately depended. Husband and wife team John and Paulette Lewis took the leads, fresh from playing the same parts for the Flookburgh Society, supplemented by such as Cyril Bond and Arnold Norman from the Barrow Society, and Jim Burdekin and Florrie Melville from Abbey.

At this time, collaboration between Societies was still not a common arrangement. Society hopping had been very much frowned upon in the past and you may recall that, back in the 1950s, Bob Bowker was heavily censured by the Barrow Society for agreeing to produce a show for Abbey. At that time however Operatic Societies were really just getting started so my guess is that it was their perceived vulnerability that made them defend their borders so vigorously. But by the 1970s, this defensiveness had been slowly giving way to a more enlightened attitude of collaboration and mutual support. It made sense.

The Sound of Music, the show staged in 1970, continued in this vein. Joyce Hill, who had previously performed for both Ulverston and Millom, took the lead role of

The von Trapp children (Sheila Cornthwaite, Valerie Rooke, Jon Fletcher, Tracey Locke, John Kent, Heather Judge and Nina Steele), *with Maria* (Joyce Till) *and Captain von Trapp* (Bill Steel)

Maria, with Bill & Noreen Steel, late of Ulverston and Abbey, playing Captain von Trapp and Elsa Shraeder, his would-be fianceé. Walney stalwarts Irene Livingstone and Frank Farish also featured. Ronald Metcalfe's press review however led to an unpleasant exchange between him and the Society through the pages of the *Barrow News*. He had accused the show of 'lacking pace' which in turn led to him being 'publically denounced' from the stage on the show's last night. We cannot know exactly what was said but it sent Mr Metcalfe into a spluttering rage in his column the following week. 'I understand I was accused of having an unfriendly bias towards Walney,' he fumed. 'I have nothing but contempt for such a remark, and have only one word to say – poppycock!' I say old boy, steady on.

Still, the Society was going through a pretty tough period which perhaps accounts for some over-sensitivity on their part. Having to rely on the support and goodwill of other Societies to survive was not a good position to be in. Then there was another blow in 1971 when the proposed production of *Pickwick* had to be cancelled due to the lack of Society membership. After much subsequent deliberation an alternative was chosen – *Annie Get Your Gun* – the source of the Society's greatest success of course back in 1954. Presumably the hope was that such a show would invigorate both the cast and the audience and remind everyone that, as Annie would sing, 'There's no business like show business!' It certainly had an effect as the Society then embarked on a regular annual output for the next 16 years – until 1988.

Several of the annual shows that followed were produced by Dorothy Hardy, a well respected and tireless force on the amateur scene, who also managed to direct shows for the Abbey Society at the same time, or at least in the same years. She was assisted by Doreen Dunlop, another well-known power-house, as her Musical Director. Together they steered *Fiddler on the Roof* (1976) and *Kiss Me Kate* (1977) to success, and then in 1978 came *Gigi*. It was a special production as it had only been released to the amateur stage that same year. There were some signs of a tightening of the budget as the scenery was specially built in-house, and many of the costumes were designed by the ubiquitous David Marcus. And indeed the end of the 1970s would herald the start of another unsettled period for the Society. It began with an unfortunate double booking with the Millom Society in 1979, when both Societies staged *Call Me Madam* within a week of each other. Sadly, Ronald Metcalfe had passed away in 1973 but, were he still around, you can imagine what he would have had to say about that.

Following Ronald Metcalfe's death Bob Bowker had taken over as Arts correspondent for the Barrow News and, like his predecessor, was finding that his critiques were not always appreciated. In 1980, when the Walney Society staged the fourth local production of *South Pacific*, he had put people's backs up when he had moaned about the frequency with which this show (along with *Oklahoma!* which Ulverston were staging that year) kept being revived. Even so, familiar as *South Pacific* may have been, it didn't stop Joan Davidson being awarded a *Barrow News* Oscar for her portrayal of Bloody Mary. Then, on a later occasion after attending a particular show, Mr Bowker found himself in a pub face to face with a drunken member of the cast who accosted him about his constant "vitriolic" reviews. 'We work damn hard', he is reported to have said. 'Give us a break!' To describe his reviews as 'vitriolic' seems a bit harsh but, at this time, even in the wake of a mildly unenthusiastic press review it was quite usual for letters of protest to appear the following week from disgruntled members of the public. As Mr Metcalfe had learned before him, a critic's lot is not a happy one

Then, in 1981, came the sad news that the Society lost one of its favourite performers, Irene Livingstone. She had been a star performer for Walney for many years, having first appeared as a dancer in the show *Wild Violets* in 1949. From then on she had appeared in a range of diverse roles for many shows produced by both Walney and the Barrow Societies. In a moving obituary Bob Bowker described 'her unfailing genius for looking stunning on the night, and her warm, sunny nature that we shall always remember.'

Another venue scare was then to unsettle everyone in 1982. The Society had taken up a comfortable residence in the new Civic Hall, using it both as their regular performance and rehearsal venue. But when Barrow councillors approved a new rate of hire charges (as much as a 25% rise for the use of the main hall) it over-stretched the Society's resources to the point where it was feared their proposed show, which ironically enough was *Half a Sixpence*, would have to be cancelled. Eventually a sort of compromise was reached when the cheaper mid-week nights were offered although, when all the logistics were taken into account, it would mean that, instead of staging the show in April as was the usual practice, the performance would have to be postponed until the following September. Eventually the crisis passed and the storm was weathered.

Things picked up again with enjoyable revivals of *Carousel* (1984) and the playful *Mr Cinders* (1985). Paulette Lewis, who you have yet to hear about in the context of the Flookburgh Society, was now a leading lady for many of these Walney Society productions. She starred in the following year's show *Hello Dolly*, (pictured left with Gerald Babbs) and for her performance was nominated for a *Barrow News* Oscar at the same time as her daughter Abigail was being awarded the Nellie English Award for 'most promising newcomer' for her performance in *Dracula Spectacular* for Walney Juniors.

In 1987 Paulette then took the lead in *Calamity Jane*, a role she had played for the Flookburgh Society 20 years earlier. David Marcus, who produced the show, remarked, 'Paulette holds the record for being both the oldest and youngest Calamity Jane in the district!' An innovative way of promoting the show whilst at the same time raising extra funds was also tried by inviting people to meet the cast at a coffee morning held at the Civic Hall on the day the box office opened.

Then, after *My Fair Lady* (1988), productions came to a halt, and the Society did not stage another show for the next 4 years. When they did finally return with *Oliver!* in 1992, there was also evidence of a loss of momentum as, despite the quality of many individual performances, overall it was reported to be a show which lacked spark and energy. I have no hard evidence to support this thought but, in accounting for the four-year gap and the subsequent loss of momentum and drive, my inference would be that the problem was every Society's constant nightmare – cash-flow and a shortage of funds. If this in turn elicited anxieties about the Society's future viability, the situation may also have been aggravated by the uncertainties surrounding the future of the Civic Hall. Extensive re-furbishment had been promised but no-one was absolutely certain of the time-scale or exactly what was being proposed. This was of course a development which affected all the amateur groups in the town, although as I say it may have compounded any internal problems the Walney Society were experiencing. As it happened the Society recovered from this gloomy period pretty quickly and, from 1993 onwards, a series of shows were produced which, as well as having enhanced production values, also re-vitalised the performers by providing good opportunities for them to showcase their vocal and dancing talents. There was *Camelot* (1993) with its sumptuous setting and romantic songs, *Guys and Dolls* (1994) with its vibrant dance routines, and *Fiddler on the Roof* (1995) with its poignant musicality and Jewish folk dancing. It seems to me that this sort of ebb and flow appears to be a feature of all the amateur Societies I have studied, no doubt in part because of the dynamic nature of their changing membership – one minute they're down, and then they bounce back and are up again.

Revival

Certainly novel ventures and attempts to improve cash-flow were in evidence in the period that followed as extra variety or 'medley' shows were added to the Society's output. Of course it was common practice for an amateur Society to stage extra shows during the summer as a way of boosting funds, since such shows cost very little to put on and required much less preparation than a full-scale musical. These Walney Society shows contained the usual blend of 'songs from the musicals' but were presented as more well-drilled, and more lavish and ambitious than usual. Through David Marcus, they were also subject to heavier promotion presumably to ensure good receipts. The said shows were dubbed *West End Memories* in 1995 and 1996, and *For Old Times Sake* in 1997 and 1998.

Having regained their confidence with a series of successful shows, the Society was now ready to take a risk with a new show, Stephen Sondheim's pastiche of early Broadway shows *Follies* which was their major production in 1996. As ever with Sondheim this is a demanding show with a complicated story, centred around two show-girls who attend a reunion at an old theatre that is about to be demolished. There are then flashbacks to their younger selves and early experiences. The leading roles were taken by Eileen Lithgow and Paulette Woodhouse, with Michelle Larcombe and Lisa Sharrock playing their younger selves. Bill Calvert and David Marcus played their husbands. In true trouper fashion Michelle, who had suffered a leg injury, had to walk through her part whilst on crutches. It was a very well-received production but, since the story maps so nicely on to what had happened a few years earlier to Barrow's Civic Hall, how much more effective it would have been to have staged it in 1990!

The story of *Crazy for You* (1997), the Society's next show, is again the story of a struggling theatre threatened with closure. A love-struck hero then saves the day by 'putting on a show'. As I've implied once or twice already I think it's quite possible that a Society's choice of show sometimes says something about its internal pre-occupations at the time. So perhaps, given their past experiences of venue disruption, and their nomadic life of the past few years as they were moved from venue to venue, the choice of *Crazy For You* may have reflected their continuing anxieties about the life span of Forum 28, their new venue. After all *Crazy for You* carries the clear message that it is only by 'putting on a show' that such venues have an assured future! Whether this is the case or not, the Committee and production team were so keen to get their hands on the show that, due to the late release of its performance licence, they were prepared to risk a shorter rehearsal period than usual. Unfortunately this showed when the show began its run as, unlike previous productions, there were reports of several technical hitches, missed cues, mistakes with the scenery, and strained silences. But for all this, it was still reviewed as 'a thoroughly entertaining and fun show.' It was also full of energetic dance routines and many of George Gershwin's best known songs, such as *I Got Rhythm* and the bitter-sweet *They Can't Take That Away From Me*.

And to finish off the century there was still lots to love in the Society's next outings. First there was *The King and I* (1998) with Craig Brown as the King and Eileen Lithgow as Anna playing, so it was said, the part she was born for. Then came *Kismet* (1999) with Russell Palmer and again Eileen

Lithgow in leading roles. 'There was much to enjoy,' reports Helen Wall in the *Evening Mail*, 'with brilliant singing and loads of laughs.' As with most of these past series of shows they had been put together by the same production team of David Marcus, Peter Dyer, Graham Barker and Deborah Brown. Peter Dyer, you may recall, was also busy working as Musical Director with the Barrow Society's productions at this time, and you will come across the names of the choreographers Deborah Brown and Graham Barker in other contexts as we proceed, all demonstrating yet again the amazing fluidity that now existed between Societies. Graham Barker is also a good example of how family traditions pass through the generations in this amateur world as he is the grandson of two of the founders of the Walney Society, Sid & Phyllis Bundy.

David Marcus

The new century could then perhaps be the marker for the start of the Walney Society's heyday, with David Marcus in charge of productions. Of course he had already firmly made his mark in the previous decade but from 2000 onwards the shows he produced seemed to take on a new character. They were in the main shows new to the district, drawing together performers from all parts, with an occasional professional recruited from further afield. The Souvenir Programme also became, perhaps for the first time, an important part of the show itself – a high quality glossy A4 booklet complete with cast biographies and first-rate photography. In 2012, the programme for *Peter Pan* was so impressive it even won the NODA award for the Best Souvenir Programme in the North West Region.

As you will have realised David Marcus' activities were by no means confined to one Society with some of his work actually going beyond the boundaries of the groups so far discussed, so perhaps now is a good time to consider his story in more detail, to put his work into context and to draw the various strands together. As far as amateur theatre is concerned his reputation is that of a man with energy, ambition and big ideas. Since he arrived on the scene in the early 1970s he has been associated with schools, colleges, and operatic societies, and has steered many productions to success.

Born David Clay in Bradford in 1949, he arrived on the Furness scene in the early 1970s. He had caught the theatrical bug early and from the ages of 8 to16 had first worked with the Bradford Playhouse Children's Theatre. He then worked for a brief spell with a theatrical costumier in Leeds before securing the post of property manager, and then stage/company manager with the Alhambra Theatre, Bradford. As an actor he had some early success in film and TV, with parts in a number of well-known series (including Coronation Street), and in the course of his early career worked with many star names.

Then comes the part of the story, which will be told in a later chapter, when he comes to Barrow at first on a holiday trip, decides to stay, and is instrumental in establishing the Barrow Savoyards in 1973. He was then chiefly involved with the productions of the Barrow and Walney Societies, but his story also goes off at something of a tangent from there. The show which could possibly be ear-marked as a turning point was the Barrow Society's production of *Jesus Christ Superstar* for which he was Artistic Director in 1984. Although the phrase can be over-used, in this case the show really did 'break all box-office records', and my guess is that it was the success that this particular show enjoyed which inspired him to tackle bigger and even more ambitious projects.

One such was the establishment of his own company "David Marcus Productions". Although destined to have a shorter life, it followed the pattern of Ronald Metcalfe's 'Furness Drama Association' in the 1960s in that it pulled together talent from all parts of the district, and functioned independently of the established local Societies. With himself again in the role of Artistic Director this company staged *West Side Story* in 1986, with Ian Honeyman as Musical Director, who was both a local musician and a well-respected performer of contemporary opera. The complex dance numbers, a major component of this particular show were directed by Liz Dunn, experienced both as an actress and choreographer with the Barrow Society. Many other familiar names, all of whom had performed in various other local Societies, can be found in the 40-strong cast, such as Chris Warby, Martin Craig, Steve Carrick, and Helen Troughton. Riff, leader of the Jets, was played by Martin Savage, an actor whose main affiliation was with the Abbey Society. As you will hear later he was to progress to a successful career both on the London stage and on film.

David Marcus' next major project, and certainly his most ambitious, was the one for which he is probably most remembered, namely The Furness Abbey Mystery Plays in 1988. The event is worth recording but how comfortably it fits in to a review of amateur theatricals is questionable. With a total cast of around 250 many amateur performers were of course involved, but many professionals were engaged too, with the overall balance of actors and services in their favour. It was generally agreed however that the Mystery Plays constituted something very special. The combination of imaginative lighting, sound, and special effects in the context of the 11th century Abbey created a haunting, emotionally-charged atmosphere which was said to hold the capacity audience spellbound. HRH Prince Edward had even accepted an invitation to attend.

Fired up with the success of the project, David Marcus attempted to go a step further with another event at the Abbey two years later, an event he called 'The Festival of Furness Abbey'. The principal idea was to present up to 12 performances of *Jesus Christ Superstar* in the Abbey grounds, with a cast of professional actors supported by amateurs from the local scene, and a succession of celebrity nights involving the likes of Ken Dodd, Humphrey Lyttleton and the revered Halle Orchestra. A catering marquee was also to be available complete with various sorts of marketing merchandise such as T-shirts, mugs etc. Overall the event, awe-inspiring, successful, and a great boost for the arts in the district as it was, also brought with it heavy financial liabilities. When all was accounted, a jaw-dropping deficit of more than £100,000 was recorded. It led to the near-prosecution of David Marcus and his company by the Crown Prosecution Service, although this was subsequently dropped. Nevertheless his health, and his reputation, took a thorough demoralising beating.

On the other hand, although there was this controversy and unpleasantness, the event was the inspiration for something much more positive. Ruth Williams of the Barbados Community Foundation (BCF) had at some point been in the audience and had been so impressed she asked if David Marcus and his company would be willing to bring *Jesus Christ Superstar* to Barbados as a fund-raising event. At the time the BCF was the island's major charitable organisation, responsible for distributing funds across a wide cross-section of charities in the community. It actually took a long while for the plans to come to fruition but eventually, in October 2002, everything finally came together.

In true David Marcus' style the cast for the production was a troupe of local performers combined with professionals from the London stage. Steve Balsamo, for example, having previously starred in the title role in a West End production of the show played Jesus. Among the performers from the South Lakes' amateurs were Martin Craig, Wayne Buckley, Bill

Calvert and Vincent Burston. David Marcus himself played his favourite role, King Herod. He also directed of course, assisted by Christopher Manoe, a professional actor and writer. Ian Honeyman was again engaged as Musical Director, assisted by Eileen Lithgow, with Kay Charnley as Head of Choreography assisted by Sally McKimm, all of whom having a sound local Operatic Society pedigree.

It was a memorable and exhilarating experience for all the cast, but also exhausting. It was a two-week trip in total but not exactly a holiday in the sun. I'm told (perhaps with some artistic licence, but who knows?) that rehearsals lasted for 12 hours a day, for 10 days. The musicians who formed The Rock Band, were again all local to the South Lakes with considerable Operatic Society experience: Andre Dannell (Keyboards), Paul Bryden (Lead Guitar), Ron Fones (Rhythm Guitar), Steve Simpson (Bass Guitar), and Andrew Sproxton (percussion). Claire Smeaton was the rehearsal pianist. With preparations over, there were then two performances, both staged in the prestigious Garfield Sobers Sports Complex, St Michael, Barbados – one performance especially for local school-children (with just the rock band), and a Gala show for everyone else, including the Governor of Barbados, the British High Commissioner to Barbados Mr John White, and other dignitaries. For the Gala show the rock band were supplemented by the Barbados Police Brass Band and the Barbados Symphony Strings. It must have been quite an event to be a part of, and I imagine the atmosphere was pretty electric. And then, when it was all over, the cast at last had the freedom and space to do whatever they wished to do with their remaining time there – sleep, I guess.

Back in Barrow, apart from his work in schools as a teacher and drama coach, David Marcus remained chiefly involved with the Walney Society and the production of their annual musical. He also set up another independent company 'Pumpkin Productions' with the primary purpose of staging an annual pantomime, details of which can be found in a later chapter. His work has not always been free of controversy and his policy of mixing the two worlds of amateur and professional theatre has not always met with universal approval, but there is no doubting the spirit of enterprise and commitment he has shown towards local community theatre. On stage he has also demonstrated an enviable versatility in his ease of movement, both as actor and director, from one musical genre to another, whether it be a Gilbert and Sullivan operetta, grand opera, a modern musical, or a pantomime. There is of course a great deal more to his story than is recorded here, but I hope there is sufficient material to at least demonstrate his contribution to the South Lakes theatre scene both as a performer, innovator, and general motive force.

The New Century

Meanwhile – returning to the story of the Walney Society, the musical *Mack and Mabel* kicked things off in 2000 with David

Marcus and Julie Lloyd playing the title roles. The same team followed this up very successfully with *West Side Story* (2002), which his own company 'David Marcus Productions' had previously staged back in 1986. Then came another production with which he was very familiar - *Jesus Christ Superstar* – the show he had previously produced for the 1990 Festival of Furness Abbey, and had then taken to Barbados. For the 2003 production Malcolm Smith, actually a Walneyite but someone who had since forged a career in the professional theatre, was engaged to play Jesus (he had also played the apostle Peter in the Barbados production), with Martin Craig as Judas, and Deborah Bird as Mary Magdalene.

In 2004, no doubt driven by David Marcus, the Society dropped the 'amateur' tag and adopted a new name, The Walney Musical Theatre Company (WMTC), and then embarked on a whole series of premieres with other guest performers occasionally drafted in from outside. The first of these was *Ragtime*, a challenging piece with a complex musical score and a plot to match, which dealt with weighty subject matter. If you haven't seen it you may be surprised to note that, in the league table of 'favourite musicals' it is often found to be in competition with *Les Miserables*. Then, in a lighter vein *Summer Holiday* followed in 2005 with all the usual suspects putting on their dancing shoes and taking you for a ride – Wayne Buckley, Martin Craig, Chris Warby, Deborah Bird, and Deborah Brown. There was even a guest appearance by Elaine Parkinson, star of many an Ulverston Society show.

But talking of *Les Miserables* (as we weren't since it is not on release to senior societies to perform) WMTC perhaps chose the next best thing in *Jekyll and Hyde* in 2006. It is an equally stirring piece with lashings of melodrama, and with the odd death scene and prostitute thrown in. (What's not to like?) Still, it was a brave venture and one that the Company pulled off with their usual aplomb. Richard Hough, who had joined the Company that year played Dr Jekyll, with a performance that actually won him the NODA award for the Best Actor in a Musical for the North West region. But if you thought it might have been an unsuitable show for those of a nervous disposition, how about *The Full Monty* in 2007? You know the one – how a group of steelworkers learn how to cope with long-term unemployment by wearing nothing but a smile. Baring all for their art were: Andrew Barrow, Richard Hough, Russ Palmer, Wayne Buckley, Craig Mitchell, and newcomer Ian Gibbs.

Following the exuberant *42nd Street* in 2008 came the equally exuberant *Singin' in the Rain* in 2009. With a mix of experienced players, younger newcomers, pre-shot film footage and a real on-stage rain shower, the famous musical was brought fully to life. Bianca Tranter, Craig Mitchell, Deborah Bird and Tom Halfpenny starred. The show also saw a new Musical Director in Donald Gillthorpe (who had succeeded Peter Dyer as Head of Music at Dowdales School, Dalton), and experienced choreographer Sue Lloyd-Roberts, who had first appeared on the scene in 1991 for the Barrow Society's production of *Cabaret*, was also recruited. For her contribution to *Singin' in the Rain* she won a NODA nomination.

The following year she was then part of the impressive creative team which, in addition to David Marcus included Eileen Lithgow & Peter Dyer, for the next revival of *Jesus Christ Superstar* in 2010. (Including the production at The Festival of Furness Abbey in 1990 this would be its fourth outing on the local scene.) Malcolm Smith played Jesus, reviving the role he had played previously in 2003, with Rob O'Hara, a recruit from the Ulverston scene playing Judas, whilst a young Emily Dodd, who had made her debut for WMTC the previous year, played Mary Magdalene. On the last night of the run, possibly inspired by the Barbados experience,

Jesus Christ Superstar, 2010

a Charity Gala Performance was staged in support of the Mayor's charities. The Mayor and Mayoress, Councillor Rory and Wendy McClure, were of course the special guests along with many other local dignitaries. It was a much appreciated nod to the past when profits from amateur productions were regularly donated to local charities. Sadly, over the years, rising production costs had made such an arrangement increasingly difficult to sustain. It proved to be a very successful initiative so was repeated the following year with the WMTC's production of Mel Brooks' comedy *The Producers*. This time the Rotary Club was the beneficiary, who in turn was responsible for distributing the returns to local charities. As for *The Producers* the show went on to win a clutch of NODA awards: Best Choreography (Sue Lloyd-Roberts & Deborah Brown), Best Actor in a Musical (Russ Palmer), and the coveted title of Best Musical.

*   *   *

Russell Palmer and Andrew Bond
as Captain Hook and Smee

In 2012 WMTC presented *Peter Pan*, which was much praised for its technical achievements in lighting, flying, and general swash-buckling – and of course for the guest appearance of Tinkerbell, who was making her Barrow-in-Furness debut direct from Disneyland. And it's worth pausing for a moment just to reflect on the amazing range of shows being staged by the other local groups at this time. For example, in addition to *Peter Pan*, during 2012 you had the opportunity to see *Annie* at the Coronation Hall in Ulverston, a variety show in Flookburgh, *Chess, Dr Dolittle, The Sound of Music* and Youth Theatre productions such as *High School Musical* and *AIDA,* all at The Forum in Barrow. And that's just one year. And talking of an amazing range, in 2013 the WMTC then went for a stark contrast to *Peter Pan* with *La Cage aux Folles*, a gay-themed musical comedy. The campness and trans-gender confusions were fully embraced by both the cast and the appreciative audience in a way that had not been the case in Ulverston 20 years earlier. They were less tolerant times then of course, but the Walney production was thoroughly unabashed and disinhibited, and ablaze with stunning make-up and costumes which had actually been worn in the original 1987 London production.

In 2013, since a fair number of young people had been inspired to join the ranks, a decision was taken to form 'Walney Musical Theatre Youth Section.' This seems a little odd since The Walney Junior Operatic Society, although an independent society in its own right, was already a well-established outlet for junior performers. But whatever the reasoning rehearsals soon got underway and their first and, as it turned out, their only full-scale production *CATS* was performed in the following year. Twenty or so youngsters aged between 13 and 20 comprised the cast, many already having previous stage experience in school or junior productions, and many of whom were later to go on to study drama and the performing arts. Among these were Meryn Nixon who played Grizabella (that's the one who gets to sing *Memory*), and who later secured professional work as a Disney Princess. She had also performed in *Peter Pan*, along with other 'Lost Boys' like Adam Walker, John Edwards, Robbie Gaffney, all of whom also starred in *CATS*.

Shimbleshanks (Tom Rutte*r), Gus* (Robbie Gaffney)
and Rumpus Cat (Adam Walker) CATS, 2014

Meanwhile the seniors were proud to present another Lloyd-Webber musical in 2014, (and by the way another premiere for the district) *Evita*, followed by the evergreen *West Side Story* in 2015. Unfortunately David Marcus' health was beginning to fail at this time so he had been forced to stand down from production duties. Nick Carson took over as Artistic Director, a local man who had previously worked both in professional theatre, on TV and in film. He had also appeared in previous Walney productions such as *Jesus Christ Superstar* in 2003, and in the Company's earlier production of *West Side Story* in 2002. Paul Blake again occupied the position of Musical Director, his 15th show incidentally for the Company, whilst Deborah Brown, another veteran of numerous previous productions, took care of the challenging choreography demanded by this show.

Eighteen-year old Mili Rich (also from *CATS*) played Maria with, so it was noted, remarkable confidence and maturity. Ryan Grainger took the part of the ill-fated Tony,

making his debut with WMTC, although he had previously appeared in the productions of the Abbey Society. Ben Lewis played Riff,

Pictured left:
Catherine Andrews, Louise Marshall and Sally McKimm as Sharks Rosalia, Consuela & Estella
West Side Story 2015

leader of the Jets, his second appearance for the Society having previously appeared in *Peter Pan* (2012). He was already a regular performer on local stages since the age of seven, when he first appeared in a Furness Youth Theatre production of *Oliver!* Subsequently he joined the Ulverston Society and took part in all their annual shows between 2008 and 2015. With few exceptions, I understand that all these young performers have ambitions to go on to study musical theatre and advance to the professional stage. In fact I can tell you that, at the time of writing, Mili Rich will soon be studying musical theatre at the Royal Conservatoire of Scotland, and Ben Lewis has been accepted by the Guildford School of Acting where he will train as an actor-musician.

So as we reach the modern day I think it's fair to say that over the past two decades the Walney Society has experienced a real developmental spurt with an impressive back catalogue of shows: from the classics to modern comedies, and from melodrama to high camp, whilst also feeling brave enough to tackle adult themes, the technically demanding, and even classic children's stories. And looking back over the history, it's clear that the Walney Society has much in common with other local amateur groups with a natural ebb and flow of fortunes and, being part of the same landscape, has had to deal with similar issues: the interruptions of war, the problems caused by disappearing theatres, rising costs and the ever-changing trends in popular music and, perhaps most crucial of all, how to keep the customer satisfied. In this respect it has certainly had its share of premieres, and has been as keen as any other group to leave its comfort zone and tackle challenging new projects. There is also plenty of evidence for the constant chasing after professional standards in the production values of all the shows it has staged.

One or two people I have spoken to have voiced a fear that, with all this similarity between local groups and the constant movement of performers from one Society to another, the boundaries between each group are becoming increasingly blurred. In consequence there is a danger that each group is losing its own particular identity. I am very doubtful myself that this is much of a problem. From what I have seen the most important blurring of boundaries going on in every Society, is the constant erosion of the boundary between what we call 'amateur' and what we call 'professional'. And the developmental march of the Walney Society is a prime example of this.

5

PANTOMIME!

Pantomime has been performed on many occasions in many venues and by many companies in the South Lakes area, and most (I hope) will be referred to in this chapter. But I think it's fair to say that it was in Ulverston, at the Coronation Hall, where the tradition of an annual pantomime really took hold, originating from the initiative of the British Legion Concert Party in 1948. Hence I have decided to insert this survey here as the next chronological stop on our journey through the years.

So this chapter is all about pantomimes. Oh yes it is! (Apologies, but I know you'll be expecting me to say that at some point, so it's important to get it out of the way.) The origins of the modern pantomime stretch far back in history but, for our purposes, can probably best be traced to the European and Music Hall influences of the 18th and 19th centuries. The term was first used to describe an entertainment advertised in a long forgotten newspaper *The Daily Courant* on 2nd March 1717, although we can assume that particular show won't have borne much resemblance to the more familiar shows of today. The modern version really stems from the late 19th century when the Music Hall stars of the day got involved in an attempt, by managers, to boost the box office.

Familiar characters appear in various guises in every pantomime tale. There is of course usually the eponymous hero, the attractive female he yearns for but whose quest for true love is thwarted by either an authoritarian father figure or some kind of villainous adversary, and the well-intentioned but hapless comic side-kick. The basis for these can be traced to the important European influence of the Italian 'Comedia dell'Arte' whose main protagonists were: Harlequin the hero, Columbine his love interest, Pantaloon the over-protective father, and Pulchinello the clown. The standard 'slapstick' sequence in every pantomime also had its origins here. Harlequin would always carry a magic sword, a sort of cross between a weapon and a magic wand, which he used to deter his adversaries. It was furnished with a hinged flap so that, when used, it would make a loud slapping sound which would give it more comic and theatrical effect. Over time, this use of the so-called 'slapstick' then became the generic term for any sort of comical knock-about encounter between characters.

The character of 'the Dame', as a cross-dressed male, emerged from the Victorian Music Halls. It was a character already familiar to these audiences but it was one of the most popular comedians of the day, Dan Leno, who helped to establish the character as a central figure in the modern Pantomime. In 1879 a certain Augustus Harris took over the management of the Theatre Royal, Drury Lane, and started the trend of adding star turns, such as Dan Leno, to his productions. The sight of a highly-rated comedian dressed as a spirited comic old lady enthralled audiences, ensured good box office returns, and of course started a trend that the many others that followed would seek to imitate.

Gender reversals and cross-dressing are both standard features of all pantomimes. So the male 'hero' is usually played by a female and even where the love interest is male, as in *Cinderella*, the character is again usually played by a female. This character has come to be known as the 'Principal Boy', and has perhaps the strangest pedigree. In the Victorian age there was nothing unusual about females taking on the role of a heroic male figure - it was another convention of the Music Hall. But for pantomime the rather wonderful and weird agreement was that, in an age when even the sight of a bare ankle was frowned upon, shapely female legs in tights *were* allowed as long as the wearer was playing a male role!

With all these elements in place the basic structure of the pantomime has probably remained the same for over 100 years now. Of course a strong story is always required and this has been ably provided by traditional fairy tales or folk legends – the more popular ones being such tales as Cinderella, Dick Whittington and Aladdin. The other essential ingredients are topical references, corny jokes and sketches, audience participation, and large helpings of song and dance. Nowadays, just as the Music Halls did with Dan Leno, larger theatres and professional companies compete to attract star names to draw in the crowds, whereas local amateur companies have to rely exclusively on local talent. On both counts it has proved to be a successful formula. The attraction of seeing a popular personality (whether Pop star, Actor, Estate Agent, or Buildings Inspector) in full Dame regalia, feckless and humiliated - who wouldn't want to see that?

As far as the South Lakes is concerned entertainments of this type may well have been brought to the long-gone theatres in Barrow and Ulverston, or by the strolling players or travelling theatres which were popular in the late 19th and early 20th centuries, but I'll begin our tour with an entertainment which was staged in Ulverston in April 1919 entitled *Hop O'My Thumb,* as it is the nearest thing I could find to our modern understanding of this genre. It is actually a show which has long been out of favour on the pantomime circuit although, way back in time, it is credited with being the first one ever to include a 'principal boy' in the cast. It was also one of Augustus Harris' 'star turn' productions at the Theatre Royal, London, when famous Music Hall star Little Tich took the title role. In Ulverston a group of amateurs staged it as one of the first productions at The Coronation Hall in 1919, when it was described as 'a bright and breezy musical revue.' Other pantomime shows appeared later, in a spasmodic sort of way, and were usually the work of a visiting professional company. One example is a production of *Aladdin*, which was staged in January 1929 by 'Jay Highley's Company' and was billed as "The greatest panto which ever visited the Furness District." Whether or not it lived up to such hype isn't known. Then, in 1948, the British Legion Concert Party took up the cause.

Their frequent concerts given around the district had already proved to be a popular and successful means of fund-raising for local charities. Then in 1948 the idea came from Gladys Cox (a member of the British Legion's Ladies Section) to put on a show aimed at raising funds for the British Legion itself. The plan was to stage the pantomime *Aladdin* which, although of course is usually a Christmas entertainment, was planned to take place in February because of the Legion's commitment to Remembrance Day duties in November. It was a major success, so much so that a second show, *Beauty and the Beast*, was staged the following year. And so the ball was set rolling and, although its pace may now be slowing, it has been moving steadily along ever since. As we will see, little has changed over the years – it has even remained as a late-January/early-February event, although the organising group has now morphed into 'Ulverston Pantomime Society.'

I say the pace may be slowing not to imply any decrease in the energy or enthusiasm of those concerned, but rather to a possible decline in interest from audiences. In the heyday of the 1950s and 60s packed houses could be assured almost every night but, nowadays, the Tuesday to Saturday run sees numbers build up only slowly after a patchy start. Don't get me wrong, it is still a popular event and an important part of Ulverston's annual programme but, as with everything in the entertainment world these days, there are many outlets competing for attention.

Following Gladys Cox as Producer came the formidable Bridget Turner, who had played leading roles herself in the early shows. The pantomime then remained in her capable hands for many years, aided by her husband Granville. The shows were all based, as usual, on the fairy tales we are all familiar with although, in these early years, some productions were Pantomime subjects rarely seen in our modern age – e.g. *Humpty Dumpty, Goody Two Shoes, Robinson Crusoe.*

The 1954 production of *Jack and the Beanstalk* (the first one I saw as a wide-eyed 6-year old) actually attracted a good luck telegram from none other than radio and TV star Max Bygraves and his Ulverston pianist Bob Dixon. 'Our best wishes have arrived, and to prove it, they're here!' it ran. 'May you have lots of success and may you always be jolly, and the box office bring in plenty of lolly. That's our message to everyone, and we think you'll agree, it's a good one, son.'

A scene from the finale of "Goldilocks", 1959

Whatever the show, there were several constant and reliable ingredients to each performance at this time: Norman Teagle marshalled the orchestra as Musical Director, whilst his wife Marjorie acted as dancing mistress, choreographing 3 dance troupes made up of different age groups (The Glamourettes, The Sunshine Girls, and The Legion Babes); Walter Howson provided the comedy as the traditional Pantomime Dame aided by the likes of Maurice Dickinson and Bill Satterthwaite; elaborate and colourful costumes graced every show which were all hand-made by the ladies of the British Legion Section; and Kathleen Harrison and her accordion always led the audience in community singing whilst the stage was prepared for the Grand Finale. After the finale on the last night, following their bows and well-earned applause, the cast would then all be presented across the footlights with gifts from family and friends, the Chairman of the Society would make a speech of thanks and everyone would go home content, feeling that little bit happier about facing the austere times they were living through.

The 1961 production *Cinderella* saw the debut of 16-year old Elaine Wilson (later to become Elaine Parkinson) who, building on her already quite substantial stage experience, was to progress to become one of the district's most enduring and popular performers, both as a dramatic actress and a star of musical theatre. Indeed she has already been referred to in the previous chapters. When I was speaking to her about her career I was struck by her passion and commitment to amateur theatre in all its forms and, I suspect like many others who have been bitten by this particular bug, she regards it as an indispensable part of her life. I particularly liked the story she told about her marriage to Jack Parkinson when, she said, she made it a condition of marrying him that he would never ask her to give up on her acting and performing. Subsequently, perhaps in a 'if you can't beat'em, join'em' kind of way, Jack was to become Assistant Stage Manager for the pantomimes, and Chair of the Society.

As well as Elaine and Jack of course many others have shown loyalty to the productions over several years. Terry Leech is one example, supported by his wife Rita, long active in the wardrobe department. Some have even progressed to the professional stage. Derek Corkhill, for example, who appeared in pantomimes during the 1960's (and who also performed with the Ulverston, Barrow, and Walney Operatic Societies) famously went on to land a part with the BBC's 'George Mitchell Black & White Minstrel Shows'. It's worth a mention I feel, but probably not something you put on your CV these days. Despite the danger of offending by omission, I will also risk mentioning the following who have been active in recent productions: there has been the frequent appearance of Ken Hindle as the traditional pantomime Dame, Bob Needham (who also later appeared as the Dame), Helen Day, Sue Little, Denise King, and Andrew Barrow, with added support from some key performers in other Societies in the district such as Russell Palmer, Martin Craig, Wayne Buckley, and young, talented, up-coming performers such as Ben Lewis, Bethany Rigg, and Phoebe & Leah Greaves. Creative input in the art of dance has been regularly provided by Sue Lloyd-Roberts, Gail Lloyd, and Jean Lancaster. Andrew Barrow also demonstrated his creativity by writing the shows for 2009 (*Dick Whittington*) and 2011 (*Robin Hood*). As you will have noted, most of these are familiar names on the local scene and are likely to be encountered in other chapters.

And last but by no means least there have been the important contributions of Paul Bryden and Gordon Crayston. Paul was recruited as Musical Director in 1998 on the 50th anniversary of the Society, and has stayed loyal to the role ever since. Both have been mentioned previously in the context of their work with other Societies, and we are sure to encounter them both again as we proceed. But just to remind you - Paul is a well known music teacher and musician in the area, and has been a member of the orchestra for the productions of almost every Musical Society in the area. Gordon Crayston has regularly produced the lighting wizardry not only for the pantomimes, but also for every stage production at the Coronation Hall, and indeed for probably every other local Society production for the past 30 years or more. He says he can't, or refuses to, remember which show was his first. (I suspect it was *The Mikado*.)

Sue Little, Terry Leech, Bob Needham, Lindsey Jackson, and Tracy Jackson in a scene from Jack & the Beanstalk, 1999

Funding a show remains an ever-present problem. For an Ulverston production costs today can rise to as much as £14,000 – lighting, sound, music, scenery, costumes, room hire, and insurance all stack up, and it is apparently getting increasingly difficult to recoup these costs. There are some local sponsors such as Glaxo, and the Fisher Foundation, but members also have to be active fund-raisers – bag-packing at Booth's Supermarket for example is one such initiative. But these are constantly changing times with ever-shifting public tastes in entertainment, and as much as Pantomime is a national tradition, the Coronation Hall pantomime has done very well to remain a local one.

This is not to say of course that it is absent in other parts of the district. For example, a group calling themselves 'Pennington Pantomimers' put on an annual show for a time, as did many Church groups, particularly during the 1960s and 70s. The Broughton Players have also been active in the past, and have experienced a revival in recent times. They were chiefly an am-dram group staging plays at Broughton's Victory Hall, before sadly disbanding in 1983. Then in 1995 Sally Ann Melia arrived in the village with her husband – they had both felt a need to leave city life behind and move to the country. By profession she was a journalist and free-lance writer, but had some performance genes in her family as her mother was a professional dancer who ran a dance school in Essex. After meeting and talking to like-minded people in the village she determined to re-generate local theatre, focussed initially on the genre of pantomime.

At first there was a dearth of both money and male volunteers – 'twas ever thus. Men did gradually begin to trickle forth and, in order to avoid such costs as performing rights fees, Sally Ann decided to write a show herself. Then it was discovered that there was still some money from the former Broughton Players account squirreled away in the Bank. And so it was that *Robin Hood* rode again through Broughton in 1995, to be followed each year not only by old favourites such as *Cinderella* and *Mother Goose*, but also by some new creations. e.g. *Alice in Blunderland*, and *Dracula ... the Pantomime* (which must have given a whole new level of terror to the phrase 'He's behind you!') Re-named the Broughton Drama Group and fired up by their successful pantos, the village players went on to stage a nine year run of comedy one-act plays. In the wake of Sally Ann, Jennifer Sadler is now Panto Organiser and Treasurer for the group.

Grange-over-Sands too has a vibrant pantomime tradition, presented currently by the youth of The Grange and District Amateur Operatic Society (of which more in Chapter 7). They have presented a steady series of highly successful shows since 1990. Prior to this the St John's Ambulance Group had organised a regular Christmas show, but in 1990 Jean Malkin of the Grange Society was invited to take over. She has produced every show since, with assistance from her husband Mick, and of course with the backing, support and resources of the senior Society.

Their back catalogue is certainly impressive with shows ranging from the traditional such as *Aladdin* and *Cinderella*, to the more technically demanding such as *Scrooge, Jack and the Beanstalk*, and *Peter Pan*. 'I count it as a privilege', says Jean Malkin, 'to work with these wonderful kids and watch them as they grow. Many of them go on to perform in the adult shows, which is great.'

Their activities are also firmly rooted in the support of charitable causes. For example, in 2014 the group supported BBC Radio Cumbria's Jigsaw appeal (Cumbria's Children's Hospice), and even took their show (*Sleeping Beauty* that year) to entertain the children and staff. In the past they have also raised money to sponsor children (their education and welfare) in such countries as India and Malawi through the World Vision Programme.

Pantomime has also been a regular feature of the theatre scene in Barrow but, unlike Ulverston's recent years, there has been no single or constant 'society' providing the entertainment. Over the years shows have been performed by a variety of groupings, which were usually visiting professional companies. For example, the Ruby Kimberley Company came to the Royalty Theatre in 1929 to stage *Cinderella*, with popular Music Hall performer Billy Kray as the host, and 4 miniature ponies to pull the coach. Then in 1958 a local amateur group, the Barrow St Mary's Pantomime Group, got in on the act with a show which had a 3-night run at Her Majesty's Theatre. The group was made up of youngsters with an average age of 18 who had been coached for several months previously by Mrs Esther Wilson. It was a one-off though, and in the 1950's it was chiefly left to Donald Sartain's repertory company, Renaissance Theatre, to stage an annual pantomime at the theatre, and they followed the St Mary's group in December 1958 with a 3-week run of *Cinderella*. His professional actors of course took the principal parts but it was also Donald Sartain's practice to recruit extras from local schools to act as dancers or 'bit part' players. Len Simm (son of Joe and Abbie Simm) recalls the 1959 production of *Aladdin* when he was invited to play the Genie of the Lamp. The role required him to be covered in ultra-violet sensitive grease-paint which was a very sticky, oily substance which proved to be extremely hard to remove. He was later told this was exactly why none of the professionals had been willing to take the part.

But young local performers weren't content to stay in the background and in the late 1960s and early 70s they were stepping confidently into the limelight in their own right. In 1965 for example Furness Youth Theatre presented *Robinson Crusoe* at Her Majesty's Theatre. Formed in 1964 the group had already staged a series of one-act plays and held various social events but this was its first full-scale production in a

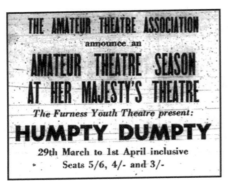

THE AMATEUR THEATRE ASSOCIATION
announce an
AMATEUR THEATRE SEASON
AT HER MAJESTY'S THEATRE

The Furness Youth Theatre present:

HUMPTY DUMPTY

29th March to 1st April inclusive
Seats 5/6, 4/- and 3/-

professional theatre. It was produced under the guiding hand of the very experienced Wyn Large, the Musical Director of many local productions at this time. Also up-coming was the Walney Junior Amateur Operatic Society, which was formed in 1968, and whose early productions had the flavour of pantomimes, although they were staged in March or April rather than during Christmas. Their story will be covered in a later chapter. Another group, who called themselves The Young Image also put on annual shows, usually in February, throughout the 1970s – from *Mother Goose* at the Public Hall to *Pinocchio* at the Civic Hall in 1977. The producer was a lady called Nellie English, who also ran her own Dancing School, with additional support from Bernard Crabtree and Dennis Wootton.

Meanwhile professional productions remained popular at the Civic Hall, with the lead roles occupied by such celebrities of the day as Alan Randall (famous George Formby impersonator) who appeared in *Dick Whittington* in 1975, and Ken Platt (mainly a radio comedian well-known for his regular opening line – *'Allo. I'll not take me coat off. I'm not stoppin'*) who starred in *Babes in the Wood* in 1977. And in more recent years, perhaps in an attempt to cater for modern tastes, this policy of engaging a professional company headed up by some well-known personality, continues. In-between times however, the most notable initiative to provide an experience of traditional panto entertainment with a much more local flavour came from one David Marcus, a name you will now be familiar with. In 1995, assisted by Yvonne Patterson, daughter of veteran Barrow entertainer Danny Patterson and professional singer and drama teacher in her own right, their own company 'Pumpkin Productions' staged *Cinderella*, and then continued to put on an annual show for the next 12 seasons until 2007, all featuring local talent. Andrew Sproxton for example, another well-known local musician, took charge as Musical Director in the latter years. David Marcus himself regularly took on the role of the Dame but, whilst many established and up-and-coming local performers took part, he remained drawn to the idea of including a 'star' attraction to pull in the crowds. So alongside Bill Calvert, Martin Craig, Wayne Buckley and experienced local performer (and sisters) Amy and Michelle Larcombe, he recruited from his contacts with the professional theatrical world. Mo Moreland came to be a regular choice. She had achieved TV fame as one of Les Dawson's dance troupe, The Roly Polys, although prior to this had performed a comedy double act with her husband known as 'The Mighty Atom and Roy'.

The David Marcus shows were nothing if not ambitious, and therefore quite costly to stage. The curtain finally came down in 2007 when Barrow Borough Council withdrew their support on the grounds that the shows were 'too old fashioned.' They went on to express their intention to book 'more commercial productions' in future. It's hard to imagine how a panto can be described as 'old fashioned' since that is surely the point, but presumably their decision also had something to do with money matters. Perhaps also the novelty of Mo Moreland was wearing a bit thin. There was something of an outcry at first as letters of protest began appearing in the *Evening Mail*, and objections were raised in the Council Chamber, but the decision remained unchanged. 'It is necessary to have variety,' said Councillor Dave Pidduck, 'rather than sticking in the same old rut every year.' So

Pumpkin Productions had had its day and Barrow moved away from pantomimes involving amateurs.

Mo Moreland, Wayne Buckley, David Marcus, and Jackie Fielding in a scene from Pumpkin Production's "Mother Goose", 2004

Today pantomimes remain as essential a part of the Christmas season as a visit from Santa Claus. They may be predominantly a Christmas treat aimed at children, but in many ways their allure crosses all generations. I also like the idea that it is become an essentially British phenomenon. As I have mentioned previously, Pantomime was my first experience of LIVE theatre at the Coronation Hall in Ulverston, and I recall it being a simply magical experience, especially when my father and sister were in the cast, and it left a lasting impression. I can still recall my father coming home in his garish make-up (which was both exciting and unsettling in equal measure), my sister in full 'Sunshine Girl' costume, Kathleen and her accordion, and Walter Howson making his pratfall-type stumble down the steps in the finale. I very much hope that the children of today, if they can be prized away from their iPhones and X-boxes, can be affected and inspired in a similar way.

Oh yes I do.

6

ABBEY MUSICAL SOCIETY (Founded 1949)

For any amateur company, as you may imagine, there is plenty of drama going on both on and off the stage. As far as the history of the Abbey Society is concerned, it is by no means alone in having endured near bankruptcy, controversies and anxieties about booking dates, producers and venues, internal wrangling, hissy fits (I have no evidence of this but I think it's a fair bet), and ego trips (ditto). But through whatever difficulties it has faced, the show has invariably gone on. By 2015, in its 66 year history, Abbey had staged 69 musical productions, 41 Summer shows, and more than a dozen 'specials'. The successful ingredients are described by one Chairman as 'tremendous interest, unbounded enthusiasm, and sustained voluntary effort.' And to that list must surely be added a large amount of local musical talent. So how did it all start?

The Abbey Musical Society is born

There were two principal founders or, since both sexes are represented, perhaps they could be called parental figures: Mr Charles A Thompson and Mrs J Maltby-Black. The story goes that a Reverend W Earl, Minister of the Abbey Road Methodist Church, was once very helpful to Mr Thompson in some major way. In order to re-pay the debt he felt he owed to the Reverend, Mr Thompson approached the Director of the Church's Ladies Choir and suggested that they should organise a fully staged show together.

Both had considerable experience to draw on. Mr Thompson was already well known on the amateur stage and had been involved in the productions of several local schools.

Mrs J Maltby-Black   *Mr Charles A Thompson*

Although an ebullient and forceful man who was also a stickler for detail, he was popular and much in demand. As well as being the original Producer for the Abbey Society, he was also responsible for the debut productions of three other local societies – Grange, Walney and Flookburgh. Mrs J Maltby-Black had been a pupil of Mrs T Bourne (Musical Director for the Barrow Society's early shows and a well-known music tutor in the town), and was a member of the Barrow Madrigal Society and the Barrow Choral Union. She had won awards in several music contests and, as a soprano in the Abbey Road Methodist Church Choral Society, had competed in music festivals throughout Lancashire. In other words, both had pretty impressive CV's.

The plan was for a production of the dependable *Mikado*, to take place in the Abbey Road Wesleyan Schoolroom – which immediately caused problems as the 1949 version of Health & Safety required that, in order to meet regulations for public safety, the entrances and exits needed both significant alteration and the fitting of special lighting. A stage set also had to be built, scenery had to be painted, costumes had to be made, and of course a cast with some musical talent (and preferably experience) had to be assembled. Gradually the group of interested parties increased. Hubert Bramhall of local firm 'Hartley and Bramhall' stepped in to manage the electrical work, Mr Thompson himself created the scenery required, and Harold and Florence Melville arrived to help with advertising, administration, and costume design/creation. Meanwhile Mrs Maltby-Black recruited and trained the singers, assembled an orchestra, and on Wednesday April 6th 1949 *The Mikado* came to life. One of the principal singers was Joseph Simm who, along with his wife Abbie, had been former members of the Barrow Operatic Society before moving over to support Mrs Maltby-Black's new initiative. Their son Len recalls, as a 7 year old, huddling under the piano stool in their semi, watching countless legs stamping out a complex dance routine whilst his Mum pounded away on the piano, and the neighbours pounded away on the wall in complaint.

The Mikado was a great success, so much so that the decision was made to formalise proceedings – a new society was formed, a steering committee appointed, and plans made for a future production. Mr Thompson could at last breathe a huge sigh of relief, safe in the knowledge that he had repaid the Reverend Earl in full. Exactly what the good Reverend had done for Mr T. isn't recorded but it must have been something pretty special – 66 years later his repayment gift is literally one that has kept on giving.

Following the success of their first venture the Society moved to the more spacious and dedicated theatre venue, His Majesty's Theatre (which of course became *Her* Majesty's

Theatre in 1953), for their second production, *The Yeomen of the Guard*. It ran for a full week from Monday, March 27 to Saturday April 1st, 1950. The *Evening Mail* responded with a glowing review of opening night. The only problem was that, just as the overture was ending, all the electricity had shorted out and the audience had to be ushered out without witnessing a single scene. The story goes that the reporter concerned had skived off for the night, and had submitted his review in advance. Massive bad luck for him, but it reflected well on the reputation of the Abbey Society. The reporter *just knew* it was going to be wonderful. And so it proved to be as audiences packed in for the remainder of the run.

Samuel Briggs as Jack Point *in* Yeomen of the Guard, 1950

Florence Melville as Queen of the Fairies *in* Iolanthe, 1952

For the next nine years, until 1957, the Society then ran the gamut of Gilbert and Sullivan operas, building up a talented cohort of reliable performers as it went. And just as an aside, to make you feel really old, the price of a ticket in the stalls at this time was 4 shillings (or 20p today) and, if you couldn't afford that, you could sit in the Gallery for 1/6d (7½p). There was an unfortunate bump in the road early on when, in 1951, the committee invited Robert 'Bob' Bowker to produce their next show *The Gondoliers*. He was in fact already an active figure in amateur theatre and a long-term member of the Barrow Society, having first appeared for them as early as 1931. As mentioned earlier, Society hopping was very much disapproved of in these days and his defection to Abbey, this new upstart Society, despite being a supposed temporary arrangement, attracted much criticism.

The upshot for Mr Bowker (pictured right) was that he was effectively drummed out of the Barrow Society, so his temporary move suddenly became permanent. He and Mrs Maltby-Black thus became established as the regular Producer/Musical Director twosome, an arrangement which lasted right up until 1963, when Mrs Maltby-Black retired, to be replaced by Jean Longbottom. Mr Bowker and Ms Long-bottom's reign then lasted till 1968 when Mr John Towler replaced Mr Bowker, again in somewhat controversial circumstances – but more of that later.

Levels of enthusiasm and optimism remained high. In October 1954, during preparations for their production of *Princess Ida*, around 2 dozen society members were treated to a weekend trip to London to gain inspiration and experience from the professionals. Their itinerary included attendance at a BBC broadcast at the Playhouse Theatre, and tickets for two theatrical events - *Macbeth* (at the Old Vic theatre), and a production of *Princess Ida* itself at the Savoy Theatre which, coincidentally, was starring the famous Barrow tenor Thomas Round.

But there were difficulties that also had to be faced in this period. Despite the boost of the London trip for example, when it came to it, the staging of their show was very nearly scuppered. Plans and preparations were proceeding well, but the financial stability of Her Majesty's was decidedly not and abrupt closure was threatened. In order to save the show, and indeed all their properties housed in the theatre, the Society had to hurriedly bring performance dates forward. This meant that frequent and intense rehearsals had to be organised to ensure everything was ready for opening night. The crisis was duly averted. Mr James Hay, Chair of the Society at the time, subsequently expressed both his sense of relief and a prophetic view of the future: "A Society which can meet such an emergency," he said, "and face up to it in such a manner, is destined to continue and thrive."

Early days and difficulties

At this point it is a risk to single out key individuals, mainly because I am bound to offend by omission. The work that goes into each production cannot be over-stated, and the success of each enterprise is clearly the result of much joint effort. Even so, among the players in this early period, the names of regular performers emerge, some of whom went on to serve the Society for many years to come. Harold and Florence Melville should be mentioned in this context, as should Esther Murphy

and her daughter Aprille Butterfield, Ben Williams, Marie Allmark (nee Worrall), Dancing Mistresses Maud Tranter and Dorothy Steel, Jim Burdekin (a King of comedy who also was to serve later as a Chairman of the Society), the afore-mentioned Joseph Simm, Bill Parkinson, Jack Davidson, Bill Steel (also a later Chairman) and his wife Noreen (pictured left), key figures both in these early days and in many later productions. Indeed both are still active supporters of the Society at the time of writing. The name of Cliff Kitto should also be mentioned – he was the constant and reliable stage manager for all of these early productions before going on to produce shows for the Walney Juniors Society.

Meanwhile financial problems had engulfed Her Majesty's Theatre and it had to close its doors. Although, on this occasion it turned out to be a temporary closure, the loss was felt keenly by all local groups as the facilities and space provided by such a purpose-built theatre had to be replaced by the more limited Public Hall in Barrow. Audience numbers were also dwindling as the town and district's appetite for Gilbert and Sullivan seemed to decrease. It was time to try something new but, for a few years at least, the formula for success was elusive.

The choice for 1958 was *Maid of the Mountains*, still a traditional operetta in the Gilbert and Sullivan mould, but this time from George Edwardes' Gaiety Theatre collection. (It had done very well in London in 1917 and ran for 1,352 performances). It was not the best choice as the Flookburgh

Society were staging the very same show that year. In future improved liaison between the various local groups would ensure such unfortunate coincidences were not repeated (which was the case until 2007 when, somehow, both the Barrow and Flookburgh Societies managed once again to stage the same show, ironically enough entitled *Anything Goes*). The following year they tried *The Rebel Maid*, a romantic light opera from the 1920's which actually hadn't done all that well in London, or indeed in Ulverston back in 1925. True to form it didn't do all that well in Barrow either, and at the end of the run the Society found itself firmly in the red. "We have had only a moderate return for a very expensive production," Mr Hay announced gravely, and in 1960, for the one and only time in its history, the Society was unable to put on a show. But, true to the spirit of theatre, rather than calling it a day, the committee and all Society members redoubled their efforts in fund-raising and recruitment. The response was very good – presumably on the basis of its earlier productions people thought it was a Society worth saving. Ultimately, on the basis of all this extra effort, the Abbey Society was able to mount a new show *The Quaker Girl*, in 1961.

Derek Roberts, Aprille Butterfield, Esther Murphy,
& Jack Davidson : The Quaker Girl, 1961

In a similar way Her Majesty's Theatre had also managed to navigate its own stormy seas and rose again in the same year. Quite how this was achieved is the basis for another story but the efforts of Donald Sartain had much to do with it. He had established an enthusiastic repertory company, the aptly named Renaissance Theatre Company, which would ensure the theatre's survival for at least a few more years. With competition from television, bingo, and Working Men's Clubs there were always going to be struggles, but at least, for the time being it meant that, for the Abbey and other local Societies, the show could go on. The audience for *The Quaker Girl* in fact was able to appreciate the show in the setting of a newly-decorated theatre which had also been equipped with new seating. Was this a turning point?

Sadly no, although things looked more positive at least for a while. But perhaps inevitably given the nature of the times, the fortunes of Her Majesty's took a downward slide again, and in 1967 the curtain came down for good. Local societies were forced to seek out a new venue, with Barrow's Public Hall being the obvious choice. Everyone was kept in an anxious limbo however as the Town Council demurred on a decision, until permission was finally granted.

Then Abbey became immediately embroiled in another controversy concerning their choice of producer for their 1968 show *Wedding in Paris*, which was to be staged at the Public Hall. Instead of Bob Bowker the job was offered to John Towler, an experienced producer of drama in the district but not, apparently, of musical theatre. The Committee asserted that, because Mr Towler had produced several plays at the Hall with Barrow's Elizabethan Players, he knew a great deal about how to manage the stage facilities and their limitations etc, conveniently forgetting that, when Her Majesty's had been out of commission previously, Bob Bowker had quite happily managed to produce the Abbey's shows at the very same

Public Hall. The whole business produced a lot of anger and ill-feeling, which was directed at Abbey's poor Committee, although I suspect that the root of it was a projection of all the frustration generated by the closure of Her Majesty's in the first place. (Interestingly, as you may recall from Barrow Society's history, there was an altercation between Ronald Metcalfe and the Barrow Society at exactly the same time, presumably driven by the same mechanism.) Anyway, order was eventually restored and, fear not, Bob Bowker's career was far from over at this point, although he never produced a show for the Abbey Society again.

The Civic Hall era

With little alternative the staging of shows in the Public Hall was acceptable but not wholly satisfactory. A new 'Civic Hall' on Duke Street, which would act as both theatre and community centre, had been planned as far back as the 1950s but by the early 60s next to nothing had been achieved. The first phase of a 'New Town Venture' had been built in the shape of the Furness House 'Tower' block but it then took another 5 years before the adjoining streets (Paxton St & John St) which were to accommodate the new buildings were demolished. There were further delays when the original contractors for the New Town Venture unexpectedly pulled out. Finally the Lyons Company stepped in and within a couple of years the new Market Hall and the Civic Hall were completed and ready for use.

In March 1972 the Abbey was the first to present a show there, which they did with *Summer Song*. The Civic Hall was actually not due to be officially opened until the following month so the show gave everyone an opportunity for an advanced viewing. The show went off alright, but the new Hall did not meet with universal approval. The stage area was disappointingly small and, from certain seats in the balcony, it was quite impossible to see the stage at all, so some rapid adjustments had to be made. In later years it would famously be described by Ken Dodd as 'this abandoned bakery' and 'this old Zeppelin hangar.'

Taken as a whole, the 70's decade proved to be a lean time for all. Remember the three-day working week and the winter of discontent? As far as audiences were concerned it appeared that the novelty of a new performance space soon wore off and support for live theatre suffered. It was perhaps not a time to take undue risks with less well-known shows, so those chosen in this period tended to be old favourites - new productions for Abbey but all of which had been staged previously by other local groups, such as *Rose Marie* (1969), *The Quaker Girl* (1971), *The Vagabond King* (1973) and *New Moon* (1975). As you have already heard, other local Societies were all experiencing similar problems. Budgets were very tight and morale was low. Abbey tried to lift their own, and everyone else's spirits by putting on extra concerts of song medleys from popular shows, but audience numbers remained disappointing.

Then in 1976 came *Showboat*, the seminal show which had first opened in America in 1927. Again previous productions had been staged in the district by both Barrow (1951) and Ulverston Operatic Societies (1963) but Abbey's run did have its own 'first' in that it was the maiden show for the new team of Dorothy Hardy, Producer, and Anne Cragg-Hine, Musical Director. The two were to stay together for the next 7 productions, complemented by Noreen's Steel's reliable choreography. Another first was the debut appearance of Colin Smith in the role of Frank Schultz. He acted in several later shows before later taking over Producer duties himself, ultimately becoming Abbey's most prolific Producer/Director.

Showboat (pictured above) was quite a gamble however, as the nature of the show places major demands on both the cast and production crew. It is no light-weight musical comedy, but one with a strong storyline described as an epic tribute to the power of undying love. The characters have depth and are so well-defined that it is they who must drive the drama forward largely through their own interpretation of the music. Great care has to be taken therefore to ensure that both the characters and plot come across sympathetically, and that the tragic elements of the tale do not overwhelm the audience. And if all that weren't enough it is a show which requires elaborate staging and, most particularly, a 'double' chorus – one black, and one white. In practice this meant that the Civic Hall stage in Barrow would need to accommodate around 70 people, pushing the available space to the limit. In the event it all proved to be a risk well worth taking and the Society pulled it all off very successfully. It drew in large audiences during its run with a complimentary press review from Bob Bowker who dished out well-deserved praise to all the cast for their strong and committed performances.

As *Showboat* had been a turning point in American musical theatre, so it proved to be for Abbey. From 1976 onwards things certainly started to improve, slowly. Having turned out successful productions of quintessentially English shows such as Noel Coward's *Bitter Sweet* (1979) and Ivor Novello's *Glamorous Night* (1980) the Society then demonstrated both confidence and ambition by producing two shows in 1982. The first of these was a reprise of their 1976 success *Showboat*. Sadly it did not reach quite the same heights and Bob Bowker's verdict was decidedly luke-warm, describing the show as 'lacking pace and drive.' Still he was impressed by the colourful staging, and the quality of many of the individual performances. There was even an unfortunate scenery collapse on one occasion which could be read as symbolic. Colin Smith was again in the cast and, at a time when it was still considered acceptable, was required to 'black up' for his part. His son was born during the show's run and he recalls dashing home after the final curtain, still in full make-up, to see him. Striking an early blow for political correctness the poor child screamed the house down.

The company came back strongly however with their second offering in the year, *The Sound of Music*. It is a much-loved favourite musical, held dear by many hearts so the pressure to do it justice, particularly after *Showboat*, must have been great. I guess it's like being entrusted with someone's baby, the last thing you want to do is injure it in any way. As it turned out, it was probably the most successful Abbey production to date. Audience response was so positive it was even possible for the Society to make a substantial donation to charity – a perennial aim of course but one that it isn't always possible to achieve. On this occasion the Barrow and District

Spastic & Handicapped Children's Society were the grateful beneficiaries.

The production for 1983 was *White Horse Inn* which featured young Leye Johns who, two years earlier, had won the Nellie English Award for 'most promising newcomer' whilst with the Walney Junior Society. But as young talents emerge old ones are lost as, also in 1983, came the sad news of the death of Florrie Melville. She had been in the Society's very first production in 1949, and had subsequently given 34 loyal years of service in many guises – as leading lady, as a member of the Ladies Chorus, as a member of the management committee, and even as wardrobe mistress. Her passing was much mourned.

Many of the shows were chosen at this time for their emphasis on the chorus work, rather than everything being built around one central star. *White Horse Inn* is perhaps a good example. A total cast can sometimes number as many as 70 or more individuals. So ponder for a moment what it must be like to garner all these resources together, to train, coordinate and rehearse all those people, and marvel at the sheer hard work and effort that goes into all these shows! More detail on this matter will be supplied in a later chapter.

Someone who knows quite a bit about all this necessary effort is Colin Smith, the Producer/Director of most of Abbey's shows since 1985 (pictured left). As mentioned earlier, his performance debut had been a few years in the 1976 production of *Showboat*. He remembers lying under his car, struggling with an oil-change, when Bill Steel appeared. I like to think that Mr Steel immediately thought to himself, 'Well there's a man who knows the value of a well-oiled machine' and invited him on the spot, but I suspect Mr Smith's reputation had somehow preceded him. A teacher by trade, he is credited with having inspired many youngsters to perform in amateur theatre, and his many successful productions for Abbey bear testament to his creativity and imagination. He taught for 25 years at Greengate Junior School which, before he arrived, had actually been destined for closure and in 2009 he was awarded "Teacher of the Year" in the Barrow Community Awards. In Colin's early performance days the Producer was the much-loved Dorothy Hardy from Morecambe, famed for her range of colourful outfits and coordinating glasses. She produced Abbey's shows from 1976 to 1983, with Anne Cragg-Hine as Musical Director, and Dennis Wootton as Accompanist (who in fact remained in this role right up to his retirement in 1997.)

But back to the early 1980's it was as if Abbey had now found its voice, and was asserting itself as a major player on the local scene. There was a sense in which, as a later starter in the local amateur scene it had perhaps been running to catch up, but now it was stretching its legs, and for a time really got out in front. Three shows exemplify this, two of which were (for the second time in Abbey's history) staged in the same year (1985), and none of which had been put on previously by any other local society. The two shows from 1985 were *The Inn of the Eighth Happiness*, which was the first to be produced by Colin Smith, and *Hans Andersen,* the live action version of the Danny Kaye film, which Tommy Steele had successfully transferred to the West End. The third was *Beyond the Rainbow* (1989), important because Abbey were only the second amateur society in Britain to be given permission to produce it. The story concerns a small Italian village which has been chosen by God to be saved when he sends his second great flood. A real dove was even recruited as an honorary

Society member for a part in the grand finale. The Voice of God was portrayed by Bill Steel who, quite coincidentally I'm sure, was also Chairman of the Society at the time.

The cast re-enact Gladys Aylward's famous trek across the Chinese mountains, leading a group of orphans to safety following China's invasion by the Japanese

Inn of the Eighth Happiness, 1985

As for *The Inn of the Eighth Happiness,* it tells the story of the courageous missionary Gladys Aylward, who in the Abbey's production was portrayed to great acclaim by Noreen Steel, and I am reliably informed that some actual artefacts which once belonged to Miss Aylward were used in the production. The production of *Hans Andersen* prompted a congratulatory and good luck message to the Society from none other than Tommy Steele himself. Martin Savage, who was referred to briefly in the history of the Barrow Society, took the lead role. He subsequently went on to forge a very successful professional theatrical career. He appeared in Mike Leigh's 1999 film *Topsy-Turvy*, the musical biography of Gilbert & Sullivan, then later toured with the original version of *Pickwick*, starring Harry Secombe. He has also appeared in several TV series such as *The Thick of It*, *Extras*, and *Foyle's War* and latterly appeared as the fussy Warden Hodges in the 2016 film of *Dad's Army*.

The 1990's and Forum 28

It was clear that the Abbey Society was now really getting into its stride – there was an annual musical production, Summer Shows and occasional concerts in aid of local charities. Everything was thrown into some chaos however in mid-1989 when the Barrow Council put plans in hand for the refurbishment of the Civic Hall. As it was unclear whether it would be available in time for the Abbey's annual show, the project generated much anxiety and uncertainty, particularly about performance dates, and indeed whether it would be possible to stage a show at all. But all's well that ends well (as they say in theatrical circles) and *Finian's Rainbow* went ahead as scheduled in Barrow's new theatre/conference centre/ tourist information centre FORUM 28. (The address was _28_ Duke Street, in case you were wondering, although nowadays it is simply known as The Forum.)

From this point onwards innovation and imagination come to dominate the Society's output, and the 1990s proves to be a decade of intense activity. One of the early highlights is the production of Ron Grainer's *Robert & Elizabeth* in 1991, the story of the love affair between the invalid poet Elizabeth Barrett and Robert Browning. It was a lavish and costly production requiring elaborate Victorian costumes, several scene changes, and the casting of a pet spaniel. Anne Woods and Keith Harrison played the two leads. Then came Lionel Bart's *Blitz!* in 1992. Much persistence was required initially on the part of Noreen Steel, having now assumed the role of Musical Director, in order to get permission to stage the show. Lionel Bart had refused this to amateur companies for many years and Noreen Steel is credited with finally getting him to change his mind. Then with a cast list of 14 principals, 35 chorus members, 28 children, 9 members of Barrow's Territorial Army, and 2 firemen it was billed as the biggest amateur production of the show in the country. It generated a huge amount of interest among other amateur societies and groups from Galashields, York, Hull, Newcastle, and Bromley (Kent) all travelled north to see it. It was staged to commemorate the 50th anniversary of the Blitz as experienced in Barrow, and played to full houses during its week's run. A second production was then staged with equal success in 2003.

Back: Julie Newby, Jacqui Richards, Christine Lander, Ann Granville
Front row: Mark Jefferson, Nick Collinge, Mark Collinge
Blitz, 1992

One bright summer day Colin Smith walked into the rehearsal room of St James Infants School to be faced with a sea of eager and enthusiastic faces. "This year we've been invited to produce the famous West End musical BARNUM," he said. "It has great songs, a bit of dancing – oh, and just a few extra things. There's some juggling involved, tight-rope walking, a few magic tricks – that type of thing. Can anyone here ride a unicycle by the way? And what about the flying trapeze? Who's good on that?" It was truly an ambitious project, but one which was heartily embraced by all, not least the management committee who were going to have to find over £11,000 to stage it. Circus skills workshops were arranged, and several local performers and a gym club helped to coach the cast in tumbling and acrobatics. Andrew Bond was cast in the lead role. He had made his debut with the Society as a chorus member in 1985, and had then taken character parts in 1989 and 1993. Now he had to master the art of juggling and tight-rope walking. He certainly put his teeth into it – two in fact which he lost in one unfortunate (amongst many) bruising falls during rehearsals. Heather Collinge, an established Abbey performer since 1976 as dancer, chorus member, and leading lady, was cast as Charity, his wife. The whole cast rose to the enormous challenges with great energy and persistence, and unsurprisingly the show was a runaway success. Among these was eighteen-year old Claire Powell who took on the challenge of the trapeze under the guidance of the Starlight Circus School in Rochdale. She brought to the show such exotic manoeuvres as 'the bird's nest,' 'the gazelle' and, my personal favourite, 'the ankle hang'. The Society was to go on to repeat the whole exercise in 2000, when *Barnum* was chosen as its Millennium production with Andrew and Heather again taking the lead roles. The show won special praise from NODA, awarding it 'best amateur theatrical production' for the year 2000. Looking back to the Society's sedate *Mikado* beginnings in a cramped

Church hall back in 1949, this was surely a long long way from Titipu.

The exuberance that was BARNUM, 2000

Following the 1994 production of *Barnum*, the cast had a quieter year in 1995 with *Half a Sixpence*, but the 'flash-bang-wallop' circus tricks were back for their 1996 show, *Carnival*. Another energetic and lively show it required jugglers, a trapeze artist (ably supplied by Amanda Craig) and human puppets – oh yes, and a magician, but since 'magical' was a frequent description of Abbey's shows at this time, that posed no major problems. Then in 1997 another first: a production of a musical version of Jane Austen's classic *Pride and Prejudice*, written by the less well-known American, Bernard J Taylor. He had 15 or so musicals to his credit which usually first appeared as concept albums. To date none of his works have ever reached the big time of Broadway or the West End, but all have had success internationally with productions in countries from Europe to Australia.

Pride and Prejudice had its world premiere in Peoria, Illinois only four years earlier so it was indeed a fresh work, and a largely unknown quantity for Abbey to take on. As it happened, it all worked really well – Abbey proving that in addition to 'energetic and lively' they could also do 'stylish and sedate'. The Society subsequently tackled another of Mr Taylor's works in 2002, adapted from Emily Brontë's more visceral novel *Wuthering Heights*. Dave Diggle, a regular performer in Ulverston's productions, took on the challenge of Heathcliff, with Sarah Johnson (who also choreographed the dancing) playing the restless and volatile Cathy. Cathy's younger self was played by 13-year old Sacha Bell who, in 2003, successfully auditioned for the National Youth Theatre. Colin Smith, as ever, produced and in this instance also adapted the libretto, whilst Noreen Steel added harmonies for the chorus. Their work won approval from no less than Mr Taylor himself who came to view the show (how often does that happen in an amateur production?) as well as from a representative from NODA who gave it a star rating. "It is a feast of musical entertainment," enthused the review, "with

Dorothy Hardy

excellent arrangements and harmonies."

Before moving into the new century it is important to record the loss of 3 people at this time who had each given devoted service to the Society over many years. One was Dorothy Hardy who passed away in 1993. At her funeral Bill Steel gave an emotional rendition of *I'll See You Again*, her favourite song from Noel Coward's musical *Bitter Sweet*. Such was the esteem in which she was held that a Memorial Concert was mounted for her at the Grand Theatre, Lancaster in January 1994. The Morecambe Operatic Society and 40 members from the Abbey Society performed selections from some of her favourite musicals. Then in 1997 one of the Abbey's founders, Mrs J Maltby-Black passed away, followed soon after by Dennis Wootton, the Society's Accompanist for many years. Along with many others, they all had made massive contributions to the Abbey Society, so the ground was well prepared for the further innovations that were to come as the year 2000 dawned.

The new century

With a revival of their hit show *Barnum* from 1994 the Society kicked off the new century with great gusto and in a spirit of high optimism. But, as is the case with all live theatre these days, audience support could still not be guaranteed. Also, a particular feature of amateur productions is that ticket sales tend to be 'last minute' so the production team are never sure exactly how things are going to work out. Performers need audiences! Post-2000, in an age of social networking, an ever-expanding range of media entertainment options, and massive competition for one's attention in general, the formula for a successful show was to say the least a challenging one. Shows had to be novel, have a large cast, have a good amount of chorus work, be humorous and entertaining, and have a good story to tell. On the whole Abbey's choices fulfilled this brief well, but the Society had to take quite a few risks in staging premieres of new and untested shows. Examples are: *Scrooge* (2001) which received a nomination in NODA's North West Theatre Awards for 'Best Musical', *The Card* (2004) with music written by Tony Hatch, *Titanic* (2009) complete with tilting platform, which received a NODA nomination for 'Best Staging', *The Likes of Us* (2010) which is the first and rarely seen work by Andrew Lloyd Webber and Tim Rice, and *Dr Dolittle* (2012) complete with (among others) a chimpanzee, a greedy pig, and a short-sighted carthorse.

Talking to the animals Dr Dolittle, 2012

The first decade of the new century was also to see some important changes in key positions. In 2007 Noreen Steel stepped down from the position of Musical Director, which was one she had fulfilled for the previous 17 years, having initially taken over from Doreen Dunlop for the 1991 production *Robert & Elizabeth*. She was succeeded by Angela Guntrip who at the time of writing remains in the role. Noreen had joined the Society in 1962 and for the next 20 years or so took on principal roles in many productions whilst also operating on other occasions as chorus mistress, production assistant, choreographer and in many other parts. Together with her husband Bill they have both been key players in the Abbey story for most of its life, with Bill also acting as a chorus master, taking many leading roles, and then becoming the

Society's Chairman in 1976. It was a position he held for the next 30 years, before finally standing down in 2007. The Vice Chair Jill Lyon stood in for a couple of years, before the position was taken up by Nick Collinge in 2010, the son of another Abbey stalwart Heather Collinge.

But we are not finished yet! The annual Summer Shows have so far received scant attention, but they have been a regular feature of the Society's annual output for over 40 years. I don't propose to scan through them all but reference must surely be made to the highly popular and innovative series which began in 2010. The first of these was the *Love Barrow Musical* which featured a group of 'tourists' who arrive in Barrow for a holiday. In the context of suitable songs and dance they visit, among other sites, Furness Abbey and the dockyards (where they 'Go Fly a Kite'), they visit the Lakes (where of course they sing in the rain), they celebrate Barrow AFC's victory in the FA Cup (you remember that surely), and they experience the 'Circle of Life' at the South Lakes Wild Animal Park. The show, and indeed the three that were to follow, were put together by the formidable production team of Colin Smith, Angela Guntrip (Musical Director), Sarah Powell (Choreographer) and Ray Martindale (scenery & sets).

Sarah Powell, Colin Smith, Angela Guntrip & Ray Martindale

In 2011 the Summer Concert was *Barrow Cluedo*, a show which combined elements of the 'Cluedo' board game, *The X Factor*, and *Britain's Got Talent*. In Barrow's Town Hall Sharon Hasbeen, Cherry Cola, and Pieman Cowell are judging the talents of Miss Scarlet, Professor Plum, and Mr ... well, you get the idea, when mystery disappearances create confusion and distress. Aided by song and dance clues, Monsieur Poirot and Miss Marple then arrive to solve the mystery. The following year 2012, was of course the year of the London Olympics so, ever topical, the Summer Show presentation was *Olympic Barrow*. The show was remarkable in revealing the little known fact that, in reality, following a strange voting accident, the games had to be staged in Barrow. Who knew?

And then finally the series was rounded off in 2013 with *Cupcake Cabaret*, derived from the popular shows *Masterchef* and *The Great British Bake Off*. Unsurprisingly it involves various competitors trying to impress judges Mary Belly and Paul Hollyoaks with a few songs and a large helping of local produce and home-grown talent thrown in. It was a riotous success and in 2014 received a NODA award for 'Best Concert/Revue of 2013'.

As far as the annual musical production is concerned, at the time of writing the three most recent presentations have seen a return to energetic dance-themed shows – *Footloose*, *Grease*, and *Hairspray* – musicals geared perhaps towards a younger cast who are prepared to throw themselves around a bit. "It's a bit like marshalling a pack of wolves," says Colin Smith. "But when their hunger and excitement is channelled, the results are wonderful to behold. At the end of each rehearsal period I am frazzled but always proud and uplifted by what we have achieved." It seems to me an apt description of the general culture of the Abbey Musical Society throughout its history. Long may it continue.

7
THE GRANGE AND DISTRICT
AMATEUR OPERATIC SOCIETY
(founded 1949)

Grange and Flookburgh

From a small fishing village to a grand Edwardian seaside resort – such was the story of Grange-over-Sands in the mid-19th century, thanks to the advent of the railways. Healthy sea air was now accessible to those from the smoky industrial towns of the north, so wealthy merchants began to arrive and to build grand houses and holiday apartments. As befitting a fledgling resort new hotels, piers, and even an outdoor lido also soon appeared. From a modern-day perspective perhaps Grange's heyday as a resort destination has now past, although the town still thrives on a brisk tourist trade and is a favoured jumping-off point for those who wish to explore Furness and the South Lakes.

About 4 miles or so up the road lies the smaller village of Flookburgh whose origins, like Grange, were again founded on fishing, notably of course through the harvesting of the eponymous 'fluke' (although there is some dispute as to whether this is actually the origin of the 'Flookburgh' name.) Nowadays a thriving fishing industry persists, though the village is perhaps more well-known for the manufacture of Cartmel's famous Sticky Toffee Pudding.

Given that barely 4 miles separate these two towns, you may think it odd that two independent Operatic Societies should have been founded at roughly the same time - Grange in 1949 and Flookburgh in 1951. I am given to understand however that, when Grange's debut show was being planned, 'a major disagreement' arose between the Grange committee and a certain Mrs Jean O'Hara, the upshot of which being that Mrs O'Hara stomped off to form her own Society up the road. The nature of this disagreement isn't clear (though may well have something to do with casting decisions) but this seems unimportant when you realise that the outcome was two Societies for the price of one or, in other words, twice the potential entertainment opportunities for the surrounding district to enjoy.

It is perhaps no surprise that the two Societies share similar characteristics. For example, both have a relatively small population from which to draw their resources, and both have modest staging areas on which to mount their productions. This has inevitably placed limits on the type of shows they are able to present. Equally however, there has been no shortage of talent or enthusiasm in either Society. If an initial rivalry ever existed this appears to have quickly dispersed as, since their founding, both have thrived for 60+ years. Unfortunately, as you will hear in the next chapter, Flookburgh's flame has recently been snuffed out, whilst that of Grange burns on.

Beginnings

There is some evidence that an Operatic Society was first founded in Grange in early Edwardian times, with the usual Gilbert & Sullivan repertoire, but (and I have to admit my information is somewhat flaky on this matter) I'm led to believe that their productions were spasmodic and that, sharing the fate of all of the early groups, they were forced to disband following the outbreak of the war. I do know for certain however that 'The Grange and District Amateur Operatic Society' as we know it today was officially founded (or perhaps it is better to say revived) in 1949, and among the founder members were: Mrs M Stoker, Mr R W Nelson, Mr H Anderson, Mr A R Thompson, and Mr F Wike. Their first show was staged at the Victoria Hall, Grange, in February

1950, and indeed this venue would become the Society's home for all their future productions. In many ways this echoes the Ulverston Society and their relationship with the Coronation Hall. The Victoria Hall *(pictured above)* was built a few years earlier than the Coronation Hall, in 1901, but like the 'Coro', which was built to commemorate the coronation of George V, the Victoria Hall was also built to commemorate a royal event - Queen Victoria's Diamond Jubilee.

As for the Society's first production - can you guess what it might have been? Well, as you must surely have gathered by now, whenever a new Society appears, it is almost the law that its first offering should be a Gilbert and Sullivan piece. The Grange Society were not about to buck this trend and, yes, the piece chosen was *The Mikado*. It was to be produced by our old friend Charles Thompson (well-known local Producer and co-founder of the Abbey Society), assisted by Musical Director Mr W Mackereth Clark. Among the cast were Robert Nelson as Pooh Bah, John Price as Nanki Poo, and Isabel Lythgoe as Yum Yum.

Two further Gilbert & Sullivan pieces were then staged in the years following – *Iolanthe* in 1951, and *Yeomen of the*

Guard in 1952 – again with Charles Thompson and Mr Mackereth Clark in charge, and with cast members who were to make regular appearances in many future productions, e.g. James Graham, Harry Tyler, John Price, and Dorothy Best. As is usually the case with the early productions of small Societies, the budget was slim and as far as was possible a show's requirements (costumes, scenery etc) had to be found from internal resources. In this respect Grange was fortunate in securing the services of local man Ben Ward who was to provide lighting expertise for many years, and the skills of a well-known artist Mr Sydney Buckley (from nearby Cartmel) who, assisted by Cyril Gaskarth, produced very professional scenery. In the press reviews the quality of both the scenery and costumes is frequently remarked upon, described by such words as 'spectacular', 'refreshing' and 'colourful'. For later shows another local artist, Mr Harold Riding RCA also won prise for his imaginative contributions.

For the year 1953, the year of Queen Elizabeth II's Coronation, the Society celebrated with two productions – *Dorothy* in February, and *HMS Pinafore* in June. The former was produced and choreographed by Jessie Barbour (who had produced several shows for the Ulverston Society), with Mr Mackereth Clark again wielding his baton over an impressive 17-piece orchestra. Clearly the Grange Society was here to stay and meant business.

More evidence of this was to be found from 1954 to 1957 when, with an implicit sense of self-confidence, they put on shows which departed from the familiar Gilbert & Sullivan comfort zone. The first of these was *The Country Girl* (1954) when the audience response and subsequent takings were described as having 'broken all records'. Perhaps this is not too surprising when you consider that live theatre was a very popular pastime in this period. Television was of course about to flex its muscles and give live theatre a right good kicking but, in the early 1950s, a staged show continued to pull in the crowds. For Grange's residents, having easy access to such novel shows courtesy of local amateurs, must have been both attractive and exciting.

This may explain the Society's somewhat odd choice of show for 1955 – *San Toy*. First performed in 1899, it was one of a series of orientally-themed pieces which had proved very popular with Edwardian audiences, such as *The Mikado, The Geisha,* and *A Chinese Honeymoon. San Toy* follows the tradition of these pieces where a convoluted love story gets placed within an oriental setting. In this case the daughter of a mandarin is disguised as a boy to evade being drafted in the Emperor's ladies Corps, with resulting complications to her love life. As things turned out the production tested Grange's resources to the limit as, on the very day the show was to open, the lead actor James Pearson fell ill and was unable to perform. Step forward Rev. J E Noel Coleman, vicar of Allithwaite. With little more than three hours to prepare, in a remarkable feat of sheer wizardry (but presumably also with God on his side) he was able to act as a stand-in, and pulled off a creditable performance.

I'm not sure if he was given a special award for such sterling work, but it had become a tradition at this time for the Society to reward performers who had been voted by members as having made a special contribution to the success of a show. This was the so-called President's Trophy and took the form of a silver rose bowl. Maud Thexton won it in 1953 for her performance in *Dorothy*, followed by Betty Graham in 1954 for her role in *A Country Girl*. Later recipients were George Bellman and Marion Pearson who by now had become regular performers.

Lilac Domino and *Merrie England* followed in 1956 and 1957, before the Society decided to revert to the familiar ground of Gilbert & Sullivan, *The Gondoliers* (1958) and

Pirates of Penzance (1959). Remember that the choice of shows was still somewhat limited at this time (certainly when compared to modern times) so it may not be too surprising that these works keep appearing. One twist however was that the copyright on Gilbert and Sullivan works was lapsing at this time which meant that it was possible for producers to be freer in their interpretation of a particular work, and thus give it a fresher feel. Accordingly, Grange appointed a new Producer for the purpose - a man who has featured large in our history, Mr Bob Bowker of Barrow, who was to remain as the Producer of Grange's shows for the next six years, until 1963. He scored a number of successes with several ambitious undertakings – especially *Pink Champagne* in 1960 (also known as *Die Fledermaus)*, with music by Johann Strauss. No Society had attempted this previously and it attracted considerable local interest with parties arriving from Morecambe. Lancaster, and Preston to see what Grange would make of it. No-one went away disappointed. The *Merry Widow* followed in 1961 and, whilst it was a popular and successful show, poor Mr R W Nelson, Chair of the Society, was taken to task in the correspondence pages of the *Barrow News* for making an over-long speech of thanks at the end of the run. I have to say that begrudging the cast a word of thanks, however verbose, seems a little peevish to me. Perhaps the correspondent had just bought a telly and was keen to get back home to catch *What's My Line?* or some such.

Following another Johann Strauss piece *Gypsy Baron* in 1962 ('ablaze with truly magnificent costumes') there came a re-staging of *The Mikado*. This was to be Bob Bowker's last production for the Society and, as it turned out, the final performance of a Gilbert & Sullivan work by the Grange Society. The cast comprised many who had appeared in several of the previous shows and in fact, having a relatively small catchment to draw from, in future productions these performers varied little from year to year. Harold Rawlins took on the role of the Mikado, with John Price reprising his role from 1950 as Nanki Poo. Harry Tyler played Pooh Bah, with the 'three little maids' played by Sheila Hemingway (Yum Yum), Doreen Wiper (Pitti-Sing) and Eileen Butler (Peep-Bo). All featured in many later productions, along with others from the chorus who were later to take on leading roles such as Hetty Lancaster, George Bellman, George Bryden, and Malcolm Higginson.

The next two shows were produced by the very experienced Joyce Warrington of Morecambe – a re-run of *The Country Girl* (1964) and *Waltz Time* (1965) – supported by the ever reliable Mr Mackereth Clark as Musical Director. A dearth of male voices had emerged however so it was necessary to secure a boost from members of the Operatic Society in nearby Kendal. It all paid off as Ronald Metcalfe's review in the *Barrow News* was one of his most enthusiastic as he singled out the performance of each lead performer for special praise. "This is the best Grange production I have seen for a very long time," he says.

The Society was now on the cusp of a new beginning as its reputation had grown and, despite the odd gap, new voices and new talent were signing up, but what's more, the years following were to see a departure from the traditional operetta, to musicals with a more 'modern' style (at least for this period).

*　　*　　*

Getting to Know You

I am aware that I have given scant attention to the important role schools play in opening up the world of music and drama to young people, yet for many this experience is so inspirational the transition from school to amateur theatre is almost seamless. In the course of researching this book I have spoken to several performers who, if not following in a family member's footsteps, will cite their experience at school as their key influence. I was discussing this point with Jean Malkin, a seasoned performer with the Grange Society who herself had joined their ranks in 1966 directly upon leaving Ulverston Grammar School (now UVHS). She went on to tell me that, as a spellbound 12-year old, she had sat on the front row of their 1960 production of *The Mikado* (what else?), and, entranced by the music and spectacle unfolding before her, had determined there and then that this was a world she somehow needed to become a part of. It was at this point that I fell off my chair.

Not really of course – it was just that, as she spoke, like an arrow thudding into my chest it struck me who Jean Malkin really was. She was Jean Copeland! Or at least that's the name she went by when I knew her, back in those heady days when we were both new arrivals at UGS. And not only that I also realised that I too had been at the very performance she was referring to, although it's only fair to note that, rather than being inspired, I found the whole experience much more disconcerting. That was when my poised and dignified French teacher Miss Winston appeared on the stage dressed as an elderly histrionic woman, wild-eyed and menacing in her scary garish make-up, threatening vengeance and execution on all those who would dare to cross her. The memory haunts me still.

But back to Jean Copeland/Malkin. She had always loved music and singing, and blessed with a lively and spirited personality, an amateur operatic society outside of school was the obvious outlet for her talent. She thus made her debut for the Grange Society in their 1966 production of *The Maid of the Mountains* and has appeared in just about all of their productions ever since, often in leading roles. Latterly, as most seasoned performers do, she has taken on the role of Producer.

In 1990 however, as described in Chapter 7, she was instrumental in establishing a thriving Youth Theatre programme within the Grange Society which stages both a pantomime and several other productions annually. She has also featured in many straight dramatic roles (i.e. non-musical) whilst finding time to lead a Brownie troop and to pursue a successful career as a teacher of children with special needs. In 2010 it is perhaps no surprise to note that she was awarded the MBE for her work with young people in the community – except she does not think of it as 'work'. I believe it was Noel Coward who said, 'The only way to enjoy life is to work. Work is much more fun than fun.' I'm sure Jean would agree with him.

The Grange Society's next two productions were works by the Austro-Hungarian composer Franz Lehar – the less well known *Land of Smiles* (1967) and perhaps his most famous piece *The Merry Widow* (1968). Both were produced by Sandy Doig of Kendal, backed by Mr Mackereth Clark, and the dance expertise of Maud Tranter. Leading roles were taken by performers familiar to the Grange audience, such as Harry Poole, Sheila Hemingway, Maureen and Malcolm Higginson, Maureen Davidson, Margaret Stockley and Derek Roberts.

Whilst these shows continued to benefit from Ben Ward's skilful lighting, the sets were painted by local man Mr C B Earnshaw, at least until he had to retire on health grounds in 1969. His contributions were always commented on in the press reviews, and usually described as vivid and impressive. In fact colour and spectacle came to be a signature feature of Grange's productions, with the quality of their sets and scenery often the envy of other local groups. On Mr Earnshaw's retirement the tradition was upheld by Colin Burrow and Adrian Wiper who continued to provide sets that were both imaginative and professionally produced. In fact, in the 1969 production of *White Horse Inn* they even went a step further by creating cardboard cows that could actually produce fresh milk! Truly magical skills.

Jim Noble & Sandy Doig at work

White Horse Inn is also notable in three other respects – firstly it featured a new Musical Director in Jim Noble because, after over-seeing 20 previous productions, Mr Mackereth Clark finally decided to hang up his baton; secondly, Derek Roberts was awarded a Barrow News Oscar for his performance in the show; and thirdly, the cast featured a real live goat named 'Fritz' (who didn't). This blatant lack of recognition could of course have been down to the fact that poor Fritz was overcome by nerves in the midst of his performance and lost control of his bowels. In an effort to make amends he turned up at Jean and Mick Malkin's wedding a few weeks later in order to extend his good wishes – which would have been fine had his nerves not got the better of him once again.

Sandy Doig remained in the Producer's chair for the next four shows as the Grange Society demonstrated their versatility with more energetic and demanding shows such as

Oklahoma! in 1971, *Carousel* in 1973, and with a repeat of a favourite show from 1960 sandwiched in between. This was *Pink Champagne* for which Jean Malkin, who was by now being regularly cast in leading roles, won a *Barrow News* Oscar. In the following year's production of *Carousel* she then played the much sought-after role of Julie Jordan opposite Derek Roberts as the ill-fated Billy Bigelow. And coincidentally it was he who had played the Mikado for Ulverston Grammar School's production back in 1960 – the very show 12-year old Jean had found so inspiring. I'm sure she couldn't have imagined that one day she would be playing alongside him in a major production.

Mary Lumb of Morecambe took over as Producer in 1975, an experienced director and choreographer who had worked extensively with other local Societies. Her time with Grange was however beset by a number of set-backs. For example the show planned for 1975 had to be changed at short notice, mainly because of the common difficulty of recruiting sufficient male voices. The upshot was a repeat of *Oklahoma!* staged only four years previously. As a result audience numbers suffered, despite an enthusiastic review in the *Evening Mail* and also, incidentally, despite the fact that the Society was at this time taking the trouble to arrange coach transport to bus people in from outlying villages, specially for the show. What a lovely idea.

This problem of recruiting sufficient willing men has been a common problem for all Societies as females appear to be much more readily attracted to the performance arts and social gatherings than males. The Grange Society did not hold back however and in many past show programmes I found a regular plea going out for male recruits. "We are in great need of new male members," pleads Margaret Stockley in one. "The Society would welcome you with open arms." Unfortunately she then goes on to say, "I am appealing to the red-bloodied men among you. Come on lads – we won't bite!" I don't know what sort of response this produced, but perhaps the implicit vampirish touch to her plea was ill-advised.

As for Mary Lumb's tenure as Producer, several other difficulties plagued her. If it was not the last remnants of bad winter weather affecting audience numbers (despite the allure of special buses) it was key cast members falling ill (as Harry Poole did in 1978 when a debilitating bout of flu meant that Adrian Wiper had to stand-in at the last minute), or it was scenery going missing (when in 1979 a hired backcloth was mistakenly left on the train and ended up in Durham.) Even so she managed to steer through a series of very successful shows ranging from *Waltzes from Vienna* (1976) to *Maid of the Mountains* (1981). Mostly she was assisted by the very experienced Jim Noble as her Musical Director, and Ruth Bowyer, who by this time had been recruited as a loyal chorus mistress. One of their productions, *The Count of Luxembourg* won the Cumbria Drama Trophy (an award presented by Cumbria County Council) in 1978. Since the trophy had been established to recognise an outstanding contribution to the development of drama in the county, it was a very special accolade for Grange.

I Could Have Danced All Night

Local producers then took charge of the shows through the 1980s, such as Arthur Wilson of Flookburgh whose sterling work with their own Society you will hear about in the next chapter. His show was perhaps a safe bet in 1982 – *The Merry Widow* – as it was the third time the Grange Society had staged it, and even starred the same two principals from the last outing in 1968, Sheila Hemingway and Harry Poole. Elaine Parkinson from Ulverston then took up the mantle for later shows such as *White Horse Inn* (1984) which, according to the *Westmorland*

Gazette was 'one of the Society's best productions in recent years', and *Viva Mexico* (1987) which not only included for the very first time in any local production a flea circus, also saw the debut of Mick Malkin, Jean's husband, who one assumes had finally yielded to the pressure and answered Margaret Stockley's call. To be fair he was already a talented musician and probably hadn't needed too much persuasion. Either that or he was tired of seeing Jean being wooed annually by the likes of Derek Roberts and Harry Poole. Actually Mick was part of a whole new batch of fresh faces joining the Society as some of the stalwart performers from previous shows finally decided to hang up their tights (or whatever it is actors do when they retire.)

But talking of new faces, seven turned up in the 1988 production of the all time favourite, *The Sound of Music*. Jean Malkin played Maria, supported by Derek Roberts as Captain von Trapp, with Rebecca Ellis, Michelle Clough, Terran Brown, Andrew Thorburn, Emma Logan, Verity Healey, and Claire Howson playing the seven von Trapp children *(pictured above with Jean Malkin)*. Meanwhile the familiar faces of Maureen and Malcom Higginson, Colin Burrow,

Adrian Wiper and Margaret Stockley all appeared in the cast list. The show was highly praised, not only for the usual high standard of performance and staging, but also for the expert touches of Colin Burrow and Adrian Wiper as scenic artists. On this occasion a special sound system was installed which included the increasingly popular 'throat microphones.' Up to now the Society's singers had managed perfectly well with the odd stand microphone.

1990 then proved to be a landmark year for the Grange Society in a number of ways. For a start the year marked the Society's 40th anniversary, celebrated with a sparkling production of Lerner and Loewe's famous musical, *My Fair Lady*. Jean Malkin relished the role of Eliza Dolittle, the cockney flower girl who learns how to talk proper (so to speak) under the tutelage of Professor Higgins, as played by Derek Roberts, and his friend Colonel Pickering, played by Malcolm Higginson *(pictured above)*. Margaret Stockley took the part of the stately Mrs Higgins and, in his first major role, Mick Malkin played Freddie, appropriately enough in love with Eliza.

The show faced the resident scenic artists and stage management team with fresh challenges, as it required as many as 18 changes of scene. And very important to note is that this production marked the debut of a new Producer – Christine Jones, a local dancing mistress and choreographer. Soon to be married and become Christine Bell, she was then to remain as the Grange Society Producer for the next 25 years, until she finally hung up whatever retired Producers hang up in 2014.

Another major event to note in 1990 is the establishment of the Grange Society's Youth Theatre which, as well as providing inspiration and experience to Grange's young people, has in turn proved invaluable as a feeder for the senior group. I have heard it referred to as 'the backbone of the Society.' The Youth Theatre's contribution to the district's pantomime tradition has already been discussed in Chapter 7 and their activities will crop up again when youth theatres as a whole are reviewed in Chapter 11.

Through the 1990's the Society presented a mix of old favourites (*Waltzes from Vienna*, 1992; *The Desert Song*, 1993; *Brigadoon*, 1995) and new challenges (*Showboat*, 1991; *Fiddler on the Roof*, 1994; *Oliver*, 1997). There was evidence of changing times however. Whereas no-one batted an eyelid in 1970 when a donkey was cast in *The Desert Song*, the powers that be vetoed this in 1993 on the grounds that the Victoria Hall was not insured for such an (apparently) high-risk venture. Costs were also rising and the Society was struggling, although if there was a loss on a particular show (as often happened) the annual pantomime was usually a sell-out to balance things out and keep the accounts in the black. It is perhaps of interest to note therefore that the choice of shows may well have been reflecting these themes e.g. how to produce beautiful music from a precarious position (*Fiddler on the Roof*, 1994) and how to remain creative in the face of difficulty and opposition (*Summer Song*, 1996, which is the story how Dvorak's New

World Symphony was borne out of hardship and oppression). All right, I know it wasn't quite that bad for Grange, but hopefully you see what I mean.

Other changes were in evidence with the Society's experience of sad losses at this time. In 1995 the loyal and long-serving chorus mistress Ruth Bowyer passed away, as did faithful front-of-house helper Norah Tallon. A few years later the loss of Jean Wiper was recorded, a one-time Vice-President and long-serving Society member from the start. Equally however, as is the way with these things, new faces were appearing, bringing renewed energy to the shows. For example, the irrepressible Doreen Dunlop ('the sparkly lady at the front') joined Christine Bell's team in 1992 for an old favourite, *Waltzes from Vienna*, previously staged in 1976. Meanwhile Sue Quarmby was waiting in the wings to serve as an accompanist for several future productions. The benefits of the Youth Theatre initiative were also soon in evidence with the choice of show for 1997. This was Lionel Bart's *Oliver*, a production obviously needing a large complement of young people. Phillip Purvis took the title role, with Rachel Muir as

Nancy, and Martin Gregory as the Artful Dodger, all Youth Theatre graduates. Helen Wall, writing in the *Evening Mail*, described the show as 'a stomach-wrenching, breath-stopping, tear-swamping experience', by which I think she meant she enjoyed it.

Phillip Purvis (pictured left with Malcolm Higginson in *Me and My Girl*) and several other members of *Oliver*'s cast then appeared in the following year's production of *Me and My Girl*, another high-energy show, who were then to be joined by more Youth Theatre graduates in the shape of Gary Upton and Lucy Dell for *Hello Dolly* in 1999. In this production Jean Malkin took the title role, a dream part for her, especially as she was partnered with husband Mick as Horace Vandergelder, the focus of her match-making but who subsequently wins her heart. It was a huge success, more than meeting the Society's traditional standards of colour and spectacle, and a fitting show to celebrate its 50th birthday.

The new century

So a new century dawned. As noted, the policy of feeding the senior group from the Youth Theatre programme was working well and enabled the Society to start things off in a well-deserved spirit of optimism. The year 2000 even marked the Society's Golden Jubilee year, which was celebrated with an exhibition of Society memorabilia in the Victoria Hall organised by Jennifer Burrow and, later in the year and with the support of the Town Council, a *Charity Cabaret* was presented in aid of Derian House Children's Hospice and St Mary's Hospice. This was so successful the Society decided to do it all again the following year as part of the centenary celebrations of the Victoria Hall (built in 1901). Sad to relate however is the sudden death of Adrian Wiper at this time, a passionate supporter of the Society, a past performer, and of course a valued scenic artist.

The annual show for that year was *Carousel*. Sue Quarmby's daughter Lucy played Julie Jordan, her first adult role, having just starred in the Youth Theatre's pantomime, *Beauty and the Beast*. She had however some previous experience with an appearance as an 8-year old in *Showboat* (1991). And following in her mother's footsteps she is also a talented pianist, winning a £100 bursary trophy at the 1999

South Cumbria Music Festival. Mark Jeffreys took on the role of Billy Bigelow with Jennifer Archibald (who had also featured in *Beauty and the Beast*) playing his 15-year old daughter. Her particular speciality was dance which she both studied and taught. Oddly enough she was to play opposite Mark the following year as his love interest in *Half a Sixpence*. Both were not only to take leading roles in many of the Society's future productions, they were also to take leading roles in each other's lives as a few years down the line they were to become Mr and Mrs Jeffreys!

Half a Sixpence (2001) was a new venture for the Society, and a special challenge, as it was a show which pushed the performance space in the Victoria Hall to the limit. With a very effective mix of youth and experience in the cast the show went down very well, and it had been promoted quite creatively by having cast members wander around the town in their Edwardian costumes. Subsequently the quality of both the performances and the production were recognised with a national NODA nomination, and a regional award for best show.

Jennifer Archibald
Gigi (2003)

The Society really was riding high on a wave of renewed energy and confidence at this time, all of which was reflected in their shows over the next few years. For example there was the exuberance of *Anything Goes* (2002), the romance of *Gigi* (2003), and the demanding plot, music, scenery and costumes of *My Fair Lady* (2004) when Derek Roberts reprised his 1990 role as Professor Higgins. This time he was sorting out the vowel sounds of Jennifer Archibald in the role of Eliza Dolittle. And in a sad acknowledgement of the passage of time, poor Jean and Mick Malkin, who had played the young lovers of 14 years earlier, were now cast as old Mrs Pearce, the housekeeper, and as Alfred Dolittle, Eliza's shiftless father. Margaret Stockley suffered a similar fate in the following year's production of *Irene*. Whereas in 1980 she had taken the lead role as the young and adventurous Irene, in 2005 she was re-cast as Irene's widowed mother Mrs O'Dare. Meanwhile Derek Roberts was happy to re-don dress and make-up to play Mme Lucy, just as he had done previously, in 1980.

It's a Hard Knock Life

You know the kind of thing that happens. The sun is shining, you're in a good mood, sailing along happily, and then someone pushes in front of you at the Post Office, you get a puncture on the way home and then it starts to bucket it down just as you get out of the car to fix it. Well that's pretty much the experience of the Grange Society in 2007 when, after a series of highly praised shows, they found themselves embroiled in a row about their choice for 2008. This was *Showboat*. Despite its revered place in the history of the Musical, anti-racist campaigners have never liked this show, claiming that it depicts an offensive and stereotyped view of black people. In other circles however it is seen as a positive statement *against* racism with an underlying sympathy towards the plight of black people, and with a message which calls for tolerance and racial harmony. In any event, for the Grange Society, a chorus of disapproval from various quarters arose when the news of its intentions was revealed. The arguments then bled into the correspondence pages of the local press, with the majority of correspondents supporting the Grange Society and refuting the racist claims as ill-informed. But possibly what upset the protestors most was Grange's intention to have white actors 'black up' for their roles, a practice which, to be fair, was rare and had become generally frowned upon. Although Christine Bell argued strongly that both the musical and the intent of the Society were being seriously misunderstood, in the end she decided to abandon the project and choose an alternative. This turned out to be the anodyne *Waltzes from Vienna*, a show which would offend no-one, except perhaps Craig Revel Horwood if he was in a particularly bad mood.

One wonders if Scottish people ever find *their* portrayal by English actors offensive but, if they do, no voices of protest were raised when Grange presented *Brigadoon* in 2009. But generally, the miserable experience of *Showboat* aside, this was a time of transition with a series of young players completing the three stage process of gaining experience in the Youth Theatre, then graduating to the chorus in the senior group, and then finally to being cast in leading roles. The production of *Carousel* in 2010 exemplified this with a number of performers who had completed this journey. Mark Jeffreys reprised the role of Billy Bigelow from 2000, whilst Caroline Fearon took on the role of Julie Jordan. I say 'newcomer' although she had graduated as a regular Pantomime player to give an impressive performance in *Brigadoon* the previous year. Grace Heap also made her debut for the senior Society in 2010 as Louise, Billy Bigelow's daughter, although in real life she was the daughter of another of Grange's regular players, Ann Heap. Grace would feature in later productions before going on to undertake professional training in London. I understand she is highly thought of there, and on the cusp of a successful career.

Samatha Grundy is another example of a performer who has worked steadily from Youth Theatre to senior Society when, after sterling work in the chorus, she undertook her first main role in the 2005 production of *Irene*. Later she was cast in such roles as the tragic Nancy in *Oliver* (2011), the boisterous title role in *Calamity Jane* (2013) and, in a complete contrast of characters, the sweet and gracious Anna in *The King and I* (2015), and the deliciously menacing Miss Hannigan in *Annie* (2016).

As for musicians, some of the trusted and locally-known Musical Directors of past decades have already been mentioned, but whilst these may sometimes have been drafted in from other parts of the district, now they were emerging home-grown. For example, Phillip Purvis who had first appeared for the Society in *Oliver* in 1997 (playing the title role), re-appeared as Musical Director to take charge of two productions – *Waltzes from Vienna* in 2008, and *Brigadoon* in 2009. He was then followed by another local talent Tom Gray, a local lad but now a graduate of the Birmingham Conservatoire. He led the orchestra from 2010 to 2014 before, as many of the young talents do, leaving the area for pastures new.

Christine Bell   *Vivienne Wilde*

Following Christine Bell's retirement in 2014, and presumably because of the reputation she had helped the Grange Society to establish, a new production team was engaged for *The King and I* (2015), each bringing a great deal of talent and experience with them. Shirley Britton was the Producer, who you may recall from her work with the Ulverston and Barrow

Societies, and John Iveson was the Musical Director, a one-time principal musician at the Royal Opera House, Covent Garden. Meanwhile Vivienne Wilde continued as accompanist/rehearsal pianist, a role she had first taken up in 2008 from Sue Quarmby. She too carried a wealth of experience, having played in numerous theatre orchestras around the country. Then, in 2016, having appeared in countless of the Society's shows, and having looked after the Youth Theatre since its inception, it seemed only right that Jean Malkin should finally get the opportunity to produce a show for the senior group. This she did with *Annie*. It was pretty much a seamless transition for her and the cast since Molly Cowley, who played Annie, and her 12 orphan conspirators had all emerged from the Youth Theatre, so of course were very familiar with Jean Malkin. It must have given them all added confidence, as well as proving yet again that the Youth Theatre was indeed 'the backbone of the Society.' Jean was also supported by a new Musical Director, Jane Thedham, leader of the Bay Community Singers, and, proving a worthy successor to Colin Burrow, by Helen Lawler who took over as set designer and scenic artist.

Since the focus of this book is musical theatre, there is unfortunately no space to talk about the other amateur drama productions which are a feature of Grange's year, nor has it been possible to say much about the popular Edwardian Festival. And what about the Society's Spring and Summer Concerts, and the ad hoc entertainments provided in local retirement homes etc? There is indeed a long tradition of local performance or home-grown entertainment in the town, perhaps because of its location and, although I hesitate to use the word, isolation – in other words people have had to make their own entertainment. Also important in the Society's longevity is the presence of a fixed performance venue in the Victoria Hall and the fact that it has been freer from the tyranny of cinema competition, and damaging theatre closures, which have had such an impact on many of the district's other amateur groups. So far so good, but what of the Society's future?

The recent production of *Annie* (2016) was the most 'modern' musical the Society had ever staged. When you think of the efforts of the bigger Societies to tackle the newer, more

Annie (Molly Cowley) *with Sandy her dog (as played by Rosie) and her orphan friends as played by* Elisia Carter, Alice Payne, Zoe Tunnadine, Martha Rand, Daisy McLoughlin, Becky McCleery, Nerissa Blatchley, Samantha Myers, Megan Hargan, Hannah Tunnadine, Faye Hill and Emily Kate Unsworth

ambitious productions and when you read (in the next chapter) about the fate of the Flookburgh Society, you might wonder whether Grange is in danger of being left behind, and you may possibly have a judder of anxiety about the Society's future. There is no need. Certainly the Society's members and patrons don't share such concerns. In fact, when I asked Jean Malkin if she was worried about the future, she gave me a bemused, bewildered look, as if I'd asked her if she was worried about the earth falling into the sun. No, what comes across clearly is that the members of the Grange Society have sufficient confidence in the consistent quality of their production values that they feel they will always succeed in making any 'old standard' feel new and fresh. And equally they have confidence in their ability to nurture and foster emerging talent to keep the Society alive.

In this respect the establishment of a Youth Theatre group in 1990 was clearly a masterstroke. Not only does it offer the youth of the area inspiration and experience, it provides a fresh supply of talent when the senior members run out of puff. Moreover, from a financial point of view (always a concern for every Society) the annual Pantomime is a reliable source of additional income if the musical fails to pull in the crowds.

And finally, having said all that, it would appear that the amount of support from the Grange audience is currently as steady and strong as the continuing energy and enthusiasm of the Society's performers and helpers. The members of the Grange Society may be ploughing their own furrow, but they appear to have hit on a winning formula. Daddy Warbucks from *Annie* perhaps speaks for them all when he sings, 'Why Should I Change a Thing?'

7

FLOOKBURGH AND DISTRICT AMATEUR OPERATIC SOCIETY
(Founded 1951)

Sadly the Flookburgh and District Amateur Operatic Society ceased to be in September 2015. The challenge of meeting modern demands, increased production costs, and the difficulties of recruiting sufficient numbers of new members had all conspired to bring this about. From its inception in 1951 with a performance of *The Pirates of Penzance*, the members had produced a show every subsequent year - that's a total of 64 productions. And so, despite (or maybe precisely because of) its demise, it is worth spending some time reflecting on its achievements whilst expressing the hope that its current closure is merely a temporary blip.

The Flookburgh Society has the reputation of being somewhat quirky, with its own way of doing things. Helen Wall, in one of her reviews for the *North Western Evening Mail* puts the case succinctly: 'Flookburgh's knack of taking the show seriously but not themselves makes for delightful entertainment.' Certainly when compared to its more advanced cousins in Barrow and Ulverston, its image is that of a stereotypical village am-dram company of hearty, well-meaning folk who go to rehearsals for a social get-together rather than to concentrate on creating serious theatre. The productions are staged, not in a purpose-built theatre but in the much smaller space afforded by the Lower Holker Village Hall in Cark, which has an audience capacity of no more than 120 people, and on a 'pocket-handkerchief' stage area (as it is generally described). The budget for a show is slender, perhaps less than a quarter of the amount other Societies may spend; when not hand-made, costumes are hired from a local supplier in Grange, whilst all the scenery *is* hand-made and hand-painted. And indeed, one may chuckle at the tales which are easily told of inopportune power-cuts, scenery failures, and wardrobe mal-functions. But for all this, it would be a great mistake to assume that the Flookburgh Society productions were of inferior quality. Quite the opposite. The evidence of 64 full scale musicals in as many years, with consistently competent singing and dancing performed by an enthusiastic and talented cast in the context of colourful and lively sets, all speak for themselves. I know this, not because I have had the opportunity to see any of their shows, but I have read a great many positive reviews of their back catalogue. Deborah Powell, a Society member for more than 30 years says: 'During that time I have been frustrated, challenged, excited, tired, discouraged, elated, entertained and taught much by fellow actors, but above all I have been part of a warm and supportive family who have rehearsed, acted, mourned and rejoiced together.'

Beginnings

So where do we start? As already mentioned, the modern Society was a post-war development, producing its first show, *Pirates of Penzance* in 1951. Prior to this a former Society, known as the Lower Holker and District Amateur Operatic Society had been originally set up in 1920, with Lord Richard Cavendish of Holker Hall as its President. As with many local groups the outbreak of World War Two brought its activities to an end and it was formally wound up in 1940. At the time its assets amounted to the sum of £17 (which translates to about £500 in today's value). This sum was then donated to the

'Lower Holker Club' (ie the village hall) in appreciation of the facilities and support it had previously provided.

Post-war, it was the initiative of Mrs Jean O'Hara which set the ball rolling again. She had been part of the thrust to revive the Grange Society but, as mentioned in the previous chapter, the story goes that because of 'a major disagreement' she decided to see if she could muster support for the revival of 'the old society' in Flookburgh. A Public Meeting was called at which 20 people pledged their support with backing again from the Cavendish family, this time from Richard Cavendish, the late Lord Cavendish's son. His support was crucial – in addition to his patronage, he also provided practical aid in the form of timber and material to allow the Lower Holker Club to build new stage equipment suited to operatic performances. Then, from Ulverston, Mr Charles Thompson (the same man who had been so instrumental in getting the Abbey Society underway in Barrow) was engaged to produce their first show, *Pirates of Penzance*.

Brian Greaves played Frederic, the hero, with Dorothy Hadwin as his leading lady. Jean O'Hara herself was also in the cast along with others who would appear in many later productions. The press review points the way for the future stating, 'The opera was staged with remarkable skill and intelligent stage-craft.' A number of mistakes were however commented on – such as the uncertain timing between voice and orchestra – 'but these were atoned for by … enthusiasm, warm sincerity, and colourful décor.' Much of the scenery had actually been painted by Charles Thompson himself.

At this time it was usual for newly-fledged Societies to tread the safe path of Gilbert & Sullivan works, but this new Flookburgh group was different. Quickly establishing a reputation for an idiosyncratic approach to amateur operatics the Committee chose Edward German's comic opera *Merrie*

England for its second production in 1952. To be fair, the former Holker & District Society had successfully staged this piece on two previous occasions, so they must have thought they were still on fairly safe ground. In fact, in the 1952 production, one of the players Jack Slater, was recruited to revive the role he had previously played back in 1921. 'He is not quite so nimble as he was in 1921,' says the programme notes, 'but his voice is just as good!' Also in the cast was Jean O'Hara who, perhaps fittingly, was cast as Queen Elizabeth I, and several others who were to become familiar names on future cast lists, including Alec Henderson, Jack Butler, Ernest Rylands, and the inimitable Brian Greaves.

Brian Greaves is now a genial 92-year old (commonly known as 'Chuckie' for reasons which are not clear to me) who continues to live an independent life in his Cark bungalow where I had the pleasure of meeting him. Although somewhat frail, he displayed a cheery good-humour and liveliness which I found quite inspirational. He is a retired railwayman who had once driven the Royal Train, with the Queen and Prince Phillip on board, on one leg of its journey from London to Barrow. Also present was Arthur Wilson, a local farmer and dairyman (now retired), another of Flookburgh's veterans who displayed an equal sense of fun and cheerfulness, and Graeme Livingstone, a talented local performer and songwriter who has acted with the Society over the past 20 years or so. It was easy to see why they had all been successful in their craft as I spent a privileged afternoon in their company, listening to their fund of memories and stories

about their time on the stage. For example, there was a tale concerning the old Society where a local farmer had sabotaged the electricity supply to the Hall on opening night in retaliation for his wife having being passed over for a lead role! Then, in more recent times there was the story of a cast member (who shall remain nameless) who had accidentally set fire to his costume by leaving it unattended on a radiator. Or what about the domino effect during a performance of *Half a Sixpence* (1989) when one's man's inebriated trip led to the whole line of people losing their balance, one after another?

With regard to his stage career, Brian Greaves has added his strong voice to both lead roles and the chorus of many, indeed most, of the Society's productions, and he has also performed in several shows staged by various other local groups, such as the Operatic Societies in Grange and Ulverston, and the Walney and Abbey Societies in Barrow. He has a fine tenor voice which, according to one early press review 'has no equal in the district.' "Do you want to hear me sing?" he said, and promptly put on a CD. He then referred to a small collection of past show programmes stored in his loft and which, graciously, he suggested I could retrieve. And so it was that, four men of advancing years (with an average age of around 75), in an effort that was far from co-ordinated, attempted to manoeuvre a lengthy ladder carefully, inch by inch, through his lounge whilst attempting to avoid hitting windows, mirrors and ornaments, all to the accompaniment of *Jesu, Joy of Man's Desiring* playing at full volume. It was a bit like the Chuckle Brothers meets *Last of the Summer Wine.*

Arthur Wilson told me he had joined the Society in 1956. He had served in the RAF during the war and on being de-mobbed returned to Flookburgh in 1951 to run his farm. The production that year was *The Romany Maid*, when he was first recruited to sing in the Gentlemen's Chorus, although subsequently he was to be cast in lead roles in many later productions. Since farming is a full-time occupation in itself I marvelled at his ability to combine such intensive work with a stage career. 'Being in the shows helped me to put the farm out of my mind,' he said, 'and gave me something different to concentrate on.' He had initially been encouraged to become involved by Pat Mikosz (pictured below), another key figure, whose legendary energy and commitment has played a major part in the Society's successful history. Sadly she passed away in 2014, at the grand age of 82, and she is clearly much missed.

She made her debut in 1953, in the chorus of *The Rebel Maid* and, although she regularly appeared in later productions, it was not until 1958 that her talents were recognised and brought to the fore. The production was *Maid of the Mountains* and her comedic performance was recorded as a sure fire hit. The *Barrow News* particularly noted her abilities and potential in a review which can only be described as glowing. 'Every now and then,' it runs, 'one comes across "natural" players, those who, even though they may be lacking in polished technique, are obviously born to the stage.'

The comments on the performance of several other players (such as Joe Whalley, Jack Butler, Hetty Lancaster, and Alec Henderson) were also very positive, and the quality of the chorus singing was singled out: 'They are delightfully uninhibited ... choruses which other amateur operatic societies would give their eye teeth to possess.' It was clear that the Flookburgh Society had come of age and was here to stay.

Scenes From Early Productions

**Merrie
England, 1952**

**The
Gondoliers, 1955**

**The Mikado
1957**

These early shows in the Society's history all benefited from the consistent input of such figures as Pat Mikosz, Arthur Wilson, and Brian Greaves, as well as many others, but also from regular Producers and Musical Directors. This consistency must have given everyone a chance to get to know each other well, to build up a sense of familiarity, and thus to create more productive working relationships. In this respect Charles Thompson carried out production duties from 1951 to 1955, Ronald Metcalfe from 1957 to 1961, and then George Webster from 1963 to 1969. As for the post of Musical Director, this was filled for many years by Wyn Large (1953 – 1960), before he then handed over the baton (literally) to Jolyon Dodgson (1961 – 1969).

Gaining in strength

By the mid- to late 60's the Society had gained sufficient confidence to move away from the rather dated, tried-and-tested old favourites of previous years to tackle the more modern *Oklahoma!* (1966) It had been staged very successfully already by both the Ulverston Society (1955) and Barrow (1960), but now it was Flookburgh's turn. With its rural setting and 'farmers vs cowboys' scenario it was probably not too much of a stretch for the actors to find their motivation. The principal roles of Curly and Jud, the rivals in love, were taken by John Lewis and George Bowyer, with Paulette Knox as Laurey the love interest. (Since Curly ultimately wins Laurey's heart by the way, the actors concerned must have fully embraced their roles as John Lewis, who played Curly was later to marry Paulette Knox.) *Calamity Jane* followed in 1968. Again, with its western themes and rural setting it suited the Society well, and who better to play *Calamity Jane* and her love interest Wild Bill Hickock than Paulette Knox (now Lewis!) and John Lewis.

The Society now seemed to be moving from strength to strength. For example, the 1967 production had been *The Desert Song* which was so much anticipated that pre-bookings demanded that the usual run of 4 nights be extended to 8. And love again was in the air when the Musical Director of the show fell for the Dancing Mistress, Christine Walker. They subsequently married and set up home together in Kendal.

The Gypsy Princess was chosen as the 1969 production – something of a retreat to familiar ground as the Society had staged this show previously in 1963, with several of the cast reprising their roles from the previous show. There were some new faces however. Ruth Bowyer, took up the baton as Musical Director for the first time, and Ruth Airey and Christine Jones, who were to become regular cast members and dancers, both made their debut in this production. (Yes, this is the same Christine Bell – nee Jones - who you read about in the previous chapter!) The story centres on a love match which has to overcome many obstacles in order to succeed and, in a curious case of life imitating art, that is exactly what the show had to do. Shortly before opening night an out-break of influenza (the so-called Asian flu) hit the district. First to fall victim was Ernest Rylands who had been cast in the lead role of Count Bonifaska. Heroically George Webster, who had produced the show previously, stepped into the breach. But after only one performance he too was laid low and was unable to complete the show's run. Then just as it looked as if the show would have to be cancelled (despite full bookings for the week) the remarkable Jack Fisher appeared. With no more than 3 hours to read the part and rehearse the songs and dances, he somehow managed (with one or two ad libs thrown in) to give a fantastic performance and save the day.

At the start of the next decade several changes were afoot. By this time Jack Butler, a past Chair and acting member of the Society had resigned, there was the loss of Eric Pollitt, the Society's long-serving Treasurer, Brian Greaves had taken up residence temporarily in Barrow, and as we have seen, several reliable contributors had fallen in love and left the district. Then in 1972 the long-term Patron of the Society, Mr Richard Cavendish passed away, although his son Hugh was immediately given the opportunity to take his place. New blood then arrived in the form of Joyce Warrington, who was to produce the 1971 show, *Night in Venice*. She ran a Ballet School in Morecambe and was subsequently to become a dedicated and reliable Producer of many future shows. Performers from other Societies also made guest appearances during this period. For example, husband and wife team Meril and Ron Bull played the lead roles in *Rose Marie* in 1972, and Ron Eddevane from Ulverston, and Aprille Butterfield from Barrow appeared in *Goodnight Vienna* in 1974.

A new face also appeared in the Society's 1979 production, *Salad Days*. During after-show drinks at the Rose and Crown pub Arthur Wilson was asked who it was who had played 'the la'al lad' in the show, i.e. the part of a small mute boy. Arthur took great delight in introducing him to Deborah Powell, a young woman in her early twenties, who had just joined the group - surely solid proof that a versatile new actor had come on the scene. Deborah has since become a loyal member of the Society, appearing in many of the shows which were to follow in the 80's, such as *The Boyfriend* (1980), *Divorce Me Darling* (1982), *Charlie Girl* (1986) and *Finian's Rainbow* (1988).

And despite the challenges of sudden illness, cancelled rehearsals due to bad weather, wardrobe malfunctions, or power cuts, in true show-business style the show always went on. With regard to the *Finian's Rainbow* for example in 1988, a violent thunderstorm caused major power failure throughout the district a few hours before the curtain was due to go up on opening night. Arthur Wilson, who was in the middle of milking-time, assumed that the show would necessarily have to be cancelled, so took himself off to the candle-lit pub instead. Relaxing with his pint he was horrified when someone in a panic dashed in wondering where he had got to. An emergency generator had been fixed up, the audience were in their seats, and the show was waiting to start. It took him about 15 minutes to hurtle to the Hall, get into his costume, and put on his make-up. 'Of course, with the generator, everything was a bit darker than usual, so I don't think anyone noticed,' he explained optimistically. Apparently it had been a safe bet to find him in the Rose and Crown, as Arthur had a reputation for disappearing for a quick pint, in full costume and make-up, in the middle of a show. It must have been one of the joys of living in Flookburgh at this time that the guy on stage ornately dressed as a desert prince was last seen in a flat cap and wellies driving his tractor down the street, or the man tearing your ticket and showing you to your seat was next seen bowing in front of the audience as he prepared to conduct the orchestra.

If there is a 'make do and mend' quality about such incidents, they also bear testimony, not only to the Society's ingenuity, but also to the determination and commitment which has always under-pinned their efforts. This was as true in recent times as it has always been and, as we shall see as the story continues, teamwork, enthusiasm and collaborative endeavour have always been key ingredients in Flookburgh's success. In the early 1980's for example Tom Walker, a well-known actor and director in the area, led a team which carried out much of the stage management. Considering the size of the stage they are said to have created many clever and imaginative sets, somehow manipulating the area so that it could accommodate the large cast demanded by some shows.

But there were some limitations of the Lower Holker Hall that couldn't be surmounted evident in the fact that, of the 20 shows staged between 1990 and 2010, as many as 60% of them were repeats of previous productions. As I say the underlying cause of this was by no means a lack of imagination or adventure on the Society's part. In the late 1990's Bob Somerset joined the backstage team and instigated some modern developments to both the sound and lighting, but until then such facilities were of a fairly basic standard. The larger, more modern, spectacle-based shows such as *Showboat, Chess,* or *Jesus Christ Superstar* which the larger local Societies were staging in this period were thus impossible to mount. Hence Flookburgh's output post-1990 tended to consist of the traditional, familiar shows such as *The White Horse Inn, The Gypsy Princess,* and *Oklahoma!* Nevertheless audiences stayed

Anne Woods, Andrew Barrow, Deborah Powell, and Ron Palmer
The Gypsy Princess, 1995

loyal and, familiar as they were, they were invariably successful productions. Having been part of village life for so long there was a sense of ownership of the Society among the local community which, it has to be said, the larger amateur societies do not always achieve.

New faces were however appearing on the scene from both local sources and the wider district. For example, in the shows of the late 1990's and early part of the new century, a number of new Musical Directors took charge (such as Chris Quarmby, Rebecca Perkins, and Olive Dewhurst-Maddock, who sometimes took on producing duties as well), whilst the choreography and dancers were, at various times, managed by Ruth Airey, Carole Leech, and Sonja Biggins. New performers also arrived, some of whom were to appear in several later productions. Among these were Liz & Andrew Purvin, Ron Palmer, Heather Kelly and Dorothy Pass – all supported by Flookburgh veterans such as Arthur Wilson, Brian Greaves, Deborah Powell, and Pat Miscosz.

The press reviews of the shows from this period are invariably positive, although occasionally poor sound quality is commented on. Remember however that the Flookburgh Society has always had to get by with stage microphones and has never had the luxury of the modern 'throat' microphones which allow the singer considerable more degrees of freedom in their performance.

Graeme Livingstone, a local musician and songwriter, joined the Society for the 1999 production of *Oklahoma!* and then starred in one of the Society's more memorable and ambitious offerings which followed in 2000 – *Fiddler on the Roof.* Graeme played Lazar Wolf, the butcher, alongside other familiar faces such as Deborah Powell, Heather Kelly, Carole Leech and five members of the Purvin family! The star of the show however was Arthur Wilson, a former dairyman himself,

Andrew Purvin with his sewing machine
Fiddler on the Roof, 2000

so very fittingly cast as Tevye, the poor Jewish dairyman of the story who is trying to hang on to a traditional way of life in the face of intense social upheaval. Helen Wall, reviewing the show for the *Evening Mail* hailed it a 'smash-hit', characterised by 'thoughtful set design and casting, good lighting and an accomplished orchestra.'

Graeme Livingstone
and Carole Leech
The Quaker Girl 2001

In 2001 the Society celebrated its 50th birthday with a favourite of amateur companies *The Quaker Girl*, the 1910 Lionel Monckton comedy which the Society had previously staged in 1984. It was received very favourably as 'a delightful light-hearted romp.' Penny Butler produced and directed, aided by Chris Quarmby as Musical Director (for the first time) and with Hilary MacArthur in charge of the choreography. It was also notable for a guest appearance by John Brice of the Barrow Savoyards.

With an injection of new voices and new ideas the early years of the new century definitely marked the beginning of something of a purple patch for the Society. Certainly the revived production of 2003, *Finian's Rainbow*, directed by Joyce Warrington, was hailed as one of the Society's greatest achievements. Arthur Wilson (right) again took the lead 'using all his country charm to beguile the audience' and several youngsters had also been recruited, undoubtedly giving the proceedings an extra shot of energy, and indeed they were  credited with 'lifting the show on the odd occasions when things started to flag.' Overall the show was described as 'magical' and a triumph for Joyce Warrington (Producer) and Olive Dewhurst-Maddock (Musical Director). John Twyford writing in the *Evening Mail* went so far as to honour Sonja Biggins with his personal 'special dance award' and Graeme Livingstone with a personal Oscar for 'best supporting actor.'

Presumably with increased confidence, the Society then took some risks with their subsequent productions with new and untried shows (as far as Flookburgh was concerned) which would require a fair degree of imagination to stage. Among these were *Paint Your Wagon* (2004) – the first and only time this had been produced by one of the Cumbrian amateur groups – *The Pyjama Game* (2006), *Anything Goes* (2007), *Hello*

Dolly (2008), the rarely seen and difficult to stage *Mame* (2010), and *South Pacific* (2011). In other words, within the span of a few years, Lower Holker Village Hall would have to be transformed into a mining camp during the California gold rush, a nightwear factory in Iowa, a cruise ship, the city of New York, and a South Pacific island paradise. As Helen Wall once wrote in the *Evening Mail*: 'With few resources, Flookburgh is as gutsy a little society as ever prized a gents' chorus out of the bar!'

Hello Dolly, 2008

Dolly (Lindsey Jackson) with her admirers Bill Little, Alan Pass, Brian Greaves, Paul Leach, David Birch, Steve Jackson, & Bob Needham

Despite such ambition however it was also true that the Society's membership was decreasing, and it was really only by attracting principals from the wider Cumbrian amateur circuit that they were able to carry their projects through. By now for example, Sue Little, Helen Day and Lindsey Jackson, regular performers for the Ulverston Pantomime Society (among other things), had joined the company and added their energy and sparkle to the proceedings. Sue Little in fact produced all the shows mentioned above from 2006 to 2011, supported by Carole Leech as stalwart Choreographer.

Full Circle

2011, the year *South Pacific* was staged, had been the Society's diamond anniversary year and a member of the cast was a certain Ernest Rylands. It was a cause for celebration as well as a point of some irony that he had also appeared in the Society's very first production, *Pirates of Penzance*, back in 1951. It was as if the Society had come full circle. And indeed, despite the lively exuberance evident in the show, and its very successful reception, the Society was clearly struggling. Finances were running thin, and it was proving increasingly difficult to muster sufficient numbers of players to mount their shows. In fact *Guys and Dolls*, the planned show for 2012, had to be cancelled for this very reason. Refusing to yield entirely however, under the joint leadership of Deborah Powell, Benita Finch, Pam Mellor and Carole Leech, the company staged a revue of songs and sketches entitled *Flookburgh Entertains*. It went down very well, so the venture was repeated in the following year as a *Musical Extavaganza*. Talent and enthusiasm may not have been lacking, but equally it seemed that, as a whole, the Society was losing its impetus.

There was a small revival in fortunes in 2014 and 2015 with two shows that were both brave, innovative and even symbolic in their way, but neither was sufficient to save the day. The first of these, in 2014, again driven by the team of Deborah Powell, Sue Little and Carole Leech, was *Stepping Out*, a musical version of a stage play which tells the story of a small group who meet together each week for a tap dance class. At first the members treat the classes as social occasions and a time for fun and distraction, but gradually they develop a high level of skill and cohesiveness. It perhaps could have been a symbolic re-working of the Flookburgh Society's own story.

Then, in 2015, in a complete departure from the traditional, the Society staged the premiere of Graeme

Livingstone's self-penned musical *The Adventures of Tom Dixon: Just a Little War*. It told the real-life story of local man Tom Dixon (played by Alistair Marsh) who joins the volunteer militia when Napoleon threatens England's shores, and then fights his way through the Napoleonic wars, culminating at the Battle of Waterloo. Although it attracted large audiences for its 4-night run, and was hailed as something of a triumph for both Graeme and the Society, it proved, ironically as things turned out, to mark the Flookburgh Society's own Waterloo.

The Society has clearly achieved much over the years and the valuable contribution it has made to the local community should not be under-estimated. But the sad reality, at least at the time of writing, is that the Flookburgh Society is one with more of a past than a future. Hopefully this brief survey does justice to the staunch work and effort that so many have put in over the years, and conveys a little of the enthusiasm and sense of fun which have characterised all their productions. The song may have ended but, as Irving Berlin once said, hopefully the melody lingers on.

8

WALNEY JUNIOR AMATEUR OPERATIC SOCIETY (Founded 1967)

Along with many others I suspect, my all-time favourite musical has to be *Les Miserables*. I know there are people who are happy to dismiss it as an over-wrought heap of melodrama but, for me, that's exactly why it's so great. Consider all the elements: an epic plot, a wronged man suffering grave injustice, an abused woman, prostitution, a vulnerable waif, barricades, revolution, and death, all wrapped up in stirring and emotive music. Something for everyone there, surely. I've seen it a few times now, all rather epic theatrical productions, not to mention the sweeping 2014 Hollywood film. So it was with some trepidation that I turned up in November 2015 at The Forum, in Barrow, to see what Walney Juniors were going to make of it. I knew they had previously scored a massive hit with it 10 years earlier, but could they really be trusted to do it again? Indeed they could. I have to say it was as good a piece of musical theatre as I have ever seen, equally as powerful and dramatic as you might expect from any adult or professional cast. But this was Walney Juniors – you know, where the average age is somewhere around 14? Of course, since I am supposed to be charting the history of this particular group I am starting at the wrong end of the story but, if you keep this 2015 production in mind, as I review the Society's beginnings you will discover for yourself just how much it has grown and matured over the years.

Off to see the Wizard

In 1967 four individuals who had all been working with young people in various ways, hatched the idea of forming a junior musical society. Because at that time they all had involvement with the senior group, the Walney Amateur Operatic Society, it was to be styled 'The Walney Junior Operatic Society' although from the beginning it was conceived to be independent, self-supporting and quite separate from the senior group. These four founders were Martyn Tonge, a local solicitor (and musician), Stella Willans, a professional musician who had played in the pit orchestra for many productions both at Her Majesty's Theatre and the Coliseum, Jim Myerscough, a local stationer, and Saxon Kolbe, a dance captain.

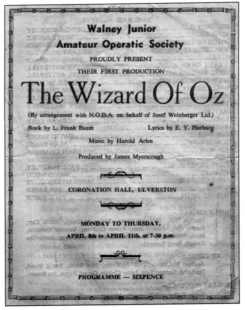

The first production, *The Wizard of Oz*, was staged in April 1968 at the Coronation Hall, Ulverston, the only venue available to them at the time. It was produced by Jim Myerscough, with Stella Willans as Musical Director, and choreography by Nellie English (remember her from the Young Image pantomimes?) As a new society resources were limited, so musical accompaniment was stripped down to the bare minimum of two pianos, drums and bass, and the scenery was borrowed from an amateur group in Eccles. (No, I don't know why either – presumably someone had a contact there.) Among the performers were Linda Cooksey who played Dorothy, and Mamie Brookes as the Wicked Witch of the West.

The show was so well received and supported it was followed in 1969, again at the Coronation Hall, by a so-called 'musical play' entitled *Tick Tock the Clock*, written and composed by Sam Wood, a well-known musician from Morecambe. Unfortunately it did not fare so well as the whole district at this time had been hit by a plague of what was called the Hong Kong flu. It was reported that at least 4 of the cast struggled through the performances under its influence, not helped by the fact that audience support was meagre, presumably because they too had been laid low. Still, Ronald Metcalfe writing in the *Barrow News* describes the overall effort as 'bright and breezy.' 'It is youngsters like this we must encourage,' he says. 'They are the future backbone of all our senior societies.' How right he was. I'll give you several examples as we proceed but, for the moment, let me mention a few who all appeared for Walney Juniors in the 1970's and who went on to be part of this 'future backbone'– Martin Craig (well-known local performer and Producer of, among other things, the afore-mentioned production of *Les Miserables* in 2015), Paul Blake (destined to become a much sought-after Musical Director), and Chris Warby and Steve Freeland (both regular Barrow Savoyards, again among other things).

A much more grown-up show was chosen for 1970, *Love From Judy*, and the venue was now moved to the Public Hall in Barrow. It saw the debut of Steven Liversedge, who was to feature in many later productions before going off to college to study Drama. He returned as Producer for several more shows, and appeared in a couple of shows for the Barrow Society (e.g *Camelot,*1977 & *Mame,*1978) before finally leaving the area in 1979 to pursue a professional career in London. As far as I am aware he is currently working with a theatre company in Essex.

Two more familiar names then crop up – Joan Eddevane (nee Park), who had actually taken the lead in Ulverston's production of *Love From Judy* in 1957 but was also by this time a well-known figure on the local amateur scene, and David Marcus. Both were involved in the 1971 production of *Babes in the Wood*, with Joan as Producer, and David Marcus making an early appearance in a Barrow show as Dame Dolly Diddlebury. Joan continued in the Producer role for the next five shows (from *Alice in Wonderland* in 1973 to *Cinderella* in 1976), supported by Stella Willans and Saxon Winship (nee Kolbe), pictured right. For those romantically inclined, you may like to note that, the King and Queen of Hearts in *Alice in Wonderland* were played by Jim Winship and Saxon Kolbe. Later that year they got married,  Saxon having become, quite literally, the Queen of Jim's heart.

By means of fund-raising activities, sponsorship, and a regular float in the annual Barrow carnival parade, the Society had now become much more firmly established. Society membership was increasing at a healthy rate and funds were improving. There was still to be a reliance on local voluntary sets and costume-makers however, and it would be a few years yet before the basic musical accompaniment of piano, drums, and bass would be augmented. The choice of shows was also becoming more bedded down, taking on the consistency of pantomime. As if to rub the point home the group actually staged two productions in 1976, both from the classical pantomime tradition – *Cinderella* in January, and *Aladdin* in the following December. The press reviews at this time are invariably positive, noting the energy, colour and 'lively movement and sparkling chorus.' Oh the exuberance of youth!

The choice for the Society's 10th anniversary show in 1977 was a revival of their debut production, *The Wizard of Oz,* with Steven Liversedge now in the Producer's chair. Two others who had taken part in the original show were again involved - Stella Willans as Musical Director and Saxon Winship, who together with Jeanne Stockbridge had performed a ballet sequence in 1968, now directed the choreography. Otherwise it was a completely new cast, as befits a developing junior society, with Dorothy now played by Sue Grey and Dennis Powell as the eponymous Wizard. It is also worth noting that Paul Blake, future Musical Director made an early appearance in this show, as did Kay Charnley who was later to succeed Saxon as head choreographer for the Juniors' shows, another example of a young fledgling dancer eventually graduating to senior choreographer. Before he left the area Steven Liversedge took care of *The Pied Piper of Hamelin*

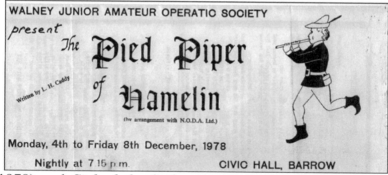

WALNEY JUNIOR AMATEUR OPERATIC SOOIETY

present

The **Pied Piper** of **Hamelin**

Written by L. H. Caddy

(by arrangement with N.O.D.A. Ltd.)

Monday, 4th to Friday 8th December, 1978

Nightly at 7.15 p.m.   CIVIC HALL, BARROW

(1978) and *Sinbad the Sailor* (1979) for his final outings as Producer, before Cliff Kitto stepped into his shoes for *Jack and the Bean-stalk* (1980). Cliff Kitto was an experienced Stage Manager (see the Abbey Society), and had also served as Chairman of Walney Juniors for more than 10 years previously. He was to produce and direct several subsequent shows.

The pantomime character of Walney Juniors' shows continued with such follow-ons as *Dick Whittington* in 1981 and *Sleeping Beauty* in 1983, but after *Cinderella* in 1984 there was a definite gear shift. This was partly driven by a necessary change in the dates of their show week. Whereas previously this had been in early December, for various reasons it had to be shifted to October – not usually a time associated with the pantomime season. But equally, since its beginnings, the Society had been in a constant state of development: new talents had emerged, new skills in make-up, wardrobe and stage management had been acquired, all of which meant that, change of dates or not, there was a sense that it was the right time for the group to consider more ambitious shows with more mature themes.

Follow the Yellow Brick Road

Bugsy Malone (1985) was the perfect choice for such a change of gear, as it can be read as a statement about this transition. It had started life as a film with an all-child cast, but with adult voices taking over the musical numbers by being dubbed in. Adult singers were again featured even when it was adapted for the West End stage. Walney Juniors' young cast were having none of that. They were quite happy to sing for themselves, and it was time for the grown-ups to move over. Consider their choice of shows from this point onwards – they were a mix of the classical and the dramatic and, after *Bugsy*, were often shows traditionally associated with an adult cast.

As for *Bugsy Malone* itself, Bob Bowker described it as 'as lively a piece of youthful "show-biz" as we could have wished for.' It was produced by Shirley Britton and, now with minimal musical accompaniment a thing of the past, Doreen

Dunlop wielded her baton over a full orchestra who were all decked out for a trip to Fat Sam's speakeasy. Kay Charnley's snappy dance routines also proved a great attraction.

This same team were then behind *Dracula Spectacular* in 1986, with Andrew Bond in the title role. It was meant to be a send-up of the Dracula story but the possibility of ghouls and blood, although great for the kids, must have put the adults off as audience support was disappointing. This was a shame as the press review was very enthusiastic.

Then in 1987, perhaps also to demonstrate how far they had come, the Society once again revived *The Wizard of Oz*. Overall production values and the confidence of the young cast had clearly improved significantly, and the show played to sell-out houses for its entire run. Lisa Sharrock played Dorothy (soon to graduate to the seniors), supported by Rebecca Carrick as the Scarecrow (both of whom had excelled in *Bugsy*), together with Nicholas Carson as the Tin Man, and David Baxter as the Lion. Judith Barrow as Stage Manager also made an impressive contribution to the show with her stunning scenery creations, and the memorable multi-coloured wigs she had made for each individual Munchkin.

Her touch was again evident in the 1988 production of *The Snow Queen* with colourful, sparkly costumes which, combined with Kay Charnley's choreography and the vitality of the young cast, brought the story to life – anticipating Disney's *Frozen* by some 25 years! With the aid of an impressive costume Lisa Sharrock was transformed into an imposing Snow Queen, with Lucy Chalker as Gerda, the heroine of the piece. Two youngsters Louise Wells (later to be known as Louise Marshall) and Deborah Bird (now McGuire) also delighted the audience as two dancing crows who aid Gerda in her quest. Both had already featured in previous shows – Louise as a 7-year old for Walney Juniors in their

1984 production of *Cinderella*, and Deborah as a 6-year old 'Thumbelina' for the Abbey Society's production of *Hans Andersen* in 1985. And following these early appearances both have since progressed to lead roles in many later productions, particularly for the Barrow and Walney Societies.

A number of other familiar names crop up at this time as members of the production team. Bill Calvert, known today for his many appearances for both the Walney and Barrow Societies, produced *The Snow Queen* in 1988, Shirley Britton also directed before taking up her new post as Drama teacher in Newcastle, and the famous Doreen Dunlop could be found wielding her sparkly baton as Musical Director. She was part of the creative team for *Hans Andersen* (1989) when David Marcus was engaged as Producer, adding to the Society's growing professionalism with his own brand of expertise. Because this was the time of the Civic Hall's refurbishment, this show actually had to be staged at Thorncliffe Road School. It may not have been an ideal setting but at least the Juniors were able to stage a show (which was more than the senior Society was able to do). Saxon Winship then took over to direct and choreograph *The Adventures of Mr Toad* (1990) and *Peter Pan* (1991).

For *Peter Pan* a new Musical Director took up residence in the shape of Paul Bryden (left), who was to bring out the musical best in the cast for several further productions. At this point I should perhaps say that Paul is a personal friend of mine, and has been a great source of information and support whilst I have been researching this book. A little known fact is that his grand-mother was a famous Music Hall star of her day, performing under the name of 'Little Ada Brooke'. She toured with the likes of Gracie Fields and enjoyed considerable popularity in her heyday, often topping the bill with her mix of comedy and songs. In later years she appeared in musical productions, such as *The Country Girl* and *The Quaker Girl*, when naturally she performed as the comic lead. As far as Paul is concerned therefore, a theatrical gene has clearly been passed down the generations.

I've known him since the mid-1960s when we used to walk to school together. Even then he was an accomplished musician, adept at most stringed instruments, but especially the guitar and banjo. We played guitar together occasionally, although whilst I didn't progress much past Bert Weedon's legendary *Play In A Day* books, he knew exotic chords like 'F□7+9' and 'Csus4' whilst managing to manipulate his fingers around the most intricate of tunes. He subsequently played in several local bands, possibly the most renowned being the "Bag o'Rags" who held a popular residency for a time at the Coot Restaurant in Urswick. Then he went off to the Leeds College of Music where, so he modestly told me, he learned 'tons of stuff', and has since been a regular orchestra member of local Society productions for more years than he cares to remember. In addition to Walney Juniors he has also served as Musical Director for the Ulverston Pantomime Society, the Furness Youth Theatre, CAST, and the A590 Theatre Group. In-between times he teaches music both privately and in schools, drinks a lot of coffee (roasting his own beans by the way), and likes curries.

As for *Peter Pan*, Michelle Larcombe played the title role (pictured overleaf), a 12-year old at the time who in her later years was to establish a successful career in the performing arts. She had first appeared 3 years earlier in *The*

Snow Queen and went on to feature in many later productions.

On leaving the Society she studied at the Welsh College of Music and Dance in Cardiff, and subsequently starred in a number of touring operatic productions. In 2002 she was part of the local group David Marcus took to Barbados, and was a frequent performer in the Pumpkin Productions' pantomimes in Barrow. As for Walney Juniors, after *Peter Pan*, her next role was one of the lead characters in *A Midsummer Night's Dream*. Not really Shakespeare, but almost.

Michelle Larcombe as Peter Pan

This was a musical production, based on the classic play, but adapted and composed by local man Andrew Sproxton. At this time he had not long been involved with musical theatre although, like Paul Bryden, was a well-known local musician. His first appearance in the pit orchestra (so to speak) was in 1990 for *The Adventures of Mr Toad*. Since then he has been a regular presence in the orchestra for numerous local productions, and for probably every local Society. During the day he taught drums and guitar in local schools. As for his Shakespeare-based musical this was very well received – 'thoroughly enjoyable with much modern appeal and charm' – with Brett Turner stealing the show in the role of Bottom. Shakespeare of course has him as a member of Peter Quince's mechanicals, whereas this version reinvents him as the lead singer of 'Bottom and the Pits', the rock group hired to entertain the Duke and the Duchess. I'm sure you get the idea.

From 1993 to 1996 the shows continued to be enhanced by the creative talents of Paul Bryden and Saxon Winship, each in charge of the music and the dancing respectively, complemented by Nick Carson and David Marcus as Producer/Directors. The shows chosen were those suited to a young cast such as the 1993 show *Bugsy Malone* (first performed by the Juniors in 1985), *The Lion, the Witch and*

Dandy Dan's Gang from *Bugsy Malone, 1993:*
Doodle (Lee Paton), *Laughing Boy* (Wesley McGrogan),
Bronx Charlie (David Woods), *and Shoulders* (David Neville)

the Wardrobe (1994) and *Oliver* (1995) Among the performers coming to prominence at this time (in other words taking on lead roles) were brother and sister Andrew and Claire Phipps-Jones, Ailsa McIntosh, Camille Maalawy, Tracy Livingstone and Daniel McKeating.

Then in 1996 Clare Rigg took charge. Although not a performer herself, she had been involved with the Society since its beginnings in any number of support roles, so she certainly knew how things worked. She was to produce the next 5 shows, with continuing support from Paul Bryden and Saxon

Winship. And of course members of the chorus were constantly graduating to take on minor, then ultimately lead roles. It is probably a risk to single out individuals but, acknowledging that there are many others, I mention the following merely as examples: let's just take *Alice's Adventures in Wonderland* (1998) when Amy Larcombe (sister of Michelle), past chorus member, took the lead. Rachael Jackson was the Caterpillar in this production and two years later took the lead in *Peter Pan* (2000); Ailsa McIntosh played the White Queen whilst her sister Lorna McIntosh played Tweedledee, and later featured as the Wicked Witch of the West in *The Wizard of Oz* (2003); and Paul Williamson, who played the Mock Turtle, subsequently took the lead in the Society's much acclaimed first production of *Les Miserables* (2005). Budding talents all. (In fact, in 2006, Paul went on to win a place at the prestigious London School of Musical Theatre, and is now on the professional stage in London. And whilst we're on the subject it is worth mentioning that brother and sister Daniel and Vicky Serra, who also appeared in *Alice*, have now progressed to the professional stage themselves.)

The success of all these shows meant that this Junior Society had by now established an enviable reputation and joining its ranks had become a very attractive proposition. 1987 was a bumper year with as many as 114 new recruits emerging, so that, for *The Wizard of Oz* that year (outing number 3) there were over 90 people in the cast. A line had to be drawn. The Committee decided that in future the maximum number of performers in a show would be 65, and the age span of the Society would be from 8 to 16 years. A waiting list would be kept when the maximum number had been reached. It was also agreed that all new members should be given the time and opportunity to develop initial skills in the art of stagecraft. In other words, this meant a newcomer would need at least 12 months as a Society member before being allowed to audition for a particular role.

Another issue which needed a response at this time was the increasing emphasis on child protection. It was a time when awareness of child exploitation and abuse had become heightened and new rules and legislation were appearing. None of these were unreasonable but they did place extra demands on the Society for a while until routines were established. All adults now had to be checked by the Criminal Records Office for example, and those with direct contact with children had to be officially approved as 'matrons' or 'chaperones' by the local council. It also became a requirement that there should be an approved number of adults present at every rehearsal, with at least two always present in dressing rooms. Permission for photography was also required from parents, and the use of any such photographs was strictly limited.

The Society's success also inevitably meant rising costs in order that standards might be maintained, if not raised. Clare Rigg, as well as an active Producer (as we have seen) has also been Treasurer of the Society for many years, knows all about this. 'We used to build our own sets,' she told me, 'but in order to keep raising our game, they eventually had to be hired. Now we hire everything, including the costumes. All the senior Societies are doing the same thing, and we don't want to look like an amateurish poor relation.' And what about audience support? It perhaps goes without saying that this is crucial to any amateur group, indeed they are entirely dependent on it. With one or two exceptions Walney Juniors were enjoying loyal support for its shows at this time – the support of family members perhaps being a particular advantage for a junior society – but there is never room for complacency.

"I've a feeling we're not in Kansas any more"

Back to the shows. The new century began on a high note with a revival of *Peter Pan*. Advertised as 'Fun, Flying and Fantasy' the cast displayed all the usual elements of exuberance, high energy levels, and enthusiasm. Even so, it was staged under

something of a cloud in that Martyn Tonge (left), one of the founding fathers and President of the Society, had been taken ill. Sadly he passed away not long after the production ended. Much gratitude was extended to him at his passing in exactly the same way he himself would, in his annual President's Letter, extend his own thanks to all the Society's officers, committee and members 'for their loyal support in helping us to maintain the tradition of music and drama among our young people.'

For 2001 Clare Rigg teamed up with two new accomplices, Ian Bird (Musical Director) and Graham Barker (Choreographer), for the Society's third production of *Bugsy Malone*. Ian Bird, you may recall, was an experienced performer with the Barrow Society having first achieved fame for his performance in *Jesus Christ Superstar* in 1984. His wife and daughters were, and still are well known on the amateur scene. Similar family involvement is also true for Graham Barker, another experienced local performer. His grand-parents had been founder members of the Walney senior society back in 1947, and he now runs his own youth theatre group (as you will discover in a later chapter) in which several members of his immediate family are involved. As far as *Bugsy* is concerned, the efforts of all the performers were praised in the press reviews: 'fine performances, stunning choreography, and great singing.' The cast included many already mentioned, plus at least two others who were to later make their mark professionally: Jack Hawitt, currently working as part of the entertainment team on a luxury cruise liner, and Paige Cook, currently working in the West End. Barrow's got talent (in case you were still in any doubt.)

Two of the productions that followed broke new ground in that they were shows usually reserved for an exclusively adult cast, e.g. *Calamity Jane* (2002) and *Around the World in 80 Days* (2004). Shirley Britton directed *Calamity Jane* on her return to Barrow, the production being described as 'a marvellous advertisement for the amount of young talent this area has to offer.' The leading roles had been won by Amy Larcombe and Paul Jones, a hit as P T Barnum the previous year. Lisa Sharrock directed *Around the World*, a previous Walney Junior herself for many years, and at the time at work in professional theatre. The sets were very impressive, having to range from London to India, Japan, and the Wild West, with the additional requirements of an elephant and a hot air balloon. How they were achieved I will leave to your imagination.

In between there was a return visit to the land of Oz, which cannot go without a mention since it featured what may be described (at least at this point in time) as Walney Juniors' dream cast. The leading role of Dorothy again went to Amy Larcombe with Paige Cook as a Witch (pictured overleaf), and Jack Hawitt, Daniel Serra (who had recently played the title role in *Oliver!* for the Ulverston Society) and Paul Williamson as Scarecrow, Tin Man and Cowardly Lion. All would go on to perform on the professional stage. Even before it opened in Barrow the cast were invited to give a special performance at the annual dinner of the Northern Association of Building Societies, which was held at the Marriott Hotel in Newcastle.

The Wizard of Oz, 2003

Above: *The Tin Man (*Daniel Serra) *with Dorothy* (Amy Larcombe)

Right: *Wicked Witch of the West* (Paige Cook)

But since I've mentioned shows usually performed by adults, the Society reached its high-water mark in 2005 when it secured the rights to perform *Les Miserables*. It was a landmark show, a definite coup, and confirmation if any were needed that this Junior Society had entered a completely new phase in its development. It is a show every senior society yearns to perform but can't – since licences are only granted to junior casts, i.e. where no performer is over 16 years of age. Then a licence is granted to perform the so-called 'School Edition' of *Les Mis*, although you have to know the musical inside out to be able to spot where the differences lie. Perhaps driven by jealousy there were of course the doom-sayers who were certain the show could not be done by a junior cast, that the themes were too gritty and adult, and that the technical demands were too great. But if I mention some members of the cast, and if you've kept up with the story so far, you will recognise the talent and experience they all brought to their performances. Paul Williamson played Jean Valjean with Scott Harper as his relentless pursuer Javert, Jack Hawitt played Marius, Amy Larcombe was Fantine, with Paige Cook as Éponine.

*Inspector Javert (*Scott Harper*) and Jean Valjean (*Paul Williamson*)*

The chorus numbers, always important in a junior society where experience and confidence may be gained, were also strong, featuring up-coming performers such as Aydn Blake (Paul Blake's son), Bronte and Bianca Tranter, Luke Mooney, and Tiffany Charnley (Kay Charnley's daughter). Clare Rigg and Graham Barker were in charge of production, with Ian Bird directing the music. And it wasn't just the capacity audiences who appreciated the show. It went on to win not just the NODA award for the Best Musical Production for the North West region, but also the award for the Best *National* Youth Production.

Gavroche (Adam Barker), *Thénardier* (Daniel Serra), *Madam Thénardier* (Caleigh Blake) *and Éponine* (Paige Cook)

There were some changes the following year as experienced cast members moved on, many to drama/music college, and Sylvia Rees was appointed as the Society's new Chair, but there was no change to the policy of staging modern, dramatic shows. *The King and I* was the choice for 2006, with the King of Siam played by Christopher Barker (Graham Barker's son), who went so far as to shave his head for his role, and Anna played by Paige Cook (who didn't.) It was hailed as 'a dazzling production' with a superb set (provided by Border Studios.) It was a first time production for the Juniors, and was chosen for the contrast it afforded to *Les Mis*, with its sprightly, light-hearted numbers and, if you don't count the fate of the King of Siam, its uplifting story.

This was also true of *Annie* (2007), with Tiffany Charnley (left) as Annie, Christopher Barker (with head still shaven) as Daddy Warbucks, and Paige Cook shifting effortlessly from the responsible and kindly Anna to the boozy, child-hating Miss Hannigan. Tracy Warby had been recruited to take care of the choreography for these two shows, and if the loss of some of the regular performers raised doubts about the remaining talents and versatility of the Walney Juniors Society, here was evidence enough to dispel them.

Then came *Barnum* (2008), the Society's 40th anniversary production. If you recall, this was the show which had been staged to great acclaim on two previous occasions by the Abbey Society, so there was a lot to live up to. In a sense that was now the Walney Juniors' constant burden after the outstanding success of *Les Mis*. They had set the bar high for themselves, and could not now afford to let standards fall. Of course they rose to the challenge. A tightrope was borrowed from Blackpool Tower Circus and set up at the Griffin Community Centre, off Ainslie Street in Barrow, to allow for frequent practice sessions. 'Toni' of the Euphoric Circus of Appleby was engaged to teach the cast tightrope and trapeze skills, and a professional performer Joel Dickinson taught juggling skills. Pictured overleaf is Anna Twyford, one of four trapeze artists, and I am happy to report that no child was harmed in the production of this show. Luke Mooney, who incidentally had just been offered a place in the National Youth Theatre, took the title role. And again it won the NODA award for the Best Youth Production – the first time any Society had won it twice!

War had been declared on societies and, as if to rub the Juniors' skills in gang the other senior point home, Walney warfare were ably demonstrated in their revival of *Bugsy Malone* (2009). Not really of course. But the audience were in no doubt that they were about to enter the dangerous world of gangsters, molls and patsies when Ian Bird oozed over to his podium at the start of the show in black shirt, trilby and shades, carrying a menacing-looking violin case. Inside it was …. his baton. After that the only violence in the show was whatever the cast could mete out with splurge guns and custard pies.

Clare Rigg returned as Director for *Oliver* (2010) supported as usual by Ian Bird and Tracy Warby. And assuming leading roles from their previous work in the chorus were such new performers as Catherine Andrews, Amy Turner, Mili Rich, and Aydn Blake. All subsequently progressed to starring roles for the senior Societies, providing yet more examples of Ronald Metcalfe's foresight back in 1969 when he asserted that the Juniors 'are the future backbone of all our senior Societies.' Indeed it is worth repeating the examples of Martin Craig and Paul Blake, both ex-Walney Juniors who went on to feature in many productions for such local senior Societies, because both crop up in our story now, returning to Walney Juniors in 2011 as the new members of the creative team.

The more recent shows have all been brave incursions into familiar, well-known musicals – brave since their very familiarity brings with it an audience with clear expectations. *Me and My Girl* (2011), *The Sound of Music* (2012) and *Joseph and the Amazing Technicolour Dreamcoat* (2013) are the shows in question. But with the challenges come gains of course, as it is shows like these which carry with them the essence of musical theatre, so they provide marvellous opportunities for the cast to extend their skills in stage-craft, showmanship and characterisation. But after such a steady stream of successes, where is there to go next? Why, to one of the most famous, record-breaking, mega-musicals of all time of course – *The Phantom of the Opera*.

Like *Les Miserables* this is another show not yet released to the senior societies so the question again arose as to whether 'the kids' could rise to the challenge. Martin Craig carried the responsibility of Producer/Director, supported by *Joseph*'s choreographer Cathy Fidler, and Musical Director Paul Blake. Lewis Devitt, a Society member since his first appearance in *Annie* in 2007 was cast as the Phantom, with Cameron Barlow as Raoul, and Caris Kerr playing Christine. Catherine Andrews, having first appeared at the age of 8 in *Barnum* (2008) and as a main cast member in later shows, played Carlotta, the opera diva. The show, to coin a phrase, really did break all box office records, and achieved no fewer than 7 NODA nominations (which included the performance of both the leads), and yet again took the award for Best Show. Paul Blake also won the award for Best Musical Director.

How then to follow this? There was surely only one possibility. And so we arrive at the brilliant second production of *Les Miserables* (2015). It was, unsurprisingly perhaps, a sell-out. Cameron Barlow took the role of Jean Valjean ('as good as any Valjean I have seen' wrote Trevor Jones in the *Evening Mail,* a sentiment to be later endorsed by NODA when he was awarded 'Best Leading Male in a Musical'), with Lewis Devitt as Javert (for me, masterfully erasing all memories of

Russell Crowe's tortured effort in the film). Both were ably supported by Connor Wood as Marius (who had already made his mark in several previous productions, having won consecutive NODA nominations in 2013 and 2014), and several other experienced players such as Thomas Lowes, Sarah McDougall, Dylan Phelps, Caris Kerr and Hannah Featham-Jackson. As ever, leading players such as these point the way for the younger talent following on behind, such as Caitlin McIntosh (pictured) who played Young Cosette. As Clare Rigg observed when I spoke to her, 'It's amazing how year after year, when we lose our talented players to college, university, or just through natural progression, there is always another group ready to come through.' Even so, I must acknowledge that there is an inevitable unfairness in picking out individuals by name since each show is the combined efforts of one group ensemble – from cast to production team.

Master of the House: Thénardier (Thomas Lowes) *and Madame Thénardier*
(Sarah McDougall)

Over the Rainbow

This production of *Les Miserables* of course now takes us back
to where this chapter began. But, as far as Walney Juniors are
concerned, we are a long, long way from where *they* began
with *The Wizard of Oz* in 1968 - a time of uncertainty,
unpredictability and limited resources. Looking back through
the back catalogue of the Society's shows in the years
following however, I think it is perhaps possible to discern a
progression from a faltering childhood to confident adulthood
in terms of its identity as a local musical theatre group. In this
respect 1968-1984, with its lively, playful pantomimes, could
be regarded as its early childhood, to be followed by the period
1985-2001 when the shows became more experimental, and
displayed the search for identity and sense of belonging which
is usually associated with adolescence. And then finally, from

2001 onwards, the society's shows demonstrate the maturity, professionalism, and experience one would associate with a society that is all grown-up.

Even so, we must remember that this is still a Junior Society, and shows suited to a junior cast are probably always going to figure in their repertoire – hence, since 1968, their have been 5 productions of *The Wizard of Oz* and 4 of *Bugsy Malone*. Both shows are highly suited as, not only do they provide great opportunities for dance ensembles and chorus work, they also give every cast member an opportunity to shine. And as far as *Oz* is concerned I also like to think there is a covert reason for its frequent choice. Isn't it just possible to think that the *Oz* story of disparate characters searching for things they already have is exactly the story of Walney Juniors? That is to say that, for each show, a diverse group of people come together to face challenges and struggles in order to uncover the qualities that, hidden somewhere inside themselves, they already have, i.e. intelligence, heart, and the courage to inspire, to develop new talent and, of course, to entertain.

9

THE BARROW SAVOYARDS (Founded 1973)

"... I'm teeming with a lot o'news...
With many cheerful facts ..."

Amateur performers in the South Lakes have been staging the works of Gilbert & Sullivan for more than 100 years. In fact, almost from the word 'go' – i.e. in the 1880's when their operas were first made available to amateur groups – a local group began performing. This was **The Furness Dramatic and Operatic Society** who staged their first production, *The Yeomen of the Guard*, in 1894. I say 'their first' which is true according to the evidence I have, although it is possible they started even earlier than this. The Society had actually been around in some form or other since 1877, though at this time press reports of their productions were not routinely provided. What is known however is that this group regularly staged a Gilbert & Sullivan piece right up until 1903 when, before finally disbanding, they performed *The Grand Duke* at His Majesty's Theatre, in Barrow.

It's important to remember that the Gilbert & Sullivan operas, being so immensely popular in their day (as indeed they remain so today), are usually credited with sparking off the whole amateur operatic movement and, at the turn of the century, many local groups were being established all across the country. Locally, in addition to the Furness Society (which re-emerged in 1911 as the Barrow Amateur Operatic Society) groups had been formed in Lancaster and Ulverston specifically to perform, at least initially, Gilbert & Sullivan works.

With their choral traditions it is perhaps inevitable that some of the new groups would be established through local churches. A group calling itself **'The St Mary's Operatic Society'** appeared in 1925 for example, presenting their first full-scale production *Iolanthe* at His Majesty's Theatre in October of that year. It was a huge success and is notable for the debut of Joseph Simm, playing his first leading role as The Lord Chancellor. 'He just revelled in his part,' enthuses the *North Western Daily Mail*, 'and garnished it with the little niceties of a finished actor.' *The Yeomen of the Guard* followed in 1926, with Mr Simm now in the role of Jack Point. He was to become a well-known local performer and took the lead in many later productions, and with other local Societies, such as the Abbey Society (which incidentally was also born from a local church) and the Barrow Society (which wasn't). Among those in charge of the production for these operas were names familiar to our history, Mr Tom Rawsthorn, Producer of some of Barrow and Ulverston's early shows, and Mr Charles Thompson, who had helped to establish both the Abbey and the Flookburgh Societies. It is also worth noting that a Mr John Richard Metcalfe, the father of local star performer and *Barrow News* critic Ronnie Metcalfe, appeared in the Society's productions at this time. For *Floradora,* presented in 1928, he played the character of Tweedlepunch 'which was received with a great deal of laughter and chaff.'

With regard to the exact identity of St Mary's Society, there are two possible contenders as to the church in question. I suspect it is best identified as St Mary's RC Church on Duke Street, Barrow. There is also St Mary's Parish Church on Walney Island, but the records show that this church formed a society in 1932, whilst laying claim to be 'the first operatic society on the island.' It seems unlikely therefore that they were responsible for the *Iolanthe* production in 1925. At this time the usual course for church-based groups was that they burned brightly for 3 or 4 productions, and then faded away, as they struggled to establish wider support and appeal. This was presumably the fate of the St Mary's Duke Street group whereas, bucking the trend, the 1932 St Mary's group from Walney happily went from strength to strength, initially calling themselves 'The Walney Parish Church Music and Dramatic Society' before changing their name to 'The Walney Amateur Operatic Society', and then becoming the group we know today as 'The Walney Musical Theatre Company.'

Meanwhile, in **Dalton-in-Furness**, the idea of forming an operatic society had been first mooted in 1925, but levels of enthusiasm and support were tentative. A few years later a fledgling 'Operatic and Dramatic Society' did struggle to its feet with a concert version of '*Merrie England*', followed by a further series of dramatic sketches. Then in 1929 the Society felt robust enough to mount a full-scale production of the perennial favourite, *The Mikado,* in the Co-operative Hall. But despite the benefit of experienced Producer, Mr T Rawsthorn, and the musical expertise of the Dalton Orchestral Society, audience numbers were lighter than expected. Nevertheless the photographic record of the production (shown overleaf), and the very positive and enthusiastic review in the *North-Western Daily Mail,* suggest that, tentative as it may have been, it was a very accomplished production. They had better success with their later productions – *The Gondoliers* in 1930, and *Yeomen of the Guard* in 1931, but then the brief life of the Society came to an end with their last production, *Rose of the East.* Two major obstacles were reported to be responsible - the difficulty of finding suitable accommodation, and a "trade depression" in the town which meant production costs could not be met.

In other parts of the district the versatility of the larger, more senior groups was increasing. The 1920s and 30s in particular saw rapid developments as the Barrow and Ulverston Societies branched out to present musical pieces from sources other than Gilbert and Sullivan. Such developments were met with some dismay by devotees who responded in 1936 by setting up their own Society – one which would be dedicated to

The Mikado: Dalton Amateur Operatic Society, 1929

Above: *A section of the Gentleman's Chorus*

Left: M*iss Marjorie McGregor as Yum-Yum*

G & S works and which would be called **The Barrow Savoy Amateur Operatic Society**. Their first production, *The Mikado*, was staged in March 1937 at the Royalty Theatre and Opera House in Barrow. In the programme notes the Secretary Mr T G Garnett writes, presumably through gritted teeth, 'Other Societies have made the move to musical comedy to meet modern demands. We say, *Good Luck To Them*. We think there is still a place for the good old Savoy operas.'

The Mikado, 1937 *'Three Little Maids'*
Yum-Yum (Ethel Davis), *Pitti-Sing* (Florence Melville) & *Peep-Bo* (Alice Hall)

One notable performer in this production was Samuel Briggs who played Ko-Ko, the Lord High Executioner, a role he was later to revive for the Abbey Society in 1949. He was an accomplished and talented comic actor, a regular performer, and a major influence on the development of Gilbert & Sullivan's work throughout the district. One of his grand-daughters was later to marry Ben Williams, another regular performer from this period. In fact it is a matter of some interest, as you may have already noted, that the local amateur scene has brought many couples together over the years – and may have even split up a few too. (But we won't dwell on that.) As for the Savoy group, they went on to perform *The Yeomen of the Guard* in 1938 with Hubert Bramhall as Sir Richard Cholmondeley and William J Clewlow as Jack Point, and then *Ruddigore* in 1939, both at His Majesty's Theatre, before finally becoming a casualty of World War Two when their activities ceased.

The group which was to revive the G & S tradition after the war then brought a new and distinctive style to their productions. This was the **'Crosslands Former Students'**, a group hailing from Crosslands Convent School for Girls on Abbey Road, Barrow. Their distinctive feature was that, being an all-girl school, the cast was necessarily all-female. Think *Pirates of Penzance* and 'I am the very model of a modern major-general' and you get the idea why this was such a novelty. They began in 1948, modestly, with *The Gondoliers* which was staged in the school hall, but the reception they

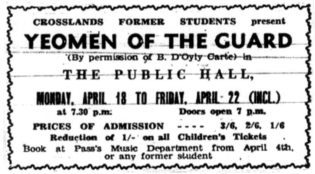

received was so positive they rapidly transferred to the Public Hall in Barrow where they staged an annual show for the next 10 years or more. Including the choruses, the total cast for each production numbered around 40, with a wide age span ranging from 15 to 30. The Producer was generally Mrs M Sharp, a member of Crosslands teaching staff, with Abbie Simm, wife of the afore-mentioned Joseph, at the piano. She was an accomplished musician in her own right and, with her husband, was a regular contributor to many local groups. I have already referred to their son Len Simm in previous chapters, who found himself regularly roped in to this local scene, and he has been kind enough to share many of his memories with me.

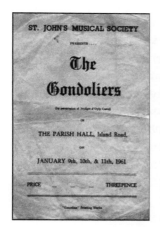

Then, in the early 1960s, as the Crosslands shows waned, a new church-based group appeared – **St John's Musical Society**, which was based on Barrow Island. It was formed at the instigation of Mabel Wade, wife of the Rev. Arthur Wade, who enlisted the support of Joseph and Abbie Simm to pull together a series of ambitious productions. The group had its moment in the sun from 1959 to 1961 when they staged, consecutively, *The Mikado*, *Iolanthe*, and *The Gondoliers*. When Mabel and Arthur Wade then retired in 1961, and moved out to Silverdale, the impetus was lost and the group folded. Undeterred however, the Simms turned their attention to the **Aldingham Church Choir Operatic Group** which, rather miraculously for such a small and remote locality, performed *Iolanthe* in 1962, *The Pirates of Penzance* in 1963, and *The Gondoliers* in 1964.

The Aldingham group was swelled somewhat by followers of Joseph and Abbie, who as well as being lovers of G & S searching still for an outlet, were also ex-performers from Crosslands School, and the Barrow and Abbey Societies. Performances took place in a converted oast house in Aldingham so the stage facilities were pretty limited. Len

Simm recalled an incident from *Iolanthe* when his piano was half-bounced off the stage by the exuberant dancing of the fairies, a group mostly made up of farmer's wives of slightly larger-than-average build. Still dancing the Fairy Queen promptly led her troupe down the steps to slide it back in position without missing a beat.

Eventually the Aldingham group morphed into a band of strolling players known as the **Savoy Opera Group** who performed concerts in church halls all over the district, taking scenery and costumes with them. For a while this was the only possibility of a Gilbert & Sullivan experience as, by now, all the other local Societies had put some distance between themselves and their G & S origins, staging musicals such as *Showboat*, *Guys and Dolls*, and *Goodnight Vienna* in an effort to meet, as Mr Garnett had sniffily observed in an earlier decade, 'modern demands'. Then, after a long illness, the prime local mover Joseph Simm passed away in 1972, and the Savoy Group floundered. Had the Gilbert and Sullivan operas finally had their day? By no means.

"If you want to know who we are ..."

The next development was to be spear-headed by David Marcus who, as you have heard, was a key influence on the entire range of amateur theatre throughout the district. The story goes that he first came to Barrow in the early 1970s for a holiday, and liked the area so much he returned a year or two later to stay. In 1972 he became involved in a fund-raising effort to send handicapped children to Lourdes, a component of which was an informal evening of Gilbert & Sullivan songs performed by, among others, former members of the Crosslands Operatic Group. The concert was such a success it was decided to stage a full production the following year. This was *The Mikado*, presented at the Civic Hall, Barrow, in 1973 and officially the first production given by this newly-formed group who called themselves "The Barrow Savoyards". Somehow or other an enterprising lady by the name of Meg Henderson was able to hand-make the 41 costumes needed for the total princely sum of £70. Following its run in Barrow it was then taken on a tour of the district with performances at the Palladium in Millom, the Coronation Hall in Ulverston, and the Brewery Theatre in Kendal.

The show had been put together by a mix of familiar and unfamiliar names. Florence Melville, a leading light from the Abbey Society, was the Producer with Abbie Simm as Musical Director and Cliff Kitto, also an Abbey stalwart, acting as Stage Manager. In addition to David Marcus, who played Ko-Ko, the Lord High Executioner, the cast members consisted of Bob Henderson as Pooh-Bah, John Twyford as the Mikado, Declan McCusker as Nanki-Poo his son, and Gwen Kenyon as Katisha,. The 'three little maids from school' were played by Wendy Jackson, Joyce Watkinson, and Christine Bretheridge. Two other ladies in the cast remain active members of the Savoyards today, namely Margaret Buckley and Aileen Jackson (nee Welch). As a point of interest Declan McCusker went on to have a career with the Scottish Opera, whilst John Twyford auditioned with the D'Oyly Carte Company, and became a regular performer of principal roles for the Savoyards over many subsequent years, most recently appearing in the 2014 production of *Pirates of Penzance*.

The Barrow Savoyards may have had modest beginnings – *The Mikado* was staged using only two pianos, hired sets and, as mentioned, home-made costumes – but they have gone on to become the most vibrant and consistent exponents of the Savoy operas currently operating in the whole of Cumbria. Loyal and consistent members have been a large part of this success, several of whom have been *Barrow News*

Oscar winners such as John Twyford, Aileen Jackson, Steve Freeland and Lorraine Carney. *The Mikado* was followed by *Iolanthe* in 1974, for example, when Terry and Kathleen Henshaw, who have since remained with the group up to the present, first joined the group. Then later, in 1978, 14-year old Karen Battersby (now Glasgow) appeared in *HMS Pinafore*, a talented performer who was subsequently to play many leading roles. In fact she took time off only when it was time to create "three little maids" of her own – Polly May, Molly Rose, and Lily Ann. In 2008, as well as playing the role of Katisha in *The Mikado* that year, she then took on the role of Choreographer. She had choreographed previous Summer concerts but this was the first time she took on a full production. It was a role she continued to perform in subsequent shows before graduating to be the Producer and Artistic Director of the 2012 production, *The Sorcerer*.

Meanwhile, back in the 1980's, the Savoyards founder David Marcus was firmly in charge, and he quickly developed a reputation for creativity and innovation. In the 1975 production of *Pirates of Penzance* for example, when Savoyard membership did not stretch to sufficient numbers of pirate

extras, he went off to the Barrow Army Cadets and rounded up a brigade of willing volunteers. I know this to be true since Peter Whalan, my brother, was one of those press-ganged into service. (He is third from the right in the picture!) And when *Pirates* was revived in 1982 he included a sequence in which the pirates and policemen were dressed as ballerinas. It received a mixed response, irritating some whilst being applauded by others as 'foolery in the grand Gilbertian tradition.' Always with an eye on high production values and visual spectacle he was responsible for imaginative décor and lighting design, and also soon made home-made costumes a thing of the past. Having worked previously in professional theatre he had contacts which he was able to use to good effect, bringing lavish costumes to the stage from leading costumiers in London. In Alice Leach's book *Our Barrovians* (1989) Eileen Lithgow, who took leading roles in the Savoyards' productions both in the 1980s and beyond, recalls that the costumes would often receive 'rapturous applause' in their own right.

In addition to Eileen Lithgow, this period saw the debut of other performers who were not only to remain with the Savoyards for many years, but were also to have considerable success as performers in other arenas. Among these were: John Brice (1982), Helen Troughton (1985), Iain Nicholson (1988), Russ Palmer (1990), Maria Mallinson (1990), Phil McIntosh (1991), and Ron Eadington (1997). Both John Brice and Eileen Lithgow have performed with Lakeland Opera and toured Cumbria with such works as Bizet's *Carmen* and Verdi's *La Traviata*. They have also been members of the Barrow-based Encore Operatic Group who perform throughout Cumbria. Helen Troughton meanwhile has played numerous roles with Ulverston, Barrow, and Walney Operatic Societies and, at the time of writing, is Chairman of the Savoyards. When not performing with the Savoyards, Ron Eadington can be found singing with the Encore Opera Group, the Furness Bach Choir, or Ulverston Choral Society. And as for Iain Nicholson and Phil McIntosh, together with Chris Warby and Mark Johnson, they have found considerable success as part of the celebrated vocal group *Voce* who regularly tour the local circuit. And as is the case within many amateur groups, the performing bug has been passed from one family member to another on many occasions. I will just cite one example – the McIntoshes. Phil's daughter Ailsa, a local vocal coach and singing teacher, first appeared as a Munchkin in Ulverston Society's 1993 production of *The Wizard of Oz*. She went on to gain a BA (Hons) in Music Studies and now, both she *and* her younger sister, Lorna are regular performers not only for the Savoyards but also for other local Societies.

In the early 90's David Marcus teamed up with Neil Metcalfe and together they created a two-man show, based on the lives of Gilbert and Sullivan, which they called 'Here's a How-de-Do'. The show was very successful, toured extensively, and was presented at the Edinburgh Festival. It then transposed into four half-hour episodes for radio, which were broadcast on BBC Radio Cumbria.

Tarantara! Tarantara!

As for the Savoyards, by the late 90's they were firmly established as the prominent Gilbert and Sullivan exponents throughout South Cumbria, with a loyal and faithful following. In fact, so secure were they in this position that they could risk offending the purists by sending up the Savoy operas with their own 'adapted' versions. It became something of a summer tradition. For example *HMS Pinafore* became a story about a luxury cruise ship, *The Pirates of Penrith* told the story of life in a greasy spoon café, and *The Gondoliers* was re-envisaged as *A Venetian Blind Date* with a holiday complex (in Venice of course) providing the setting. All were written (or re-written) by Russell Palmer and became firm favourites and much anticipated.

Meanwhile, although David Marcus had moved on to work with other projects, the future of the group was assured with a dedicated band of talented and experienced performers, and a healthy list of supporters and sponsors. In addition the group was attracting the talents of experienced Producers and Musical Directors. The 1998 production of *The Sorcerer* saw the debut of Barbara Springthorpe in the role of Artistic Director. At this time she had already been associated with amateur theatre for over 30 years, with a career that had begun in South Wales at the tender age of 11. On moving up to Furness in the early 1970s she quickly became involved in the local scene and joined the Ulverston Society, first as a dancer, then in principal roles, and later as a Producer of seven of their shows. Subsequently she appeared in and directed plays for the Ulverston Outsiders, and then played principal roles in productions staged by the Abbey Society. She has even directed two shows for the Ulverston Pantomime Society. (Oh yes she has.) She was to go on to produce a total of 10 subsequent Savoyard productions from 1998 to 2007, supported by her husband Bill, also a well-known local performer and long-serving Savoyard. Sadly he passed away in 2014.

Karen Whalley *(Melissa),* Sharon Collins *(Lady Blanche),*
Eileen Lithgow *(Princess Ida)* & Helen Canavan *(Psyche);*
Princess Ida, 2000

Barbara Springthorpe's last production, in 2007, was *Utopia Ltd*, a large-scale, and virtually unseen G & S piece. On this occasion her Musical Director was Doreen Dunlop, 'the sparkly lady at the front' who, as you may recall, has worked with pretty well every other musical company on the local scene. She teamed up with Russ Palmer and Karen Glasgow (as Producer and Choreographer) for the next production of

Doreen Dunlop   *Karen Glasgow*

The Mikado in 2008, a team which worked together for a few further years. This production was a particularly special one for another reason. It was attended by an esteemed guest, Mr Thomas Round, the renowned Barrow-born tenor.

Some years earlier he had agreed to act as the Savoyards' President, and in February 2008, prior to a performance of *The Mikado*, he was honoured with a special presentation at the Forum in Barrow, attended by the then Mayor, Councillor Ken Williams, members of the Savoyards, and others involved locally in the Arts. After unveiling a commemorative plaque acknowledging him as 'an ambassador for Barrow and the Arts', he was then presented with a specially etched glass bowl.

Thomas Round has had an extremely successful career both as an international opera singer, and as the leading tenor for the D'Oyly Carte Opera Company, and it is clear that, like many others, it is the Savoy operas which hold a special place in his affections. He has also retained a similar affection for the Furness area and over the years has given many concerts locally, often with the emphasis on the works of Gilbert and Sullivan. In September 1981, for example, he teamed up with the Savoyards to present *Gilbert and Sullivan for All* at the Civic Hall in Barrow. Ten years later he was the star attraction at a Gilbert and Sullivan Festival which was held at the Swan Hotel, Newby Bridge. "I am extremely pleased that I have the honour of becoming part of the history of Barrow," he said. "I am proud to be a Barrovian and always have been." As for the performance of *The Mikado* in 2008, despite the undoubted added nerves, it was hailed as a triumph. It was described as a 'must-see' by Richard Morris writing in the *Barrow News*, whilst observing that, 'The regular principals maintain their high standards.'

Ron Eadington, Dave Inchliffe, and Terry Henshaw

The Mikado, 2008

Then, in 2014, there was the very first departure from tradition when, rather than staging a standard G & S opera, the Savoyards presented *A Nice Dilemma*. This was a concert featuring excerpts from all 13 of the Savoy operas which aimed to tell the Gilbert and Sullivan story through their songs. It was presented by the men themselves, 'W S Gilbert' (played by Neil Metcalfe) and 'Sir Arthur Sullivan' (played by Andrew Barrow). The show involved over 30 individual performers with Doreen Dunlop as Musical Director, and Production honours falling to the McIntosh family, Phil, Ailsa, and Lorna.

Mention should also be made of the Savoyards' additional Summer shows, the occasional ad hoc charity concerts in church halls, and the *Tea at Two* events which began at the Coronation Hall in Ulverston in 2007, and which have proved very popular. Seated in cabaret style the audience are served afternoon tea whilst being entertained with excerpts from the Savoyards' Gilbert and Sullivan repertoire. (A clip of one such performance is available on *YouTube* incidentally, which clearly conveys the Savoyards' joy of singing and performing.) Also of considerable importance is the programme of workshops which are run annually for local schools. These began in the 1990's with the aims of promoting both the Savoyards and the works of Gilbert and Sullivan, and to inspire confidence and interest in the performing arts by giving the youngsters 'hands-on' experience. During the workshops the plot of the annual show is first introduced and discussed, and then the young players get to dress up and act out excerpts from the production. The workshops have toured a number of local schools and are always a great success and keenly anticipated.

Perhaps a measure of their success is the number of young people the Savoyards have been able to recruit to perform in their shows! But as is the case with other societies there continue to be struggles. A shortage of male voices is as big a problem for the Savoyards as it is for other amateur societies. The ever-spiralling costs of set and costume hire, coupled with the unreliability of audience numbers also appear to be constant sources of worry for all. I am told that the problem of balancing the budget of a production with expected income is a major dilemma every year.

"Then give three cheers, and one cheer more ..."

In summarising the Savoyards output over the last 40+ years I have, as you may have noticed, focussed on the performers rather than the shows themselves. This is mainly because the operas are so well known, and indeed the show reviews are so consistently positive there is not a lot left to say. Space does not permit me to mention everyone who has played a part of course, and I apologise to all who feel their work has not been duly recognised. In researching the history however, what is certainly striking is the consistent appearance of performers year after year. I must say quickly that it is of course true that other societies have their own band of loyal performers and reliable contributors. As far the Savoyards are concerned however this factor is undoubtedly driven by a specific love and attachment to Gilbert and Sullivan's work. Indeed, since their operas were first performed, their work has engendered this sort of devoted following globally, a devotion which has persisted for more than 100 years. Thousands from around the world flock to the annual Gilbert and Sullivan Festival in Harrogate. Why? The answer I guess boils down to the basic ingredients – clever words, great music, recognisable characters and perennial themes that have never dated. If such an attachment to Gilbert & Sullivan's works is then combined with a love of singing and performing there is perhaps some clue as to the enduring nature of the Barrow Savoyards – and also explains why their story actually goes a long way beyond their annual show.

10

YOUTH THEATRE

What is it that attracts people to take part in musical theatre, when there are so many potential obstacles to be overcome? First off there is surely the major challenge of managing one's fears of public exposure with its very real risk of public humiliation. Then, after that, it's clearly a hard slog with so much to learn and so many new skills to master. There will be lots of words to learn, unfamiliar songs to get your head around, endless hours of rehearsal, not to mention the challenge of complicated dance routines. And if the show you're in happens to be *Barnum*? Well, how are you at tight-rope walking and juggling?

So what is it that draws so many people to become involved? I guess there's no simple answer. For some it may be a means of self-expression, a way of showing off what you can do, it may be an outlet for one's creative energy, or it might simply be the sense of belonging it provides, or the benefits of bonding with others as everyone strives together towards a common goal. I would suggest however, that at the heart of it all is a basic human instinct, the desire for *play*.

I want to return to this question later but for now, I think you can at least start to get an insight into why involvement becomes so important to people when you look at the contribution of Youth Theatre Companies to the promotion of the performance arts. For some it's where it all begins. So perhaps a survey of their ethos and activities will help with a further understanding of why so many young people are attracted to take to the stage.

Early stages

Although youth theatre has only become a prominent part of the local scene in recent years, it is by no means a new enterprise. Children of all ages have always been keen to perform, and indeed have been encouraged to do so at school in choirs, concerts, nativity plays, and in the schools' own musical productions. There have also been, and still are several dance schools in and around the South Lakes area, promoting the joy of performing. If you think of any of the 'Dancing Mistresses' of any early show, say in the 1920s or 30s, it is more than likely that they were also running their own dance school.

Early evidence I have of a dedicated youth theatre group then appears in 1964, following an initiative of the erstwhile manager of Barrow's Her Majesty's Theatre, Donald Sartain. His 'Furness Youth Theatre' (FYT) was met initially with a strong feeling of optimism as to what might be achieved. Roger Hunt, Vice-Chair of the new group, is quoted as saying, 'We have great scope for doing things which professionals cannot do, in the way of experimentation.' There was even an idea that the group's outlook might be broadened to stimulate interest not just in the performing arts, but in all art forms. At this time of course the appeal of live theatre was weak and Her Majesty's Theatre itself was struggling to survive. No doubt the idea of a youth group was part of an attempt to re-stimulate interest in the flagging fortunes of live theatre, and the arts in general. There was however a sad inevitability to the theatre's demise, resulting in Mr Sartain's departure before the Youth Theatre really got started. Despite his absence the FYT did mount several successful productions, such as *Robinson Crusoe* in 1965, starring a young Saxon Kolbe (a later founder of Walney Juniors) and which was produced by another familiar character, Wyn Large. Other shows followed, but I could find no further evidence of its existence after 1972 when it was credited with a run of *The Boyfriend* at the Public Hall. At around the same time Nellie English (herself the founder of a Dance School) was producing a series of pantomimes with another youth group which she called 'The Young Image' (see the Pantomime chapter), and the Walney Junior Society was just getting going so perhaps the FYT somehow got absorbed by these groups and disappeared.

ACT & the new Furness Youth Theatre group

Following these early initiatives, in recent years the notion of a Youth Theatre Company now appears to have been re-invented with the emergence of several new groups. One of the first to appear was ACT, a group founded in 1989 in Ulverston by Liz and Brain Loveless. Its stated objectives were: *to develop the talents of its members in all aspects of theatre, from performance to scriptwriting, composition, design, prop making and publicity etc.* Their first show was a production of *Peter Pan*, staged at the Coronation Hall in Ulverston in 1990. Although based in Ulverston, it draws its membership (of 5 to 20 year-olds) from throughout the South Lakes peninsulas. Following its inception membership soon grew, and several highly-acclaimed shows became the results of its efforts over subsequent years, such as *The Hobbit* (1991 and 1995), *A Christmas Carol* (1992), and *Annie* (1996) which won the NODA award for 'Best Junior Production.' As their confidence grew, the young cast were then trusted with productions usually associated with adult players, such as *Fiddler on the Roof* (1997) and *My Fair Lady* (2000). Initially their shows were performed at the Coronation Hall in Ulverston, with others gravitating to the Forum in Barrow in the late 1990s.

The 1994 production was a piece entitled *To Death and Glory*, which was a musical about World War One and the Suffragette Movement and which had been written by one of Liz and Brian's sons, 16-year old Alex Loveless. It was a hit show and an early sign of the talent which was to be recognised two years later when he won the Promising Newcomer award at the finals of the Vivian Ellis Prize, a top national competition held at the Theatre Royal, Drury Lane, London. His pop/rock show *Sensation* was one of only 5 chosen from a pool of 144 which had been submitted for the top prize. Having then gone on to direct shows for ACT, Alex has now left the area and is currently forging a successful career in musical theatre in London.

Meanwhile his brother Chris Loveless, also a regular contributor to the success of ACT's shows both as performer and director, has also enjoyed some success beyond the boundaries of the South Lakes. He trained at the Redroofs Theatre School and with the National Youth Theatre of Great Britain. In 2001 he made his West End debut for the NYT in its highly successful production of *Nicholas Nickleby*, and later in the production's tour to The Lowry in Manchester. At the same time, because of ACT's growing reputation and evolution, it was re-named as The Furness Youth Theatre, re-claiming the name of the former group now long defunct. The aims were also modified to make it sound less like a formal Stage School with an emphasis instead on the development of confidence in performance, communication, and self-expression. To that end the new group ran summer schools, weekly drama workshops, and charity performances, as well as producing at least one major show each year. The first official FYT show was, perhaps fittingly a reprise of Alex Loveless' musical *To Death and Glory*. There then followed such major undertakings as *Annie* (2003), *Bugsy Malone* (2004), *Peter Pan* (2006), and *The Evacuees* (2007), plus fun variety shows such as *Shake*

Ripple and Roll (2008), *Dracula Rock Show* (2011), and *Skool and Crossbones* (2013). At the time of writing it continues to thrive.

Cast members from the FYT's production of The Evacuees, 2007

A590 Youth Theatre

A590 was founded at the turn of the new century by Maureen Pearson, based on some early theatrical experience and her background in Child Care. She currently serves as Chairperson of a Management Committee who together drive forward the group's activities. It all started when she attended auditions for the Barrow Society's production of *Annie* in 1996.

She was struck by the huge number of children who turned up, noted their energy and enthusiasm, and then shared in their subsequent disappointment when they were not chosen for the show. "I decided there and then," she told me, "to start up my own company, one which would take all-comers, and make the joy of dance, acting and music accessible to all, regardless of family income or background." She recruited local drama teacher Dominic McCavish and together they produced their first show, *The Jungle Book*, in 2002.

The stated aims of the A590 Theatre group are:

to provide an opportunity for young people aged 7 to 20+ to perform in musical and theatre productions, learning new skills, enhancing existing skills and providing a structured environment for their rehearsals in warm, caring surroundings. The skills learned during these rehearsals and performances can and will raise their self-esteem, confidence and promote respect for themselves and each other whilst growing into adulthood.

Notice the stress on personal and social development. A590 does not profess to be a stage school preparing students for careers in the performing arts. There is some overlap with the activities of a stage school of course, but if any of the kids do move on to the senior societies or to study drama and/or musical theatre in earnest, it will not be wholly on the basis of their enhanced performance skills. It will be on the basis of their enhanced personal development through the safe opportunities for *play* and self-expression that A590 provides.

Initially the youngsters were divided into two groups, a junior group (for 7 to 13 year-olds) and a senior group (for 13 years and up), although for the last 5 years or so they have merged into one. Mr McCavish was succeeded by Chris Loveless and Graham Barker early on also, and the latter has produced many of A590's shows ever since. He has been assisted by a reliable band of musicians usually led by Paul Bryden as Musical Director, and by the choreographic expertise of such as Pamela Duncan and Cassie Curtis-Smith.

The group enjoyed considerable early success with such shows as *Fame* (2004) and *Big Al* (2005). Then, quite unexpectedly (so much so that at first Maureen Pearson thought someone was playing an unkind joke) the company was invited to send a group to Prague to compete in "The Action Drama Festival", which had been established to promote friendship and understanding between young people of different nationalities. In 2006 their production of *Cinderella* won the Silver Award, and then in 2007 and 2008 they became outright winners of the Gold Award with their shows *Outcast* and *Honk: The Ugly Duckling*. Graham Barker was subsequently invited to sit on the judging panel although, sadly for A590, it became too expensive and too complex a trip to allow further productions to be entered.

Meanwhile at home their productions have never lacked ambition and they have tackled both playful and serious pieces, some of which might stretch the capacity of a senior society.

e.g. *Guys and Dolls* (2009), *Rent* (2009), *Fiddler on the Roof* (2011), *Aida* (2012), *The King and I* (2015) and most recently, *Whistle Down the Wind* (2016), with Leah Greaves impressively taking on her first leading role. *Rent* was a controversial choice for a youth group with its dominant themes of drug addiction, AIDS, and

Left: *Cast members of Rent, 2009*

homelessness but equally it was a very modern, contemporary piece which brought something radical and fresh to the local scene. Certainly the press review was very enthusiastic, the cast being praised for their 'real talent, infectious enthusiasm, and sensitive maturity.' It subsequently received a NODA nomination for the Best Youth Production.

2011 marked the group's 10th anniversary with *Fiddler on the Roof* in April (which incidentally also won a NODA nomination), and an anniversary concert in July. Maureen Pearson noted with some satisfaction that, 'Half of the young cast in that show weren't even born when we started out!' The concert was both a celebration and a thank you to all supporters and sponsors, and consisted of a medley of songs from their previous shows. It also announced that their 2012 show was to be a production of Elton John and Tim Rice's *AIDA*. A590 were one of the first in the country to stage it, winning a personal note of commendation from Sir Tim Rice. "Elton joins me," he said, "in wishing everybody concerned the best of luck."

Although, as I say, not the principal intention of the A590 group, it will be no surprise to note that their productions have spawned many talented performers who have gone on to be active members of the local senior societies, and others who have gone on to seek both professional training and/or careers in the performing arts. Many however attribute their start, and their first vote of confidence to the A590 group. So said some of the youngsters I met at a BODS rehearsal for their 2016 show *Legally Blonde*, such as Amy Turner, Catherine Andrews, Dave Stockton and Tom Halfpenny, whilst other A590 graduates such as Sacha Bell, Daniel and Vicki Serra, Jack Hawitt and Lee Mason have progressed to careers in the performing arts. Then there are others who have emerged from their studies to become Drama teachers themselves, e.g. Jenny Dawson and Laura Chalker. And so the world keeps turning.

Other Youth Theatre Groups

Meanwhile, whilst the Furness Youth Theatre and the A590 group have been busy, a number of other groups have appeared in the district, such as the Spotlight Youth Theatre, the Deemon Performance Academy and the CAST Theatre Company. Each has staged successful shows and each has managed, perhaps with some overlap, to recruit impressive numbers of youngsters to make up their casts. As all of their shows have proved, there has never been any shortage of either enthusiasm or talent in the South Lakes area.

The Spotlight Youth Theatre emerged in 2003 and enjoyed a short period, appropriately enough, in the spotlight before disbanding. The group staged a successful series of shows at the Recreational Hall in Urswick, which were directed and produced by Denise Stable, assisted by an energetic group of supporters and friends. Andy Sproxton acted as Musical Director, pulling together a small band of familiar local musicians such as Paul Bryden (guitar), Gary Abbott (trumpet), Steve Simpson (bass), Michelle Reed (clarinet/sax) and Joanne Sneesby (flute). Although small scale and somewhat makeshift, they could certainly not be described as slight productions, as the young cast tackled such heavy-weight shows as *Bugsy Malone* (2003), *The Wizard of Oz* (2004), *Alice in Wonderland* (2005) and *Annie* (2006).

The Deemon Performance Academy was the brainchild of Emma Fawcett, assisted by husband Dean, and was set up in or around 2005. The focus of the group's work is more specifically on the development of performance skills, so operates more like a formalised Stage School for budding performers. Since being established it has staged a run of annual shows entitled *The Show Must Go On* which creates the opportunity for the Academy to showcase the burgeoning talent of its students.

The CAST Youth Theatre Company (now known as **CAST Theatre Company**) was formed in 2008 by the Barker and Patrick families. Graham Barker, one of the founders and a familiar name in my survey of local societies, was already very active in the district, having been director, choreographer, dancer, actor, and stage manager for numerous local productions. For CAST the Barker and Patrick families made up a large proportion of the initial performers, and indeed many sons, daughters, cousins, nephews and nieces remain involved, but numbers have since grown to include a wide range of membership. CAST now stages a full-scale musical production each year, whilst also participating in fund-raising concerts and sponsored events. Their back catalogue of shows to date, which are performed at the Forum in Barrow, has included such adventurous outings as *Summer Holiday* (2011), *Guys and Dolls* (2014), and *Barnum* (2015). CAST has also been responsible for developing the performance careers of many young actors (such as Hayley Dent, Bronte Tranter, Dave

Stockton, and Karen Barker) who have since branched out to make regular appearances for other Societies in the district.

Adam Barker and Hayley Dent
Summer Holiday, 2011

The Grange and District Amateur Dramatic Society also have an active Youth Theatre which was established in

1990. As described in Chapter 7 the group has staged a family pantomime every year, produced and directed by husband and wife team Jean and Mick Malkin. It is an enthusiastic and supportive group which accepts all-comers, aiming to build confidence, encourage friendships and, of course, nurture talent. Many go on to perform for the senior Society, and ultimately move on to professional training. It is very much a community enterprise however and, as well as providing concerts and ad hoc entertainments in local retirement homes etc, the Society organises social activities and gatherings for their members in the summer months.

Having explored these various groups, and talked to many of those involved, the sense of a strong 'family' atmosphere in each of them is clear. There is a strong culture of acceptance in each group, a sense of belonging and mutual care. Naomi Shields, herself an A590 member for just over 10 years, pointed this out to me directly when she remarked that the group was 'just like another family, where everyone takes care of each other.' I may have been given the rose-tinted spectacles version but having seen more than one group in action for myself I certainly did not see any sign of petty rivalries or back-biting, just a constructive sense of teamwork and cooperation. And the importance these young performers place on their involvement is equally impressive to note. No-one complained about the hard work of it all, the time commitment or the long hours of rehearsal. Instead they said things like: 'I feel really lucky to be a part of it,' 'I've made some fab friends by coming here,' 'It's a great experience,' 'I'm ecstatic to be involved in this show.' When the run of A590's *Whistle Down the Wind* ended in April 2016, Leah Greaves (who played a lead character) said, 'These last 5 months have been the happiest of my life.'

Then I met a young man named Chris Wilson who told me his amazing story. In 2010, whilst on holiday in Tenerife, he had been subject to a vicious and unprovoked attack by some random thugs that had left him with injuries so severe he almost did not survive. He subsequently remained in a coma for a month, and then spent the next 18 months in hospital for further recovery and rehabilitation. At the end of it all he was still left with mobility problems, some memory impairment, and a reliance on a full-time support worker. Bored, depressed, and with his self-confidence severely damaged he returned home at an utter loss. And yet, the person I met in 2016 was an affable, confident young man with an outgoing manner and a cheerful sense of humour. He told me he is now an active charity worker and a national ambassador for the disabled with The Prince's Trust, taking part in a wealth of both fund-raising and awareness-raising events. He can't quite believe in such a marked transformation himself, and how his confidence and abilities have improved. And how do you imagine it has come about? The answer is through his discovery of Youth Theatre. Brought along initially to the A590 group by an aunt he was at first very reluctant to become involved. Then slowly but surely the ice began to thaw as he allowed himself to feel the energy and enthusiasm around him, and to experience a renewed sense of acceptance. Now he is a keen participant and by the time I met him he had already featured in several productions, and was about to appear as President Roosevelt in CAST's 2016 production of *Annie*. His story has naturally earned him the respect of many people who regard him as an inspiration. What better evidence can you have of the amazing benefits and transformational effects of involvement in musical theatre?

If you recall, when the Walney Junior Society first made its appearance in 1968, I quoted Ronald Metcalfe as saying, "It is youngsters like this we must encourage. They are the future backbone of all our senior societies." This may be true but, having become more aware of the district's various youth theatre groups I have become increasingly impressed not by their role as a feeder for the seniors, relevant and important as that is. As A590's stated aims affirm, and Chris Wilson's story illustrates so well, of much greater importance is their ability to create the conditions for the development of increased self-confidence, enhanced personal development, and improved social skills. In other words, by providing structured opportunities where all the developmental benefits of *play* can be realised.

It is well recognised that play is a crucial part of healthy growth, promoting cognitive development, social skills, and emotional well-being. But even as we grow and are supposed to knuckle down and get serious, the importance of play does not diminish and can even keep us young. As no less a person that George Bernard Shaw pointed out, 'We don't stop playing because we get old; we grow old as we stop playing.' In other words, if you lose the capacity for play, you also weaken your ability to learn from new experiences, your imagination will solidify, and you will have lost the capacity to dream.

So what is it that attracts people to musical theatre? Whichever side of the footlights you happen to be on I suspect it boils down to the opportunity for *play* within safe boundaries. As far as the performers are concerned these Youth Theatre groups provide ample evidence for the benefits of play particularly in terms of personal and social development. And as far as those of us in the audience are concerned, for a few short hours a musical production allows us to exercise our imagination, it frees up our capacity to play with ideas and feelings and, ultimately, even increases our capacity to dream. As Bloody Mary in *South Pacific* reminds us all, "If you don't have a dream, how you gonna have a dream come true?"

PART THREE

You Can't Stop the Beat

11

ANOTHER OPENING, ANOTHER SHOW ....

It is perhaps no coincidence that the plot of many famous Musicals charts the journey of some heroic figure as he or she strives to overcome seemingly over-whelming odds in order to achieve what they desire. Why? Because that is exactly the situation the Producer of a Musical finds himself in when he comes to stage one! I have come to realise that all the time, effort and work required is really quite staggering. For so many Societies in this South Lakes area to have doggedly staged new shows year after year over such long periods of time is quite some achievement. In this section therefore, in order to ram that point home, I thought it would be worthwhile to review all the various phases that must be worked through in order to arrive at a final product.

First steps

The first step of course is to choose a suitable show. This in itself is no easy task as there is the immediate question of what will best appeal to the audience - how to strike a balance between the familiar and the untried. And remember that the field is not an open one as there are restrictions on what can be staged. Right out of the frame are any shows that are either currently running in the West End or in touring productions, any that are in the process of being revived, and any (like *Les Miserables*) that are only licensed to youth groups. When shows do become available there might then be competition from other local Societies as to who gets the performing rights first. Before the days of the internet a small group of good men and true (and/or women) would have been able to research the field behind closed doors, keeping their final decision secret until a contract was signed with the licensing agent. That way they might steal the march on any other Society with designs on the same show. Nowadays, with open access to all via the internet, I understand the process is a much more transparent one.

The production team

Once the show is chosen, a production team is then appointed consisting of a Producer/Director, a Musical Director, an Accompanist, and a Choreographer. These are roles that have been referred to many times in our story so far, but it's worth pausing for a second to unpack what these people actually do in more detail. The Producer is El Supremo, the person in charge of everything that happens on stage in terms of set design, costumes, and staging, and indeed all that happens off-stage in terms of costs, marketing, publicity, room hire etc. – in other words, the one who has the final say on all aspects of the final production. Of course help, support and advice is provided by a whole team of people who take responsibility for many of these business aspects, but all are ultimately accountable to the Producer, who is in turn accountable to the Society Committee or Management Board. If you're thinking of applying you will need to be able to demonstrate that you have the qualities of an artist, a diplomat, a dictator, and a psychologist.

The Music: At the start of a show, when the theatre darkens, the first thing that will happen is that someone will emerge from one side, walk slowly over to a podium and, as the audience bursts into applause, will take a bow. This is of course the conductor of the orchestra, the Musical Director or

MD (who, for simplicity I will refer to as male, although I am very aware that many Musical Directors of the local productions I have discussed have been female.) He will raise his arms, check that he has the attention of all his musicians, and then, with one swift downward swipe of his baton will bring the orchestra to life.

Without wishing to offend front-of-house staff, the back-stage team, the lighting and sound technicians, or the wardrobe department, it seems to me that the members of the orchestra are very much the unsung heroes of the musical. With the exception of the MD they are rarely credited in the souvenir programmes and yet these talented musicians set the mood and atmosphere of a piece, provide the linkage between scenes, and complement the dramatic or romantic performances of the cast. As one of my musician friends pointed out, without the music a musical is just a play. By 'just a play' I'm certain he didn't mean to devalue the importance of drama, which is of course powerful in its own way. But consider the power of music when added to words - there's no doubt that the music adds a whole new dimension. In a musical a song can say things that the words alone cannot convey. Think of Fantine's wounded "I Dreamed a Dream" in *Les Miserables* – the music heightens her pain at her shattered hopes and dreams in a most compelling way, conveying an immediate and powerful experience of her suffering and heart-break to the audience. (It gets me every time.)

At a show's first rehearsals, with the help of the Producer, the cast practice their parts to the piano accompaniment of the MD's main accomplice, the so-called Accompanist. It is here that the performers first learn their pieces, and how to coordinate their dialogue, songs and dance with the show's music. Later the MD will attend many rehearsals himself to fine-tune this early work and ensure everyone has a thorough knowledge of how everything fits together. In the meantime of course he has to assemble his orchestra, ensure that all the necessary instruments are represented and, most important, confirm everyone's availability. In addition to all this the MD is also the orchestra's business manager, negotiating and organising the payment of individual musician's fees, all of which by the way may be described as nominal. 'It's not enough to make a living,' one musician told me glumly, 'but we accept that costs have to be kept low.'

But it is then only about a month before opening night that the individual orchestra parts arrive, so each musician actually has a limited amount of time to become familiar with their part before the MD organises his first 'Band Call'. This will take place without the cast and is the opportunity for the orchestra to play the piece through together for the first time. A second Band Call will then take place soon afterwards *with* the cast, which is actually the one and only opportunity before the final dress rehearsal for everyone to ensure that music, song, dance, action and dialogue are all coordinated. In other words that's only three occasions when the orchestra have actually played together as a whole ensemble before opening night. That seems pretty impressive to me.

So don't imagine that the MD just turns up at the start of each show to conduct the orchestra. He has already been fully involved in the show's preparation, has been working with the cast either individually or in a group, has formed his orchestra, and ensured that everyone knows their part. In other words he has been fully engaged in coordinating everything to do with the music. To give you some idea of the effort and commitment required, Ian Bird showed me a file which was stuffed with a thick wadge of printed emails – a record of a small part of the various communications between himself, the producer, cast members, and fellow musicians which had been necessary to pull everything together for one particular show. I happened to glance at one email in which he was making an arrangement for the first Band Call. 'It will require a full evening,' it said. 'So you will need to bring sandwiches, sleeping bags etc.' I don't think he was joking.

Choreography: All the dance routines are obviously the concern of the Choreographer. These routines are not, as you might imagine, copied from previous professional productions, but are created as it were on a blank canvas. And remember that, in many musical productions, dance sequences can be a very important part of the story-telling, so cannot be treated lightly. Sally McKimm, an experienced Choreographer with both the Barrow and the Walney Societies, told me that one minute of dance might take at least an hour, and often more, to create. The coordination of an actor's movements and positioning with the musical numbers clearly has to look fluid and effortless in the final production, so again, a few minutes of action on stage can take a great deal of time to perfect.

Casting: The production team of course needs a cast. A series of workshops are held initially to familiarise would-be performers with the show, the musical numbers, and to build the characters. This is the time for everyone to try things out for size and experiment, and even to set up audition pieces. Open auditions are then held (in other words anyone can watch) with the selection panel headed up by the Producer and others with appropriate expertise and experience. There are no red buzzers involved, no spinning chairs, and no mean-spirited critics, but I'm assured that these events are always fun, lively, and constructive. 'The hardest thing,' Steve Carrick told me, 'is having to sometimes turn people down after they've already worked so hard.'

Rehearsals and preparations: Once the show has been cast, that's when the work really starts! A rehearsal schedule is drawn up which basically divides the show into manageable portions or 'building blocks' which will then gradually be put back together into a whole piece. It is an intense period, usually lasting about 6 months, which involves as many diagrams, spreadsheets, and emails as it does sessions of physical activity. As rehearsals can be held up to 3 times a week, the pull on people's time is demanding, and although the arrangements for each individual session may be fluid, the work to be covered is tightly organised. A typical session for example may focus on the songs, the dialogue, or the dance either as individual segments or as a whole piece, and may involve particular actors, small groups, or the whole cast. As show week nears the frequency of rehearsals increases! In 1994 Ellis Butcher of the *Evening Mail* threw herself into the mix for the Walney Society's production of *Guys and Dolls* in order to experience the thrill of amateur musical theatre for herself. She went through the entire process from auditions to opening night, emerging safely at the other side but full of admiration for the levels of commitment, imagination and energy that 'being in a show' demands. 'One thing you must realise,' she says, 'if you commit yourself to a show the rest of your life takes a back seat.'

I was privileged to be invited by the Barrow Society Producer, Steve Carrick, to watch rehearsals for their 2016 production of *Legally Blonde*. What struck me most was the warm and cheerful nature of the overall atmosphere. The cast members were all working hard with obvious energy and spirit, yet were clearly having fun without any loss of resolve or discipline. I found the mechanics of the process oddly absorbing as it was by no means the linear process I had imagined. Scenes are basically de-constructed before being acted out, to allow individual positions to be scrutinised, the timing of the music with the dialogue to be perfected, and any additional choreography to be rehearsed. Eventually of course it is then all blended together into an impressive whole.

I talked to some of the performers between scenes and their dedication to the art of musical theatre was evident. All had previous experience either in previous productions or with youth groups (often with both), and one or two had even come straight out of one show into another. As discussed in the previous chapter, when I asked what the draw was it seemed that the camaraderie of being involved was as important as the opportunity for performance and self-expression. And watching them as they worked I could see that it's not just a question of having a wish to perform, or even being able to sing reasonably well, performing in a musical is both a physical and an emotional activity – it not only requires talent and the ability to perform and project, it also helps if you have determination, reliability and a healthy helping of self-discipline.

Sets and costumes: Whilst the rehearsals continue apace the sets of course need to be prepared. Most will be hired these days but, since hire companies are geared to providing sets for larger venues than those available locally, some local construction work may still be required. And that's easier said than done as a large set will need a large space for its construction and subsequent storage. For the Barrow Society their rehearsal rooms at Storey Square were once ideal, but now they have to improvise. For the Abbey Society Ray Martindale continues to beaver away in his workshop, as he has done for many years, and for Ulverston I'm told that, at one time, as soon as breakfast was over in Ken and Brenda Hindle's former B&B at Virginia House, the dining room was immediately transformed into a makeshift workshop.

Costumes too are generally hired. Gone are the days when an army of willing seamstresses would slog away over their hot sewing machines as demands are now simply too high. The availability of necessary props then has to be checked as, even if a set is hired, not everything will be provided. Lists are drawn up, which will include everything from a newspaper or vase to a bed or a television, and all members will be asked to source whatever they can. And once all this has been sorted out, all the cast will then be involved in a photo-call. Fitted out in their regalia, a setting that is relevant to the particular musical production is chosen, and a professional photographer is engaged. All manner of locations have been used from railway stations to Blackpool Tower Circus. The resulting pictures will then be used for publicity purposes, with some ending up in the Souvenir Programme which also has to be designed and organised.

The run up to Show Week

As Show Week draws near, there are three crucial events which need to be worked through. The first of these will be the two 'Band Calls' already mentioned, which is when the cast first gets to rehearse with the full orchestra. Remember that, up to this point, the cast will have performed with one keyboard accompanist only. Having spoken to several performers I am told that a Band Call is one of the most exciting times for the cast as it is a time when, for everyone, the show finally comes to life.

The second crucial event is the so-called 'Technical Rehearsal'. By now the set has been delivered and constructed, so each scene can now be rehearsed in situ, the lighting can be organised, the fluidity of scene changes and any moving parts of the set can be checked out, and all the actors' movements, entrances and exits can be tried out and, if necessary, adjusted. And finally, when all that has been thoroughly checked and refined, there is the last chance to make any further improvements with the Dress Rehearsal – the final run through of the show in its entirety before opening night.

And when it's all over? It was once traditional for cast members to receive gifts across the footlights, usually in the form of bouquets for the leading ladies, or small gifts from family, friends and a grateful Society. Friends and relatives were also allowed on to the stage to offer their congratulations. These practices were eventually discouraged however as it always resulted in a very congested stage, and hampered the work of the stage hands who were keen to get on with their job of dismantling the set. Of course being involved in a production is deemed to be reward in itself but, in case I have given the impression that it is all work, let me add that each Society has a very active social programme with quiz nights, dinners and parties (which no doubt involve a lot of singing and dressing up!) And of course, every year there is always the NODA Annual Awards ceremony to look forward to.

Costs

As you have laboured through this, you have probably not been keeping a tally on the costs of all this effort, as they mount up. Well neither have I to be honest, so let's just consider for a moment the various items that make up the final bill:

- the fee required by the licensing agent for a performance licence,
- the writers/composers of any show which has been granted a performance licence require either a set fee

for each performance, or a percentage of the income from ticket sales,

- the local production team, members of the orchestra (during show week only), and the Stage Manager are all paid nominal fees (which are nowhere near a reflection of the time and energy they spend on each production),
- the costs of hiring librettos and orchestral scores,
- the costs of hiring the set – usually one of the largest expenses, especially when additional transport costs are included,
- the hire of costumes and wigs,
- the cost of producing the Souvenir Programme,
- the costs of publicity and advertising,
- the hire of the performance venue for the technical and dress rehearsals, and of course for Show Week itself,
- the costs incurred for the use of stage lighting, microphones and stage equipment.

I am told that, when all this is put together, the average total cost for any amateur production is in the region of £22,000. And that is only achieved by keeping costs as low as possible with the support of a huge amount of voluntary effort, and the goodwill of others in allowing the free loan of props or costume extras, the free provision of transport and, in some cases, the free provision of publicity and advertising space.

But even after all that, the final unpleasant reality is that these costs cannot be met entirely by the income produced by - to use the usual theatrical cliché - 'bums on seats.' To take The Forum in Barrow as an example with its seating capacity of around 400, even if every show is sold out for the full run, the maximum income a show can generate is no more than £20,000. And of course, although the shows generally do well, many do not achieve such capacity crowds. Income has to be boosted therefore by other initiatives such as Summer Concerts or fund-raising events like Supermarket 'bag packs', coffee mornings, sponsored sings, tombolas and raffles. These are by no means new ideas and all Societies have long been creative in their search for novel initiatives. In 1987 for example, on the day the box office opened for *Calamity Jane*, the Walney Society provided the opportunity for patrons to share in a coffee morning with the cast, and in the fashion-conscious days of the 1960's the Barrow Society once held a mannequin parade in order to raise some cash-in-hand for their next production.

Monies are also raised from the annual subscription fees paid by Society members and via the financial support provided by the many patrons of the Society who, in exchange for their donations, receive various benefits such as newsletters, discounted show tickets, and opportunities to meet the company or attend an open rehearsal. And finally, of crucial importance is the support given to the Societies through the sponsorship of local businesses and organisations.

If this all sounds like, in terms of finance, a life lived on the edge one needs to remember that no Society is in it for the money. Amateur musical societies do not aim to become successful corporations generating fat profits for their owners and staff. Each Society is a Registered Charity, accountable to the Charity Commission, which means that they are duty bound to demonstrate that they are serving their community in ways that are, by definition, non-profit making. If income exceeds outgoings in any particular year, a Society will report, in Charity Commission-speak, not a profit but 'a surplus', and the Commission requires that any such surplus should be used entirely for the benefit of the local community. As far as finances are concerned, total transparency is required so that, annually, a Society's accounts must be formally presented to the Commission, be subject to regular audit, and be available (via the Commission's website) for public inspection.

And finally ....

In the Souvenir Programme for any show, it is usual for the Society Chairman to include warm words of appreciation to colleagues, sponsors and cast members, for their continued support and for all the hard work and effort expended over the many months of preparation. Hopefully this chapter gives some sense of what that phrase *'all the hard work and effort'* really means. Even so, my survey is still just a broad description of all that is required – a more detailed analysis would require a great deal more space. But at the very least, if you are ever lucky enough to get a ticket to go to an amateur production, you can now feel much more certain that you are getting value for money.

12

THE SMELL OF THE GREASEPAINT, AND THE ROAR OF THE CROWD

As you may have gathered I am a fan of musical theatre. Having said that, I know it can sometimes be an irritation when other people bang on about something they really like, and then almost demand that you to feel the same way. TV presenters are the worst. It doesn't matter how many times they parade them before me, I'm afraid I'm never going to share Paul O'Grady's love of dogs, or understand Robson Green's obsession with deep-sea fishing. But, as far as musical theatre is concerned, if I bang on about its pleasures a little more I am probably on safe ground – I mean, if you have stayed with me this far, it must mean that it holds a special attraction for you too.

Music and song are a basic part of life. It is just not possible to live through a day without hearing music of some sort, somewhere, and a world without music is unimaginable – no Beatles, no Christmas carols, no music-while-you-work, no concerts, and of course no such thing as musical theatre. One of the great benefits of course is the feeling that, through music and song, we are engaging in a shared communal experience - hence the pleasures of community singing, and why music plays such an integral part in important national events, like a Royal Wedding or the FA Cup Final. You're never truly alone if music is playing, and this is even more true if someone is actually singing *to* you. We have all even been assured that, if you ever happen to be stranded on a desert island, your best bet is to have eight 'gramophone records' to hand – in other words access to music is considered to be one of the most important keys to survival. (The others by the way are the Bible, the complete works of Shakespeare, and one other luxury – like a boat presumably).

Music has almost magical properties in its ability to stir both memories and emotion in a most powerful way. *Keep On Runnin'* by The Spencer Davis Group transports me right back to the 1960s and Barrow's first 'discotheque' at the Duke of Edinburgh Hotel on Abbey Road. I can't listen to the Everly Brothers singing *Ebony Eyes* without feeling a prickling sensation behind my eyes, and listening to Paul Simon's *Homeward Bound* always makes me feel like a homesick traveller even when I'm sitting in my front room. In short, music gets under your skin.

We are all introduced to the joys of music at a very young age. For example, you may well have been lucky enough to have felt soothed by lullabies sung to you at the cradle. But even if you missed out on that, you would soon have been exposed to music at nursery or infant school, where singing is a crucial part of the daily curriculum. How else would you know which piggy went to market, what the wheels on the bus do, or where the farmer lives, if not through the power of song? And what about your experience of school choirs, the nativity plays, and the concerts staged for the benefit of proud parents?

I once went to a junior school's production of *The Lion, the Witch, and the Wardrobe* – which might have been more accurately called *The Puppet, the Scary Little Girl, and the Very Big Cardboard Box*. In other words, the production values weren't perhaps the best, nor (if I'm going to be picky) was the singing. But that's not the point. What struck me most was the sheer joy of singing, dancing and performing that the young cast were able to communicate to the audience. They were all totally committed to what they were doing, and putting so much gusto and energy into it, you would have to have had a heart of stone not to be affected. In short, because they were enjoying it so much, so were we. I think this joy of performing for its own sake is also the thing that marks out one of the key strengths of amateur musical theatre. Of course professional actors are committed too, and no doubt enjoy what they do, but there must be an added dimension to performance when you do it, not because it's your job, but for the sheer love of doing it.

Sadly, as you grow older, this joy of singing is in danger of being lost as inhibitions set in and we worry more about being judged. As I noted in the chapter on Youth Theatre, although we are supposed to get serious as we get older, the importance of *play* in one's life should not diminish. And for some of course this might take the form of acting or singing, which can in turn become a favoured way of self-expression.

Tracey Thorn writes eloquently about both the challenges and joys of singing in her book *Naked at the Albert Hall*. She suggests that, if you ask anyone what sort of talent they would like to have, most people will say that they wished they could sing. And certainly, if you have seen any of the TV programmes presented by Choirmaster extraordinaire Gareth Malone, in which he demonstrates the life-changing properties of singing - self-expression, release of energy, connection to others, growth of self-confidence – you cannot be left in any doubt about its power.

So why is musical theatre so appealing and so important? The draw of the theatre in general, is that it allows us to enter a different sort of world, it can give us an experience of situations we rarely if ever encounter and, if we are open to it, it can trigger strong emotions which can then be managed within safe boundaries. At the simplest level musical theatre entertain us – yes, of course it does, but there is also the more grandiose claim that it can have an impact on our view of ourselves and the world we live in. I think this is true. The musicals that endure are often those that either challenge our view of the world or deal with universal themes of living – race relations, struggles against adversity and injustice, the pain of broken dreams, the power of love, the strength of the human spirit, and so on. I would argue that there is as much a message about the power of honesty and integrity over abuse and injustice in the pantomimic *Matilda*, as there is in the weightier *Les Miserables*. Let me say it again - the musical is an art form which can harness the power of music and song and stir a depth of emotional experience like no other, and in doing so, can even set the confusing things about life in order for us. No wonder they have endured for so long and, through changing social times, have always retained their popularity and appeal.

From my brief survey of the various local Societies, it seems clear that there are many more similarities between them than differences. They have all shared similar ups and downs and, whilst each can be credited with their own individual achievements, together they have shared the common goals of stimulating interest in live theatre, fostering and encouraging local talent, providing an outlet for the area's creative energy, whilst being agents and supporters of many charitable causes. It is also impressive to note how the theatrical bug, in whatever form it may take, is passed through families from one generation to the next. Some of these family connections have already been referred to, but I have encountered many more in the course of my research that, in all honesty, it has been difficult to keep up. Of course this is how it should be – the passing of the torch from one generation to the next is another of the reasons amateur theatre continues to survive.

It is the case however that the Societies I have reviewed are all operating in a relatively small geographical area, and some members I spoke to expressed their concerns about 'a flooded market' and wondered whether it would be sensible for some official mergers to take place. Others I spoke to were, possibly quite rightly, horrified at such a suggestion, arguing that it is the very combination of cross-pollination and friendly rivalry that fuels creativity and encourages a constant raising of standards. In other words, since today's performers are granted freedom of movement between the Societies, this is of great benefit to all in enhancing versatility and creativity. Yet on the other hand such an arrangement also erodes the sense of ownership and belonging which was such a characteristic feature of Societies in the early years and, without this, it can prove difficult to get younger members to sign up to the more mundane administrative and management roles. As ever, who knows the correct way forward?

What is clear is that these are challenging times for all amateur groups especially as, in the professional world, the emphasis is now on spectacle, mega-productions, and so-called Juke-Box musicals, features which the amateurs cannot emulate. But let's not imagine that the future of the amateur world is entirely dependent on the professional theatre leading the way. The future of amateur theatre is surely much more dependent on the amount of public support it is able to generate from the communities they serve.

According to John Kenrick in his book *Musical Theatre: A History* musical productions thrive in communities which meet the following criteria:

1. There is a population large enough and prosperous enough to support an active theatrical culture.
2. There is a thriving artistic community that nurtures successive generations of creative and performing talent.

3. There is a shared sense of optimism regarding the community and its future.
4. There is freedom from government censorship or political oppression.

It is interesting to apply these criteria to the South Lakes area. Judging by the Societies I have reviewed in detail, and taking into account the others that have come and gone, there can be little doubt about the presence of a 'thriving artistic community' here. And it is true that, in times past, the activities of all of these Societies were under most threat when levels of prosperity fell, or the sense of optimism about the future was weak. As for criterion number 4, as far as I know 'government censorship or political oppression' has never been a major problem, unless we count the 1992 disturbance in Ulverston when the threat of censorship hung over *La Cage aux Folles* for a while, or the political manoeuvres in Barrow resulting in theatre closures and the accompanying disruptions to performance venues. Certainly the viability of musical productions was again under threat at such times.

But perhaps there is a fifth criterion to be added to Kenrick's list, which is specific to the South Lakes peninsula – namely, the nature of its geography. A peninsula by definition is a projection of land into the sea, thereby affording some potential for a sense of separation from the mainstream. The comedian Mike Harding once famously described Barrow as 'a town at the end of a 20 mile cul-de-sac' and Bill Bryson (remember him?) referred to it as 'out on a limb' and 'miles from anywhere'. In our modern age of transport links and communication networks the idea of any such sense of isolation is rendered meaningless but, in years past, the fact that these links were less well developed may well have given rise to a culture of 'let's-make-our-own-entertainment'. Looking back through the history of the Societies there is surely evidence that their efforts have brought many productions to a local audience that would otherwise have been quite inaccessible. Indeed one of the initial driving forces of any amateur operatic group was to bring what was happening on the distant professional stage to the lives of local communities – and indeed, at a much cheaper price for a ticket!

So - to summarise – in a relatively small geographical area this book has identified and reviewed the history and activities of 11 (7 senior and 4 junior) contemporary Operatic Societies or Musical Theatre groups, and 3 currently active Pantomime groups (Ulverston, Broughton, and Grange). From the viewpoint of the year 2016 most of these have a history stretching back in excess of 70 years, with two having already reached their centenary. The fact that they are all continuing to thrive (albeit in the constant company of threats and challenges) is a testament both to the enduring value of 'play' in our lives, and to the generations of performers, musicians, sponsors and supporters who have worked so hard to keep amateur theatre alive in this area. And by the way, what a vast army over the years this has been. My reviews have tended to give an emphasis to the performers, but there is a veritable legion of helpers who have contributed hugely to all the Societies' enduring success – from set builders to programme sellers through all points in-between. I salute them all.

Now, enough of all this. There's only one thing left to say:

Go and see a show!

APPENDIX : Past productions

1908
The Mikado (UAOS)

1909
The Gondoliers (UAOS)

1910
Pirates of Penzance (UAOS)

1911
HMS Pinafore (UAOS)
Yeomen of the Guard (Barrow)
  The Mikado (Barrow)

1912
The Emerald Isle (UAOS)
The Gondoliers (Barrow)

1913
Dorothy (UAOS)
Les Cloches de Corneville
                (Barrow)
1914
Haddon Hall (UAOS)
Tom Jones (Barrow)

1916
Iolanthe (Barrow)

1917
Dorothy (Barrow)

1918
The Mikado (UAOS)
Yeomen of the Guard (Barrow)

1919
Merrie England (Barrow)

1920
Princess Caprice (UAOS)
The Mikado (Barrow)

1921
The Gondoliers (UAOS)
The Gondoliers (Barrow)

1922
Yeomen of the Guard (UAOS)

1923
Dorothy (UAOS)

1924
Merrie England (UAOS)
Trial by Jury/Pirates of
                Penzance (Barrow)
1925
The Rebel Maid (UAOS)
Tom Jones (Barrow)

1926
The Emerald Isle (UAOS)
Merrie England (Barrow)

1927
Iolanthe (UAOS)
Toreador (Barrow)

1928
The Dogs of Devon
   The Quaker Girl (UAOS)
The Country Girl (Barrow)

1929
The Runaway Girl (UAOS)
The Balkan Princess (Barrow)

1930
Chinese Honeymoon (UAOS)
Miss Hook of Holland (Barrow)

1931
The Belle of New York (UAOS)
The Marriage Market (Barrow)

1932
The Arcadians (UAOS)
The Geisha (Barrow)
The Mandarin (WALNEY)

1933
Floradora (UAOS)
Katinka (Barrow)
The Rose of Araby (WALNEY)

1934
Princess Charming (UAOS)
The Desert Song (Barrow)
The Sunshine Girl (WALNEY)

1935
Mr Cinders (UAOS)
Victoria & Her Hussar (Barrow)
No No Nanette (WALNEY)

1936
Sally (UAOS)
Maid of the Mountains (Barrow)
Sunny (WALNEY)

1937
The Cabaret Girl (UAOS)
The Street Singer (Barrow)
The Girlfriend (WALNEY)

1938
The Marriage Market (UAOS)
The New Moon (Barrow)
Rio Rita (WALNEY)

1939
Goodnight Vienna (WALNEY)

1940 - 1946
No productions

1947
The Country Girl (UAOS)
Tulip Time (WALNEY)

1948
The Earl & The Girl (UAOS)
Maritza (WALNEY)

1949
The Desert Song (UAOS)
Wild Violets (WALNEY)
The Mikado (Abbey)

1950
Rose Marie (UAOS)
The Vagabond King (Barrow)
Magyar Melody (WALNEY)
Yeomen of the Guard (Abbey)
The Mikado (Grange)

1951
The New Moon (UAOS)
Showboat (Barrow)
Rio Rita (WALNEY)
The Gondoliers (Abbey)
Iolanthe (Grange)
Pirates of Penzance
                (Flookburgh)

1952
Katinka (UAOS)
Glamorous Nights (Barrow)
Balalaika (WALNEY)
Iolanthe (Abbey)
Yeomen of the Guard (Grange)
Merrie England (Flookburgh)

1953
The Belle of New York (UAOS)
The Arcadians (Barrow)
Floradora (WALNEY)
Trial by Jury/Pirates (Abbey)
Dorothy/HMS Pinafore (Grange)
The Rebel Maid (Flookburgh)

1954
Chu Chin Chow (UAOS)
The Dancing Years (Barrow)
Annie Get Your Gun
                (WALNEY)
The Mikado (Abbey)
The Country Girl (Grange)
The Rose of Araby (Flookburgh)

1955
Goodnight Vienna (UAOS)
Oklahoma (Barrow)
Tulip Time (WALNEY)
Princess Ida (Abbey)
San Toy (Grange)
The Gondoliers (Flookburgh)

1956
Zip Goes A Million (UAOS)
The Dubarry (Barrow)
South Pacific (WALNEY)
HMS Pinafore (Abbey)
Lilac Domino (Grange)
Romany Maid (Flookburgh)

1957
Love From Judy (UAOS)
Perchance to Dream (Barrow)
Carousel (WALNEY)
Yeomen of the Guard (Abbey)
Merrie England (Grange)
The Mikado (Flookburgh)

1958
The Quaker Girl (UAOS)

1958 (cont'd)
White Horse Inn (Barrow)
The King & I (WALNEY)
The Maid of the Mountains
                (Abbey)
The Gondoliers (Grange)
The Maid of the Mountains
                (Flookburgh)
1959
The Arcadians (UAOS)
The Merry Widow (Barrow)
The Gypsy Princess (WALNEY)
The Rebel Maid (Abbey)
Pirates of Penzance (Grange)
The Geisha (Flookburgh)

1960
Oklahoma (UAOS)
The Desert Song (Barrow)
Rose Marie (WALNEY)
Pink Champagne (Grange)
Goodnight Vienna (Flookburgh)

1961
The Vagabond King (UAOS)
The New Moon (Barrow)
The Pyjama Game (WALNEY)
The Quaker Girl (Abbey)
The Merry Widow (Grange)
Miss Hook of Holland
                (Flookburgh)
1962
Annie Get Your Gun (UAOS)
The Boyfriend (Barrow)
Flower Drum Song (WALNEY)

1962 (cont'd)
The Geisha (Abbey)
Gypsy Baron (Grange)
Night in Venice (Flookburgh)

1963
Showboat (UAOS)
Me & My Girl
Salad Days (Barrow)
The Music Man (WALNEY)
Lilac Domino (Abbey)
The Mikado (Grange)
The Gypsy Princess
                (Flookburgh)
1964
The Student Prince (UAOS)
Naughty Marietta (Abbey)
The Country Girl (Grange)
White Horse Inn (Flookburgh)

1965
The Desert Song (UAOS)
Calamity Jane (WALNEY)
Goodnight Vienna (Abbey)
Waltz Time (Grange)
The New Moon (Flookburgh)

1966
South Pacific (UAOS)
No No Nanette (Barrow)
Sweethearts (Abbey)
Maid of the Mountains
                (Grange)
Oklahoma (Flookburgh)

1967
Bless the Bride (UAOS)
Guys & Dolls (Barrow)
White Horse Inn (Abbey)
Land of Smiles (Grange)
The Desert Song (Flookburgh)

1968
The New Moon (UAOS)
The Most Happy Fella (Barrow)
Oklahoma (WALNEY)
Wedding in Paris (Abbey)
Calamity Jane (Flookburgh)
The Merry Widow (Grange)
Wizard of Oz (Walney Juniors)

1969
The Belle of New York (UAOS)
My Fair Lady (Barrow)
Oliver (WALNEY)
Rose Marie (Abbey)
White Horse Inn (Grange)
The Gypsy Princess
            (Flookburgh)
Tick Tock (Walney Juniors)

1970
Half a Sixpence (UAOS)
Call Me Madam (Barrow)
Sound of Music (WALNEY)
Maritza (Abbey)
The Desert Song (Grange)
Love From Judy (Walney
            Juniors)

1971
Brigadoon (UAOS)
How to Succeed in Business
            (Barrow)
The Quaker Girl (Abbey)
Oklahoma (Grange)
Night in Venice (Flookburgh)
Babes in the Wood (Walney
            Juniors)

1972
Fiddler on the Roof (UAOS)
The King & I (Barrow)
Annie Get YourGun(WALNEY)
Summer Song (Abbey)
Pink Champagne (Grange)
Rose Marie (Flookburgh)

1973
White Horse Inn (UAOS)
South Pacific (Barrow)
Charlie Girl (WALNEY)
The Vagabond King (Abbey)
Carousel (Grange)
Count of Luxembourg (Flook'h)
Alice in Wonderl'd (Walney Jrs)

1974
No No Nanette (UAOS)
Sweet Charity (Barrow)
Guys & Dolls (WALNEY)
Viva Mexico (Abbey)
Annie Get Your Gun (Grange)
Goodnight Vienna (Flookburgh)
Sleeping Beauty (Walney J'nrs)

1975
Wild Violets (UAOS)
Carousel (Barrow)
My Fair Lady (WALNEY)
The New Moon (Abbey)
Oklahoma (Grange)
Me & My Girl (Flookburgh)
The Rose & The Ring (Walney Juniors)

1976
Rio Rita (UAOS)
Hello Dolly (Barrow)
Fiddler on the Roof (WALNEY)
Showboat (Abbey)
Waltzes from Vienna (Grange)
Call Me Madam (Flookburgh)
Aladdin/Cinderella (Walney Juniors)

1977
Carousel (UAOS)
Camelot (Barrow)
Kiss Me Kate (WALNEY)
The Desert Song (Abbey)
Charlie Girl (Grange)
Free As Air (Flookburgh)
Wizard of Oz (Walney Juniors)

1978
Finian's Rainbow (UAOS)
Mame (Barrow)
Gigi (WALNEY)
The Merry Widow (Abbey)
Count of Luxembourg (Grange)
Calamity Jane (Flookburgh)

1978 (cont'd)
The Pied Piper (Walney J'rs)

1979
My Fair Lady (UAOS)
Oliver (Barrow)
Call Me Madam (WALNEY)
Bitter Sweet (Abbey)
Brigadoon (Grange)
Salad Days (Flookburgh)
Sinbad the Sailor (Walney J'rs)

1980
Oklahoma (UAOS)
The King & I (Barrow)
South Pacific (WALNEY)
Glamorous Nights (Abbey)
Irene (Grange)
The Boyfriend (Flookburgh)
Jack & the Beanstalk (Walney (Juniors)

1981
Brigadoon (UAOS)
Fiddler on the Roof (Barrow)
Oklahoma (WALNEY)
Goodnight Vienna (Abbey)
Maid of the Mountains (Grange)
No No Nanette (Flookburgh)
Dick Whittington (Walney J'rs)

1982
Zip Goes A Million (UAOS)
Man of La Mancha (Barrow)
Half a Sixpence (WALNEY)
Showboat (Abbey)

1982 (cont'd)
Sound of Music (Abbey)
The Merry Widow (Grange)
Divorce Me Darling (Flookb'gh)
Sing a Song of Sixpence
(Walney Juniors)

1983
Hello Dolly (UAOS)
My Fair Lady (Barrow)
Irene (WALNEY)
White Horse Inn (Abbey)
Calamity Jane (Grange)
Oklahoma (Flookburgh)
Sleeping Beauty (Walney J'rs)

1984
Annie Get Your Gun (UAOS)
Jesus Christ Superstar (Barrow)
Carousel (WALNEY)
Viva Mexico (Abbey)
White Horse Inn (Grange)
The Quaker Girl (Flookburgh)
Cinderella (Walney Juniors)

1985
Sound of Music
Camelot (UAOS)
Annie (Barrow)
Mr Cinders (WALNEY)
Hans Andersen
Inn of 8th Happiness (Abbey)
Variety Show (Grange)
Irene (Flookburgh)
Bugsy Malone (Walney Juniors)

1986
South Pacific
Kiss Me Kate (UAOS)
Sugar (Barrow)
Hello Dolly (WALNEY)
The Desert Song (Abbey)
Oliver (Grange)
Charlie Girl (Flookburgh)
Dracula Spectacular (Walney
Juniors)

1987
Guys & Dolls
The Pyjama Game (UAOS)
Pirates of Penzance
Andy Capp (Barrow)
Calamity Jane (WALNEY)
Kismet (Abbey)
Viva Mexico (Grange)
Annie Get Your Gun (Flook'gh)
Wizard of Oz (Walney Juniors)

1988
The King & I
The Merry Widow (UAOS)
Sweeney Todd (Barrow)
My Fair Lady (WALNEY)
The Great Waltz (Abbey)
Sound of Music (Grange)
Finian's rainbow (Flookburgh)
The Snow Queen (Walney J'rs)

1989
Oliver
Die Fledermaus (UAOS)
Funny Girl (Barrow)

1989 (cont'd)
Beyond The Rainbow (Abbey)
Rose Marie (Grange)
Half a Sixpence (Flookburgh)
Hans Andersen
          (Walney Juniors)

1990
Oklahoma
   Fiddler on the Roof (UAOS)
Double Feature Show (Barrow)
Finian's Rainbow (Abbey)
My Fair Lady (Grange)
Salad Days (Flookburgh)
Mr Toad (Walney Juniors)

1991
Carousel
   Kismet (UAOS)
Cabaret
   Anything Goes (Barrow)
Robert & Elizabeth (Abbey)
Showboat (Grange)
White Horse Inn (Flookburgh)
Peter Pan (Walney Juniors)

1992
La Cage aux Folles
   High Society (UAOS)
Little Shop of Horrors (Barrow)
Oliver (WALNEY)
Blitz (Abbey)
Waltzes from Vienna (Grange)
Calamity Jane (Flookburgh)

1992 (cont'd)
A Musical Midsummer Night's
      Dream (Walney Juniors)
1993
Wizard of Oz
   Annie (UAOS)
The Pyjama Game (Barrow)
Camelot (Walney)
Call Me Madam (Abbey)
The Desert Song (Grange)
Viva Mexico (Flookburgh)
Bugsy Malone (Walney Juniors)

1994
My Fair lady
   The Music Man (UAOS)
Chess (Barrow)
Buys & Dolls (WALNEY)
Barnum (Abbey)
Fiddler on the Roof (Grange)
The Merry Widow (Flookburgh)
The Lion, the Witch, & the
      Wardrobe (Walney Juniors)

1995
Showboat
   Calamity Jane (UAOS)
42nd Street (Barrow)
Fiddler on the Roof (WALNEY)
Half a Sixpence (Abbey)
Brigadoon (Grange)
The Gypsy Princess
      (Flookburgh)
Oliver (Walney Juniors)

1996
South Pacific
  Singin' in the Rain (UAOS)
Man of La Mancha (Barrow)
Follies (WALNEY)
Carnival (Abbey)
Summer Song (Grange)
Carousel (Flookburgh)
Wizard of Oz (Walney Juniors)

1997
Hunchback of Notre Dame
  Brigadoon (UAOS)
Me & My Girl (Barrow)
Crazy For You (WALNEY)
Pride & Prejudice (Abbey)
Oliver (Grange)
The New Moon (Flookburgh)
The Snow Queen (Walney J'rs)

1998
Gentlemen Prefer Blondes
  Children of Eden (UAOS)
Moll Flanders (Barrow)
The King & I (WALNEY)
Pickwick (Abbey)
Me & My Girl (Grange)
Irene (Flookburgh)
Alice in Wonderland (Walney
                    Juniors)

1999
Sound of Music
  Wizard of Oz (UAOS)
Annie (Barrow)
Kismet (WALNEY)

1999 (cont'd)
State Fair (Abbey)
Hello Dolly (Grange)
Oklahoma (Flookburgh)
Dazzle (Walney Juniors)

2000
Oliver (UAOS)
Oklahoma (Barrow)
Mack & Mabel (WALNEY)
Barnum (Abbey)
Carousel (Grange)
Fiddler on the Roof (Flookb'rgh)
Peter Pan (Walney Juniors)

2001
Me & My Girl (UAOS)
Carousel (Barrow)
42nd Street (WALNEY)
Scrooge (Abbey)
Half a Sixpence (Grange)
The Quaker Girl (Flookburgh)
Bugsy Malone (Walney J'rs)

2002
Kiss Me Kate (UAOS)
Little Shop of Horrors (Barrow)
West Side Story (WALNEY)
Wuthering Heights (Abbey)
Anything Goes (Grange)
Call Me Madam (Flookburgh)
Calamity Jane (Walney Juniors)

2003
Guys & Dolls (UAOS)

2003 (cont'd)
Hello Dolly (Barrow)
Jesus Christ S'pstar (WALNEY)
Blitz (Abbey)
Gigi (Grange)
Finian's Rainbow (Flookburgh)
Wizard of Oz (Walney Juniors)

2004
The Secret Garden (UAOS)
Comedy Drama Dance (Barrow)
The Boyfriend
   Ragtime (WALNEY)
The Card (Abbey)
My Fair Lady (Grange)
Paint Your Wagon (Flookburgh)
Around the World in 80 Day
                (Walney Juniors)

2005
My Fair Lady (UAOS)
Oliver (Barrow)
Summer Holiday (WALNEY)
Me & My Girl (Abbey)
Irene (Grange)
Viva Mexico (Flookburgh)
Les Miserables (Walney Juniors)

2006
Goodnight Mr Tom (UAOS)
Rush (Barrow)
Jekyll & Hyde (WALNEY)
Oklahoma (Abbey)
Fiddler on the Roof (Grange)
The Pyjama Game (Flookburgh)
The King & I (Walney Juniors)

2007
Meet Me in St Louis (UAOS)
Anything Goes (Barrow)
The Full Monty (WALNEY)
The Bells Are Ringing (Abbey)
Oklahoma (Grange)
Anything Goes (Flookburgh)
Annie (Walney Juniors)

2008
Scrooge (UAOS)
Sweeney Todd (Barrow)
42nd Street (WALNEY)
Fiddler on the Roof (Abbey)
Waltzes from Vienna (Grange)
Hello Dolly (Flookburgh)
Barnum (Walney Juniors)

2009
When It Rains (UAOS)
The Music Man (Barrow)
Singin' in the Rain (WALNEY)
Titanic (Abbey)
Brigadoon (Grange)
Calamity Jane (Flookburgh)
Bugsy Malone (Walney Juniors)

2010
The King & I (UAOS)
Beauty & the Beast (Barrow)
Jesus Christ S'pstar (WALNEY)
The Likes of Us (Abbey)
Carousel (Grange)
Mame (Flookburgh)
Oliver (Walney Juniors)

2011
Camelot (UAOS)
100 Not Out
    Wizard of Oz (Barrow)
The Producers (WALNEY)
The Wedding Singer (Abbey)
Oliver (Grange)
South Pacific (Flookburgh)
Me & My Girl (Walney Juniors)

2012
Annie (UAOS)
Chess (Barrow)
Peter Pan (WALNEY)
Dr Dolittle (Abbey)
Me & My Girl (Grange)
Flookburgh Entertains (F'burgh)
Sound of Music (Walney J'rs)

2013
Whistle Down the Wind
            (UAOS)
Witches of Eastwick (Barrow)
La Cage aux Folles (WALNEY)
Footloose (Abbey)
Calamity Jane (Grange)
Musical Extravaganza (F'burgh)
Joseph & His Technicolour
    Dreamcoat (Walney Juniors)

2014
Fiddler on the Roof (UAOS)
Jekyll & Hyde (Barrow)
Evita
    Cats (WALNEY)

2014 (cont'd)
Grease (Abbey)
Blitz (Grange)
Stepping Out (Flookburgh)
Phantom of the Opera (Walney
                Juniors)

2015
42nd Street (UAOS)
Sister Act (Barrow)
West Side Story (WALNEY)
Hairspray (Abbey)
The King & I (Grange)
Just a Little War (Flookburgh)
Les Miserables (Walney Juniors)

2016
Wizard of Oz (UAOS)
Legally Blonde
    Spamalot (Barrow)
Made in Dagenham
            (WALNEY)
White Christmas (Abbey)
Annie (Grange)
Grease (Walney Juniors)

    *   *   *

BARROW SAVOYARDS

1973 The Mikado
1974 Iolanthe
1975 Pirates of Penzance
1976 Yeomen of the Guard
1977 The Gondoliers
1978 HMS Pinafore/Trial by
Jury
1979 Princess Ida
1980 The Mikado
1981 Patience

1982 Pirates of Penzance
1983 Ruddigore
1984 Yeomen of the Guard
1985 Iolanthe
1986 The Gondoliers
1987 The Sorcerer
1988 The Mikado
1989 Patience
1990 HMS Pinafore
1991 Princess Ida
1992 Pirates of Penzance
1993 Yeomen of the Guard
1994 Iolanthe
1995 The Gondoliers
1996 Ruddigore
1997 The Mikado
1998 The Sorcerer
1999 Pirates of Penzance
2000 Princess Ida
2001 HMS Pinafore/Trial by
Jury
2002 Patience
2003 30th Anniversary Show
2004 Yeomen of the Guard

2005 The Gondoliers
2006 Iolanthe
2007 Utopia Ltd
2008 The Mikado
2009 Pirates of Penzance
2010 Ruddigore
2011 HMS Pinafore/Trial by
Jury
2012 The Sorcerer
2013 The Gondoliers
2014 'A Nice Dilemma'
2015 Pirates of Penzance
2016 Yeomen of the Guard

YOUTH THEATRE

ACT
1990 Peter Pan
1991 The Hobbit
The Xmas Show
1992 Smith
A Christmas Carol
1993 Murder at
Hallowe'en
1994 The Pied Piper
To Death & Glory
1995 The Hobbit
1996 Annie
1997 Gold Rush
Peter Pan
1998 The Evacuees
Fiddler on the Roof
Sleeping Beauty

1999 Bugsy Malone
     A Christmas Carol
2000 My Fair Lady
     The Hobbit

Furness Youth Theatre

2001 To Death & Glory
     Peter Pan
2002 Oliver
     Aladdin
2003 Annie
2004 Bugsy Malone
2005 Sleeping Beauty

2006 Peter Pan
2007 The Evacuees
2008 Shake Ripple & Roll
2009 Sleeping Beauty
2010 Peter Pan
2011 Dracula Rock Show
     A Christmas Carol
2012 Spring Show
2013 Skool & Crossbones
2014 Young King Arthur
2015 Wind in the Willows
2016 Alice

A590 Theatre Group

2002 The Jungle Book
2004 Fame
     Dracula Spectacular
2005 Big Al
     Shake Ripple & Roll
2006 Cinderella

2006 Peter Pan
2007 Disco Inferno
     Pandemonium
2008 Back to the 80's
     Honk
2009 Cruisin'
2009 Guys and Dolls
     A Christmas Carol
     Rent
2010 Forbidden Planet
     Aladdin
2011 Fiddler on the Roof
     That's Entertainment
2012 Aida
2013 Last Daze of St
               Swithuns
2014 Oliver
2015 The King & I
2016 Whistle Down the
               Wind

CAST Theatre Company

2009 Godspell
2010 Little Shop of Horrors
2011 Summer Holiday
2012 High School Musical
2013 Seussical
2014 Guys and Dolls
     Avenue Q
2015 Barnum
2016 Annie

PICTURE CREDITS

I am most grateful to the following for their kind permission to publish their photographs:

Paul Bryden 250, Steve Carrick 130, Brian Greaves 228, Elaine Parkinson 42, 165, 166, Bill & Noreen Steel 182; *The North Western Evening Mail* (76, 83, 84, 86, 88, 89, 127, 140, 155, 157, 168, 174, 187, 191, 193, 195, 198, 210, 213, 214, 216, 218, 238, 239, 240, 253, 258, 259, 260, 262, 265, 279); BODS (32, 56, 96, 100, 104, 106, 113, 116, 118, 123, 124; UAOS (63, 66, 68, 69, 71, 72, 73, 77); Walney Theatre Company (132, 133, 135, 143, 147, 151, 156, 158); Abbey Musical Society (177, 179, 180, 183, 189, 196, 199); Flookburgh & District Operatic Society (230, 231, 236); Grange & District Amateur Operatic Society (221, 223); Walney Junior Amateur Operatic Society (244, 246, 252, 256, 261, 264); Barrow Savoyards (270, 271, 280, 281); Furness Youth Theatre 288; A590 Theatre Group 290; CAST Theatre Company 293; Barrow Archive Centre 49, 51, 120.
(Other images are from the author's personal collection)

SELECT BIBLIOGRAPHY

FROW, G. (1985) *Oh Yes It Is! A History of Pantomime*. BBC Books: London.

GIBBON, W. M. (1986) *A Change of Scene: A Nostalgic Appreciation of Barrow's Theatres and Cinemas*. Gibbon: Barrow.

HISCHAK, Thomas. (2008) *The Oxford Companion to the American Musical*. Oxford University Press: New York.

KENRICK, John. (2008) *Musical Theatre: A History*. Continuum Publishing Group: New York.

LEACH, Alice. (1989) *Our Barrovians*. Furness Heritage Press: Ulverston.

LEACH, Alice. (ed) (2008) *Voices from Barrow-in-Furness*. The History Press: Stroud, Gloucs.

PARKER, D and Julia. (1979) *The Story and the Song*. Chappell & Company Ltd., London.

TAYLOR, G. (1977) *History of the Amateur Theatre*. Uffington Press: Melksham, Wilts.

THORN, Tracey. (2016) *Naked at the Albert Hall: The Inside Story of Singing*. Virago Press: London.

TRESCATHERIC, B. (2013) *The Barrow Story*. The Dock Museum: Barrow-in-Furness.

WILSON, G. (1985) *The Psychology of the Performing Arts*. Croom Helm Ltd, Kent.